ROBERT EVANS NYE

School of Music
University of Oregon

VERNICE TROUSDALE NYE

College of Education
University of Oregon

Essentials of

Teaching

Elementary School

Music

PRENTICE-HALL, INC., ENGLEWOOD CLIFFS, NEW JERSEY

Library of Congress Cataloging in Publication Data

NYE, ROBERT EVANS, date.
   Essentials of teaching elementary school music.

   Includes bibliographies.
   1. Music—Manuals, text-books, etc. 2. School
music—Instruction and study—United States. I. Nye,
Vernice Trousdale, joint author.   II. Title.
MT10.N97   372.8'7'044   73–21512
ISBN 0–13–289280–4
ISBN 0–13–289272–3 (pbk.)

PRENTICE-HALL INTERNATIONAL, INC., London
PRENTICE-HALL OF AUSTRALIA, PTY. LTD., Sydney
PRENTICE-HALL OF CANADA, LTD., Toronto
PRENTICE-HALL OF INDIA PRIVATE LIMITED, New Delhi
PRENTICE-HALL OF JAPAN, INC., Tokyo

contents

to the college teacher,

part one, 1

1

children and music—an introduction, 3

ESTABLISHING CONDITIONS FOR LEARNING, 4
ORGANIZING THE CLASSROOM FOR LEARNING, 4
Types of Class Organization, 8 General Principles, 4

2

teaching children music, 16

AREAS OF OBJECTIVES, 16 SELECTING MUSIC CONTENT, 18
MUSIC CONCEPTS AND GENERALIZATIONS, 21
Cognitive Process Skills, 30 LESSON PLAN, 32 Music Skills Objectives, 34
Objectives in Music Attitudes, Values, Behaviors, 36
DESIGNING PLANS FOR TEACHING AND EVALUATING, 38
Performance Objectives, 39 Designing Lesson Plans, 42
EVALUATION, 46 SUMMARY, 48

part two, 51

3

an introduction to teaching strategies, 53

SOUNDS AND TONE QUALITIES, 54
Manhattanville Music Curriculum Program, 57 RHYTHM, 68
Dynamics and Tempo, 69 Beat, Divisions of the Beat, Rhythm Patterns, 70
Accent and Meter, 87 MELODY, 87 Pitch and Singing, 87
Hand Signs, 91 Notation of Pitch, 99 Scales and the Tonal Center, 100
Melody and Harmony, 104 FORM, 107 SUMMARY, 109

4

learning music with songs and instruments, 112

SONGS, 112 TONE QUALITY, 115 The Child Voice, 115 DYNAMICS, 116
TEMPO, 116 RHYTHM-RELATED EXPERIENCES, 116
Less Common Meter Organization, 123 Meter and Music of the World, 125
MUSIC FUNDAMENTALS, 127
SOME ACTIVITIES WITH SONGS IN PRIMARY GRADES, 137
TEACHING ROTE SONGS, 138
MUSIC CONCEPTS AND ROTE TEACHING, 141
GENERAL DIRECTIONS, 143 Polyphony, 145 Harmony, 147
Harmonic Part Singing, 149 Seeing What We Hear, 156
Using Recordings of Songs, 157 The Piano and Other Substitutes, 159
INSTRUMENTS, 160 MELODY INSTRUMENTS, 162 The Recorder, 168
HARMONY INSTRUMENTS, 173 The Autoharp, 173
Ukulele and Guitar, 180 Piano Chording, 184
Chording With Bells, 189 The Singing Classroom Orchestra, 189
TEACHING WITH INSTRUMENTS, 191 ADDING PARTS, 197
FORM, 207 LEARNING NOTATION, 208
MORE ABOUT COMPOSING MUSIC, 211 SUMMARY, 215

5

learning music with recordings and films, 218

FILMS AND FILMSTRIPS, 218 TRANSPARENCIES, 220
SELECTING RECORDINGS, 221 LISTENING TO PROGRAM MUSIC, 226
LISTENING TO ABSOLUTE MUSIC, 227
LISTENING TO CONTEMPORARY MUSIC, 227 RECORDINGS TODAY, 229
Sounds and Tone Qualities, 230 MUSIC AND MOVEMENT, 240
Fundamental Movements, 241 Rhythmic Dramatization, 245
Other Rhythm-Related Concepts, 248
Miscellaneous Rhythm References, 251 Exemplary Films, 254
MUSIC-ART RELATIONSHIPS, 255
POLYPHONY, HARMONY, AND TEXTURE, 255 Exemplary Films, 258
Form in Music, 259 Forms of Music, 261 Exemplary Films, 268
MUSIC OF OTHER CULTURES, 269 SUMMARY, 275

appendix A, 277

BOOKS THAT HARMONIZE WITH ELEMENTARY SCHOOL CHILDREN

appendix B, 289

ALPHABETICAL LISTING OF COMPOSERS IN
ADVENTURES IN MUSIC

appendix C, 295

COMPLETE LISTING OF THE BOWMAR ORCHESTRAL
LIBRARY, Series 1, 2, and 3

appendix D, 304

PUBLISHERS OF MUSIC SERIES

index of songs, 305

general index, 306

to the college teacher

Essentials of Teaching Elementary School Music was written in response to requests to provide a concise but adequate textbook. It is not, therefore, a comprehensive book in the full sense; that distinction is reserved for *Music in the Elementary School*, third edition (Prentice-Hall, Inc., 1970). However, the same general approach described below can be used with the earlier book.

Part One is brief, but it contains much information of relevance to the beginning teacher. It is concerned with establishing conditions for learning, the four areas of music objectives, music concepts and generalizations, cognitive process skills, performance objectives, lesson plans, and a list of criteria for evaluating lesson plans. Part Two, the larger portion of the book, is concerned with music learning experiences—those dealing with tone qualities, tempo, dynamics, rhythm, melody, harmony, form, and the various music skills. The college teacher has the choice of beginning with Part One, or beginning with Part Two and referring to the material in Part One as needed.

It is popular today to emphasize the contributions of Dalcroze, Orff, and Kodaly. Since this book reflects the eclectic approach of the mainstream of American music education, elements of the methods of these distinguished educators are incorporated into the organization of the book, but no lengthy sections will be found concerned solely with those methods.

In this volume the authors address themselves to the desire of college students to be actively involved in the proceedings of the elementary music methods class. In Part Two the students can be assigned either as members of small groups or as individuals to develop and present aspects of the course. Thus, the book makes it possible for students to become involved in the process of teaching and learning music by its being so organized that they will use both deductive and inductive methods. Through this organization they are freed to explore, to gather data, to compare, to experiment, contrast, interpret, analyze, and formulate concepts and generalizations in music.

The college teacher's role is a supportive one. Such support includes being a resource of knowledge available to the students, treating student questions with interest and concern, being a fellow-seeker of knowledge who participates in class learning experiences, responding with genuine appreciation to students' efforts, and giving assistance, encouragement, and approval. Thus, we present the college teacher as a director of learning and a co-inquirer in the classroom.

It is assumed that there will be occasions when the college teacher instructs the class and plans with the class for activities to follow. There may be small group presentations of how to teach children aspects of music outlined in this book, often using the college class as a substitute for children. (Whenever possible, children should be used in the demonstrations.) There may be lesson plan demonstrations and reports by individuals.

When small groups or individuals are assigned sections of Part Two from which to plan demonstrations, experiments, and lesson plans, it is suggested that in the beginning they select from the many learning experiences those that they can develop satisfactorily at this point. The student needs to experience success in order to build confidence. He needs an environment in which he feels free to explore, to experiment, and to make mistakes. The activities too difficult for him at this stage of his musical development can be left for the college teacher to explain and demonstrate whenever necessary. In this way the students have the opportunity to build faith in their own competencies and to find success by selecting those learning experiences they know they can do reasonably well. The approach to teaching presented here can be integrated into a teaching philosophy which will allow the college students the flexibility to organize their teaching procedures in light of their unique personalities and their individual musical competencies.

The approach in this volume is a very simple one. The learning experiences in Part Two are listed in an order that begins with the more simple and proceeds to the more complex. At first the students are involved with music teaching strategies that require the use of neither songbooks nor recordings. Most of these are relatively easy, and they learn that they can succeed with them before a class. By beginning with these successful experiences, they can develop confidence and a desire to organize more complex teaching plans that require more advanced music skills. They next turn to Chapter Four, in which they find that they can teach the same concepts by using selected songs and pitched instruments. In Chapter Five they add to their growing resources recordings and films that can reinforce, introduce, or emphasize many of the same concepts. Finally, by drawing upon all of these resources they are able to design a well-balanced music program for children.

For the past quarter-century the grade level approach has been found to be inadequate in United States education. It is now time for teachers to find out where the children are musically and to organize and implement music programs that will help them to move sequentially to higher levels of performance.

The authors are indebted to many persons, including students and co-workers, who have given them assistance and encouragement in compiling this volume.

R. E. N.

V. T. N.

part one

part one

1

children and music
—an introduction

The prominent early twentieth-century American music educator Osbourne McConathy feared that some teachers become more interested in musical results than in the development of individual children. He said, "We must appreciate that we are not teaching the subjects of the school curriculum but the children who are studying these subjects." Teachers are to help children to learn music, and must therefore know the developmental characteristics of each child and how he learns in order to be able to teach him. It is assumed that the reader is versed in recent research in theories of child development and learning and their implications for teaching music. Knowledge of the developmental growth patterns of children and recent theories or principles of learning are basic to organizing an effective music program.[1] Since the purpose of this book is to emphasize the essentials of teaching elementary school music, child development patterns and learning principles as they relate to this task will not be developed in detail. Should the reader need more information of this nature, he can refer to the footnote on this page and to the reference list at the end of this chapter.

[1] Robert Nye and Vernice Nye, *Music in the Elementary School*, 3rd ed. (Englewood Cliffs, N.J.: Prentice-Hall, Inc., 1970), chap. iii.

Establishing Conditions for Learning

In order for children to become involved in the excitement and process of learning, they must have access to a learning environment that makes it possible for them to discover their interests, potentials, and problems.

THE EMOTIONAL SETTING

Children must become involved in working with both peers and adults in a positive and accepting atmosphere. The environment must be planned and organized so as to provide time to make it possible for children to inquire into the various elements of music. In order to do this, they will need to be taught the skills of how to explore, experiment, hypothesize, contrast, compare, interpret, analyze, generalize, evaluate, value, create, and apply acquired knowledge to the solution and exploration of new and related music problems. For this type of learning to result, children need to know that they have the respect, acceptance, encouragement, and support of both their peers and their teacher(s). Children are thus encouraged to accept uncertainty about knowledge—to gather, process, and evaluate supportive data from various sources. Experimentation is encouraged. Positive reinforcement and acceptance are needed to encourage children to persist until they have explored a problem to its fullest and successfully solved it. They should participate in the formulation of criteria to use in judging their own music performance. "We know the song could be improved; what do you think we can do to make it sound better?" "In what ways have we made real progress with this music?" "Are there places where we can do better?" "How?" Music teachers need to provide a great diversity of ways in which children can succeed. Fortunately, music's many facets make this easily possible. When a teacher plans a music lesson there should be activities included whereby the students are challenged but at the same time successful.

It should be noted that in music classes some types of learning may not be comprehended if lecturing and discussion predominate, since the skills of musical performance and many understandings about music are acquired by actively participating in making music.

Organizing the Classroom for Learning

A teacher's knowledge and skill in music are of value in the classroom only in terms of his ability to organize and manage the music activities in that classroom so that they strike a balance between the routine and the creative, between stability and change. Efficient routine is necessary to avoid overlooking detail; the main reason for taking care of detail is to provide more pupil-teacher time and energy for creative and problem-solving types of learning and teaching. A teacher needs to know procedures that should and should not be routinized. The children should have a part in planning classroom routines and in using them to facilitate learning; they should understand the value of these procedures, exactly how they are to be done, and then they should evaluate the degree of efficiency resulting from them.

While overroutinization can stifle creativity, a proper amount saves time and assists the orderly procedures of events in the music period. Experienced teachers have found these ideas helpful.

A chord played on piano or Autoharp, or a tone played on the bells can be a signal for a change of activity. Such musical means for giving directions are more conducive to pleasant feelings than the teacher's voice directing children to do something.

Materials used in a lesson should be assembled in advance. Teachers often have some of these on carts that can be wheeled from room to room. When a teacher makes advance preparations for a lesson by doing such routine things as assembling materials, writing on the chalkboard the titles and page numbers of the songs, words of rote songs, notation for class study, the order of music activities, and other directions, he promotes general efficiency. Through pupil discussion, evaluation, and modification of the order and directions of activities indicated, children have a part in the planning, and see meaning and purpose in the sequences of activities included in the lesson. When verbal directions are given they are stated clearly and concisely, thus lessening the need for repeating them. The teacher should make certain that every child can see and hear what is spoken, sung, played, danced, or dramatized.

A music learning center can be located out of traffic lines and in a place in the room which is both relatively secluded, yet accessible. It may be located in a booth off the main classroom or it may consist of one large table or several smaller ones upon which can be placed interesting materials such as books, bells and other small instruments, music to play on the instruments, recordings, record player with headsets, a viewer, filmstrips, and filmstrip machine, a tape recorder and various sound-producing materials, and machines for experimentation. The center could include bulletin boards on which can be mounted information about community musical events, composers, recommended radio and television programs, musical achievements of students, charts, musical symbols, cartoons, jackets from books about music and from recordings, newspaper and magazine clippings, notation of unnamed familiar songs which are to be identified by studying this notation, favorite songs, rhythm patterns, and pictures relating to musical subjects. However, the bulletin board must be arranged attractively and changed frequently if it is to accomplish its mission of attracting maximum interest. Soft mallets for the bells and headsets with the record player can eliminate interference with other activities in the room. By teacher-pupil planning, criteria for the use of the music materials and equipment are established. These criteria should also indicate when and how children are to work in the music learning center.

EXPANDING CLASSROOM WALLS

Music teachers of today are utilizing work space other than the classroom. They also use cultural resources in the community to enrich learning in music. The expansion of the learning environment makes it necessary for the teacher to become familiar with all areas and facilities of the school plant and community which can be useful for music instruction. When students explore the musical resources of the community, and when parents and other community resource people contribute to the school music program, the musical learning laboratory is thereby expanded.

PHYSICAL FACTORS OF THE ROOM ENVIRONMENT

It is obvious that learning is difficult when attempted in impure air, uncomfortable temperatures, and improper lighting. The busy teacher who is in the same classroom all day will sometimes fail to notice insufficient ventilation, unhealthy temperatures, and faulty lighting because of the gradual changes in the room as the day progresses. While teachers should be alert to these factors, children should assume part of the responsibility. Classroom committees can be established to give children experience in assuming responsibility and to relieve the teacher of part of this routine task.

The arrangement of the furniture influences the type of learning that takes place. Seating for the entire class should be appropriately arranged to make it possible for students to participate in discussion as well as in individual and small group work, and to provide opportunity for listening effectively and courteously to any class member who is speaking, singing, or playing an instrument.

The varied activities in music make movable furniture a necessity. Seating (or temporary standing) will be changed at times for singing in large and small groups, playing instruments, creative interpretations, rhythmic responses, and dance. Special seating may be needed if some of the children have difficulty hearing or seeing. The manner in which the children will move from one activity to another is established by clear instructions from the teacher and by teacher-pupil planning. Well-planned questions from the teacher that stimulate the children to plan and take responsibility for this part of classroom routine are needed. Leaving and entering, going to and from a music room or assembly room, and moving books, instruments, and other materials are additional aspects of school routine that need planning, reminders, and repetition so that good habits are formed that may prevent problems from arising. The teacher should circulate freely among the students to observe and assist them.

Another use of the room is in connection with listening to recordings, when, to reflect the mood of compositions, shades might be drawn, lights turned on, color employed, or objects placed in a way to heighten the aural effect.

SELECTION AND HANDLING OF MATERIALS

When series books are selected, the teacher considers such things as print, size, clarity of notation, a good grade of paper that is free from eye-straining high gloss, ease of handling by children, color, illustrations, absence of clutter, general attractiveness, well-organized and comprehensive indices, content that appeals to the age group, quality of content, general durability, quality of the cover, simplicity and musicality of accompaniments, helpfulness of the teachers' manuals, quality and usefulness of the recordings.

When instruments and equipment are selected, the teacher chooses those that produce excellent tone quality, that are durable, attractive, and easy to store, that are suitable for the age group; instruments meeting these qualifications are often those designed and sold for school use. Chairs and desks should be selected to fit the varying sizes of children found in a class.

When songs are selected, the teacher looks for simplicity and variety in the melody, repeated parts that assist rapid learning, content interesting to the age group, proper range for the voices, appropriate length for the maturity level, rhythmic appeal, and a suitable, attractive accompaniment. He examines the song to find what teaching purpose it can serve. It must pass these tests: "Is this song worth learning?" "Is it a worthy art, folk, or popular song?" and "Does it contribute to the realization of the stated objectives?"

Teachers should have the required materials assembled, should know how to use them, and should plan the necessary routine with the children. A system of distributing materials and collecting them should be planned with and executed by the children, who should know where and how to store them. For example, if Tonettes are used, each should be labeled with the child's name; they should be placed in the plastic bags that are made for them in order to keep them clean; they should not be taken home until the child can play reasonably well; a place should be selected to store them, such as a box on a shelf, and they should be played and treated as musical instruments, not as noisemakers. For sanitary reasons children should not exchange instruments, but if this is necessary, a disinfectant for plastic must be used; the instruments must be cleaned periodically with disinfectant applied with a small brush or cotton swab.

Criteria must be established, preferably with the children, for proper use of the room in viewing television and films, listening to radio programs, and using the music learning center. A classified card file of recordings, a card file of available books about music, and a vertical file of pictures should be part of the teacher's equipment, placed for his convenience. Teachers who are well prepared, and who have made provision for proper directions and routine, usually exude a feeling of confidence and security that is reflected in the behavior of the child. Children sense insecurity in teachers, and they are disturbed by it.

TYPES OF CLASS ORGANIZATION

In today's classrooms one often finds children learning through independent study, as members of small groups, and in the total classroom group. Regardless of the type of learning situation it is the teacher's task to so organize the classroom environment that the needs of the individual learner are met. To individualize instruction means that the teacher plans learning experiences appropriate for each learner whether or not he is in a group. It does not demand a one-to-one teacher-pupil relationship, although this may operate at times.

In the effort to accommodate the needs of each child, there has arisen the concept of the nongraded or ungraded school where groupings are made in accordance with achievement levels and interests rather than in accordance with age or grade levels. Also, the concept of the open classroom has come into focus. On a purely architectural basis this new classroom is a large open space—a school without walls. (According to many music teachers who have experienced this, there is still a need for a music room and practice rooms.) However, this concept operates in traditional buildings as well. The open classroom is planned so that much of what takes place during the school day is child-managed, and the learner is assumed to be motivated by his personal interests and objectives to a far greater degree than in the traditional type of school.

However, with the great emphasis being placed upon the individualization of instruction today, let us not forget that children generally desire to participate in music making as members of a group.

GROUPING

In the effort to provide for individual differences and the unique ways students learn, teachers group children in order to accommodate varied interests, abilities, and rates of learning. These groups usually consist of two to eight students, depending upon age, experience, and the activity. The groups work in designated areas of the room, in the hall, the library, in conference rooms or other nearby areas. The activities with which the groups are engaged could include composing music, planning accompaniments, evaluating different interpretations, practicing difficult sections of music being performed, learning songs from recordings, or any number of things. While grouping can be done at any level, it can be more effectively utilized at the intermediate level. When children have not participated in group work, the teacher should begin by carefully organizing one small group while the remainder of the students work as a class or as individuals. The teacher then *gradually* organizes additional groups until the time comes when most or all of the class can be involved in small group work whenever this is appropriate.

When organized groups are kept flexible with each child having an opportunity to work in several types of groups for varied reasons, they can be viewed as laboratories for firsthand learning of music. Both individual and small group inquiry can be stimulated and enhanced through interacting with others.

Concepts can be clarified, hypotheses stated, generalizations formed and evaluated. Feelings of belonging, security, acceptance, respect, and mutual trust can be developed. . . . A constructive and experimental approach to learning can be nurtured, and the excitement of discovery and sharing of ideas with the group can increase the depth and breadth of children's learning.

Teachers should know the limitations as well as the values of group work. *First,* group work should be limited to activities with some purpose that members of the group can share. Without commonly shared purposes, individuals in the group will waste time and derive little or no benefit from the activity. *Second,* group work should be limited to activities in which the children possess or can be taught the skills needed to carry out the group activities. . . . *Third,* group work should be limited to activities in which cooperative action is required to achieve stated purposes. If an activity can be completed by an individual, or by several individuals working independently, there is no need to organize a working group. *Fourth,* group work should be limited to activities in which effective working relationships can be maintained. If interpersonal conflicts and differences in points of view cannot be reconciled, progress cannot be made by forcing individuals to work in a group. *Fifth,* group work should be limited to situations in which the diverse talents of children can be put to use. If each child is required to do the same thing in an activity, individual differences will be neglected and unique contributions will not be obtained from each child.[2]

In a session at the 1972 Music Educators' National Conference, the Baltimore Public Schools contributed an outline of the grouping process which the authors have expanded somewhat.

1. *In the total class group* the teacher:
   Introduces a music concept or skill.
   Introduces one or more problems related to the concept or skill.
   Clarifies and plans with the children the problem to be solved by each small group.
   Identifies and groups children who can work well together.
   Locates materials to be used by each group.
   Designates the area of operation for each group.
   Establishes time limits.
   Plans with the children ways for them to work effectively in the groups.
   Identifies the signal for returning to the large class group to share small group and individual accomplishments when appropriate.

2. *In the small group* the students:
   Clarify their purpose.
   Decide upon a tenative plan.
   Identify the responsibilities of each individual.
   Do research and processing.
   Interpret and summarize their findings.
   Make value judgments.
   Decide if and how they will share their findings with the larger class group.

3. *In the total class group* the members of the small groups:
   Report to and/or perform for the total group.
   Answer questions asked by classmates.

[2]John U. Michaelis, *Social Studies for Children in a Democracy,* 5th ed. (Englewood Cliffs, N.J.: Prentice-Hall, Inc., 1972), pp. 332–33. Reprinted by permission of Prentice-Hall, Inc., the copyright owner.

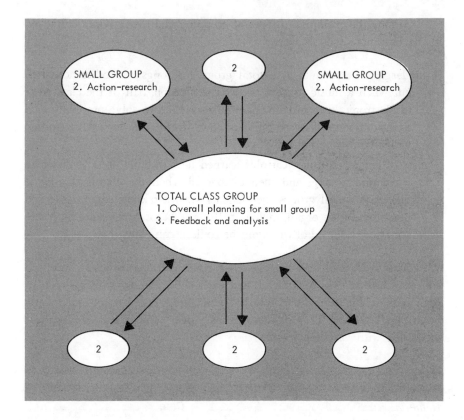

Receive suggestions from peers and teacher as to ways to improve.
Record data from small groups and analyze and interpret the information; draw conclusions.
Evaluate in terms of their purpose.

The teacher moves from group to group, giving assistance where needed. He will find that close supervision is usually necessary for productive learning to take place. However, it will soon be obvious that some groups need only a minimum amount of supervision whereas others need considerable guidance. It is also the teacher's role to offer suggestions, ask questions, commend children for good work, be a coinquirer and a resource to them whenever needed. If the teacher finds that some children lack skills to complete a task, he may organize a skills group and help its members master these skills as tools before putting them back into the original small group. Not all children must work in groups. Some may need to work as individuals.

Among the examples of types of grouping and the activities employed in the Baltimore schools were:

A kindergarten class met as a total group for songs and other activities, but when a music concept needed clarification, half of the class went to electronic keyboards to manipulate pitches to solve problems such as the difference between high and low. Meanwhile, the teacher worked with the other half of the class.

A class of eight- and nine-year-olds learned how to build chords needed to harmonize a song, and then discovered when the chords should be played. In small groups the students put their knowledge to use and practiced on the organ, melody bells, Autoharps, and piano. Each student kept a record of the songs he could accompany.

After a class of ten- and eleven-year-olds clarified a music concept, a *learning contract* was distributed, and each child decided which option or options he would contract to fulfill. These were worked upon individually or in small groups. The following is part of a sample learning contract concerned with variation form.

THEME AND VARIATIONS #1

Name _____
Completion
Date _____

I WILL:

___ 1. Show two variations of "Canoe Round" by changing the rhythm.

___ 2. Make three music variations of my own choice in the song, "Johnny Has Gone For a Soldier."

___ 3. Play this theme as a march, a waltz, and a funeral dirge.

___ 4. Show a variation in "Hot Cross Buns" by changing it from major to minor.

Learning packages have become commercially available as another approach to individualizing instruction; some teachers are making their own. While most of these are designed to be used during school, some of them can be taken home by children. Tapes are coming into wider use as another kind of learning package. Emphasis is on musical experiences rather than on uninteresting and isolated facts such as, "A quarter note in moderate tempo receives one beat." With tapes, melodies are identified; the listener tells in what ways melodies are varied; the listener tells whether the music is now faster or slower, higher or lower, and whether the rhythm is even or uneven; he tells whether the music moves in two's or three's; he identifies instruments. Other packages may be concerned with types of scales, building scales with the knowledge of their structure, writing a descant, and identifying phrases. There is work for individuals, pairs, and small groups.

More examples from the Baltimore schools include:

Seven- and eight-year-olds had a learning activity packet from which they learned to recognize the sound and name of instruments. They listened to the tape, then placed the pictures of the instruments in correct order as they heard their sounds.

Nine-, ten-, and eleven-year-olds worked in pairs with a record player and a sound filmstrip for instruction in music reading. Each child's record was charted by the teacher. In the same room there was a matching game, directions for playing melody bells, and taped lessons for electronic organ.

Many of the individual, small group, and learning package activities take place in the music learning center. See page 5.

GENERAL PRINCIPLES

Some general principles to use as guides for teaching and learning music follow. All teachers need to be aware of them and to use them as guides in developing music programs.

1. Music activities are selected that are on the child's physical, intellectual, and social maturity levels.

2. The teacher has obvious confidence in the child's ability to learn music.

3. The teacher employs a variety of activities and materials. She provides for individual, small-group, and whole-class activities.

4. The teacher arranges for musical problems to be solved by the children.

5. The children have musical experiences that are satisfying to them.

6. The children have good models with which to identify (other children, parents, teachers, other adults).

7. There is a planned, sequential, but flexible program of music instruction from level to level.

8. There is meaningful, varied, and frequent practice that is essential for learning music skills.

9. Teachers and parents work together to help children learn music; the musical and cultural environment influences to a significant degree children's musical perceptions and values.

10. Individual differences and levels of musical proficiency and aptitude are recognized, diagnosed, and accommodated.

11. The children see meaning and relevance in what they are doing as they make immediate functional applications of these skills and procedures, as they become involved in establishing purposes, in the selection of appropriate activities and materials, and in assessing the degree to which the purposes (objectives) have been realized.

12. The teacher is able to select and state what he or she is going to teach and the subsequent pupil-learning behaviors (objectives), how he is going to accomplish this (methods and materials), and then determine how well he has taught it (evaluation).

13. Children are taught the skill of asking different types and levels of questions and are encouraged and given opportunity to utilize this skill.

14. The teacher is an active guide to learning, a co-learner, and a resource person who shares in class activities.

15. The children's musical experiences are successful to them. The teacher plans activities in which children can succeed, in which they are interested, and through which they can progress in learning music.

16. The children develop favorable self-concepts through successful individual, small groups, and class musical experiences.

17. The learning of music is enhanced when the learner is motivated and personally involved in what is to be learned.

18. Children learn more readily when they begin their study with music content related to everyday life situations. An outgrowth of this can be the study of music of the past.

19. The learner needs to be in an accepting and understanding learning environment in which he is free to explore, experiment, question, discuss, hypothesize, contrast, compare, analyze, interpret, generalize, and apply knowledge to the solution of musical problems. Through these processes he learns musical knowledge, skills, and values.

REFERENCES

LEONHARD, CHARLES, and ROBERT W. HOUSE, *Foundations and Principles of Music Education*, 2nd. ed. New York: McGraw-Hill Book Co. Chap. 5.

Music Educators Journal, November, 1972. Pages 21–54 are concerned with individualization of instruction, the open classroom, and related teaching problems. Also see the April, 1974, issue.

NYE, ROBERT E., and VERNICE T. NYE, *Music in the Elementary School*, 3rd ed. Englewood Cliffs, N.J.: Prentice-Hall, Inc., 1970. Chap. 3.

2

teaching children music

In order to develop musical learning in the fullest sense, it will be necessary for the teacher to select and develop objectives in these four major areas:

1. Music knowledges or content (data, concepts, and generalizations).
2. Cognitive process skills (inquiry skills).
3. Music skills.
4. Music attitudes and values.

While the teacher may choose to emphasize any one of the four areas on any given daily lesson or unit plan, it is likely that elements of all four will be present in most plans. The four areas of objectives are outlined below.

I. Music Knowledges or Content (data, concepts, generalizations)

    A. The Subject Matter Content of Music
       1. Expressive Elements
          a. tone qualities

       b.   tempo
       c.   dynamics
    2.   Constituent Elements
       a.   rhythm (duration)
       b.   melody (pitch)
       c.   harmony
       d.   form
  B.   The Structure of Music (concepts, generalizations)

II. Cognitive Process Skills Applied to Music

    A. Observing
    B. Comparing
    C. Classifying
    D. Collecting and Organizing Data
    E. Summarizing
    F. Generalizing
    G. Creative Thinking (synthesizing)
    H. Inferring from Data and Interpreting Data
    I. Hypothesizing
    J. Analyzing
    K. Evaluating
    L. Application

III. Music Skills

    A. Listening
    B. Moving to Music
    C. Singing
    D. Playing Instruments
    E. Reading Music
    F. Creative Skills

IV. Musical Attitudes and Values

    A. Choosing
    B. Prizing
    C. Acting on Decisions

The Pictorial Description of Music Learning indicates the four major categories of music teaching: the components of music as a discipline (content); music skills; musical thinking; attitudes, values, and behaviors. These form the framework from which the teacher selects justifiable objectives, then plans learning experiences which serve to promote them.

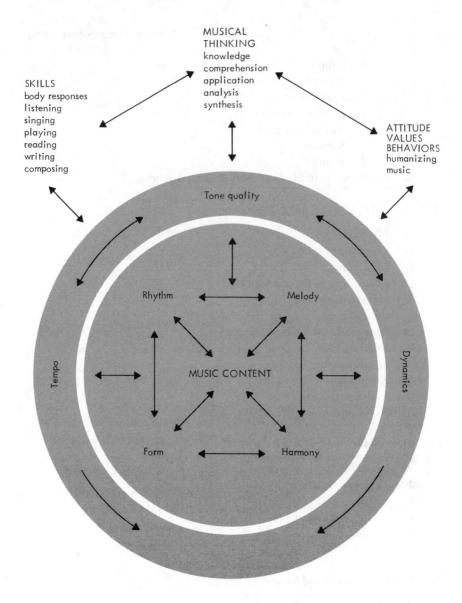

A Pictorial Description of Music Learning

Selecting Music Content

One of the major tasks confronting any teacher is the selection, organization, and sequencing of content of a music program for children. The teacher must choose portions of knowledge from the vast amount in existence. He will endeavor to select the most important and relevant information that will bring about maximum musical learning. This music content consists of data, concepts, and generalizations that make up the subject matter content of music, which Jerome Bruner calls the *structure* of a discipline. These three categories of knowledge are explained below.

DATA

Data refer to particulars rather than to universals. They are propositions or statements that include things or situations of the present or of the past. Data can be tested and proved to be true or false.

Examples of musical data (facts) are:

Bach died in 1750.

A sharp placed before a note raises its pitch one-half step.

In the same meter, a quarter note has the same duration as two eighth notes.

Some teachers place major emphasis on the learning of facts as ends within themselves. They fail to see the importance of using them as a foundation for organizing information into higher levels of knowledge. As a result, they may emphasize information of only minor import. Whether or not a fact is important to learn is usually determined by the context in which it is used. It is therefore important that students participate in learning experiences that help them tie together the facts they acquire to form more meaningful relationships.

If teachers wish to help students understand music more fully, they must do more than merely help them learn facts; they must also help them use facts to acquire a further understanding of knowledge at higher levels of conceptualization such as exist in concepts and generalizations.

CONCEPTS

Fraenkel states that concepts, unlike facts, "are definitional in nature. They represent those characteristics that are common to a group of experiences. Concepts do not exist in reality; they represent our attempts to give order to reality—to order that information from our environment that we receive through our senses. We attempt to bring order to this sensory input by attaching symbols (word-labels) to certain similarities we perceive in our experience.... Notice, however, that concepts are invented rather than discovered.... Concepts thus are mental constructions devised by man to describe the characteristics that are common to a number of experiences" which include those with musical phenomena heard, seen, and felt. "They facilitate understanding, for they make communication easier," thus reducing the complexity of the musical environment into manageable proportions.[1]

All concepts are not indicated verbally. Verbal or aural dimensions may lead one to experience a particular emotion or feeling that, although unnamed, is a concept. Perhaps later on the learner (perhaps a music listener) can analyze his reaction and name it, thus forming a concept that is more accessible and usable.

GENERALIZATIONS

Generalizations are statements that contain two or more concepts and that show relationships among concepts. Like facts, generalizations can be substantiated or disproved by referring to concrete or obvious evidence. Both concepts and generalizations aid children in organizing and seeing relationships in music.

Alfred North Whitehead stresses the importance of "main ideas" (generalizations) of subjects. He states that:

> The result of teaching small parts of a large number of subjects is the passive reception of disconnected ideas, not illumined with any spark of vitality. Let the main ideas which are introduced into a child's education be few and important and let them be thrown into every combination possible. The child should make them his own and should understand their application [to present and future music problems].[2]

From the very beginning of a child's musical experiences there should be the joy of discovery of knowledge. The discovery he needs to make is the mind-expanding generalization that he can use in the solution of his musical problems. Such main ideas or generalizations suggest relationships and offer insights into the way music is produced and into the ways it affects the life of man. They not only describe facts (data) but they give structure to them. Thus, careful consideration must be given by the teacher in the selection of valid and significant content objectives which include data, concepts, and generalizations. An example of concepts and generalizations from which to develop knowledge and/or content objectives follows:

[1]Jack R. Fraenkel, *Helping Students Think and Value* (Englewood Cliffs, N.J.: Prentice-Hall, Inc., 1973), see pp. 94–96.
[2]Alfred North Whitehead, *The Aims of Education and Other Essays* (New York: The Macmillan Co., 1929). Free Press paperback edition, 1967, p. 2.

MUSIC CONCEPTS AND GENERALIZATIONS

(This example is highly condensed; there are *many* more generalizations than are stated in it. The teacher seldom recites them to the children nor does he expect the children to form them in these words. In most cases they are to formulate concepts and generalizations from the data and express them in their own ways. The teacher uses the following primarily as guides to planning music lessons.)

Sounds and Tone Qualities

Generalizations: Some kind of sound can be produced by almost every object in the environment.

Tone quality (timbre, tone color) is the difference between tones of the same pitch produced by different voices and instruments; it distinguishes the sound of one voice or instrument from another.

Subgeneralization: Sounds, voices, and instruments can be classified according to tone quality, range, physical characteristics, and the means employed to produce them.

Concepts Classification of unconventional sound sources
  paper
  rubber
  glass
  wood
  metal
  plastic
  food
  materials found in nature
  body sounds
  other

Classification of conventional sounds sources
  voices
    soprano
    alto
    tenor
    bass

  instruments
    strings
      plucked
      stroked
      bowed
      keyboard

> woodwinds
>   flue
>   reed
> percussion
> brass
> organ
> electronic

Subgeneralization: Instruments can be played in ways that produce different sounds.

Concepts legato
          staccato
          spiccato, as concerns bowing
          mute, as concerns strings, trumpets, French horn, trombone
          vibrato
          use of extreme ranges of high or low
          stop, as concerns the organ
          glissando, as concerns the harp and other instruments
          experimental ways

Subgeneralization: Voices and instruments may be combined to produce an infinite variety of tone colors.

Subgeneralization: Composers and arrangers select different voices, instruments, and tone colors for specific reasons.

Subgeneralization: The difference in tone qualities can be explained scientifically.

Concepts resonance
          harmonics
          overtone series
          partials
          vibrato

Tempo

Generalization: Tempo (degrees of fast and slow) is found in all organized music.

Concepts

lento	(slow)
largo	(broad and slow)
andante	(moderately slow)
allegretto	(moderately fast)
allegro	(lively)
vivace	(spirited)
presto	(very fast)

a tempo	(in original tempo)
accelerando	(gradually faster)
rallentando	(gradually slower)
ritardando	(gradually slower)

Dynamics

Generalization: Dynamics (degrees of loud and soft) is a characteristic of most music.

Concepts			
accent > – ∧			(more than usual stress)
pianissimo	pp		(very soft)
piano	p		(soft)
mezzo piano	mp		(medium soft)
mezzo forte	mf		(medium loud)
forte	f		(loud)
fortissimo	ff		(very loud)
sforzato or			
sforzando	sf		(heavy accent)
crescendo	cresc.		(gradually increasing loudness)
decrescendo	decresc.		(gradually decreasing loudness)
diminuendo	dim.		(gradually decreasing loudness)
sign for crescendo:		——◁	
sign for decrescendo:		▷——	

Subgeneralization: There are relationships between changes of dynamics and tempo, and melody, harmony, and texture.

Rhythm

Generalization: Rhythm in music is a grouping of sounds and silences of varying duration, usually controlled by a regular beat.

Concepts beat
equal divisions of the beat
unequal divisions of the beat
one-to-two relation of note values
one-to-three relation of note values
one-to-four relation of note values
notated rhythm
dotted notes

rests
speech-rhythm
notated speech-rhythm
articulation such as staccato and legato
fermata ⌢

Subgeneralization: Musical sound has duration and pitch.

Concepts   word-rhythms related to duration
word-rhythms related to duration and pitch
notation of word-rhythms
notation of melody

Subgeneralization: Accent or lack of accent governs types of rhythm.

Concepts   metrical rhythm
meter, bar line, measure, upbeat (anacrusis),
downbeat, meter signature, duple meter, triple
meter, primary accent, secondary accent, rhythm pattern
asymmetrical rhythm ($\frac{5}{4}$, $\frac{7}{8}$, etc.)
"measured" rhythm (no regular recurring beat, such
as in Gregorian chant)
free rhythm
rallentando (rall.)
accelerando (accel.)
rubato
no common metrical beat (such as some Oriental, Indian,
and Hungarian music which cannot be expressed in traditional notation)
syncopation as a disturbance of the normal pulse of
meter, accent, and rhythm

Subgeneralization: Devices related to rhythm are used by composers to
add interest to their compositions.

Concepts   rhythm patterns
rhythmic ostinati
augmentation
diminution
canonic imitation
polyrhythm
free rhythm (rit., rall., accel., rubato, syncopation)
syncopation

Subgeneralization: There are rhythms which are characteristic of peoples
and nations.

Concepts   distinctive rhythms in national songs
distinctive rhythms in national dances
   (minuet, waltz, polka, schottische, square dance, etc.)
distinctive rhythms associated with ethnic groups

Generalization: Rhythm is universal and has meanings beyond music.

Concepts Rhythm in—
     the seasons
     waves of the ocean
     the grain of wood
     architecture
     painting
     the heartbeat
     day and night
     life cycles of plants and animals
     the speech and movement of man

Melody

Generalization: A melody is a linear succession of tones which are rhythmically controlled and are perceived by the human ear as a meaningful grouping of tones. (Children might say, "A melody is a line of tones in rhythm that sounds right.")

Subgeneralization: Direction: The tones of melodies may go up, down, or remain the same in pitch.

Concepts pitch and vibration
high and low
contour
relation to tension, climax, and release
notation of pitch
   staff, note, clef, numerals, and syllables to identify pitches

Subgeneralization: Duration: Melodies are formed by a union of pitch and rhythm.

Concepts relation of song melodies to word rhythms
note values (see Rhythm)
rhythm patterns in, or related to, melodies

Subgeneralization: The tones of melodies may have adjacent (scale-line) pitches or skips (chord-line pitches).

Concepts   scale (major, minor, diatonic, modal, pentatonic, chromatic, the tone row derived from the chromatic, wholetone, ethnic, invented)

passive and active scale tones (tension and release)

tonal centers

home tone

key

key signature

accidental

intervals

relation to chords (see Harmony)

Subgeneralization: Form: Melodies are usually formed of distinct parts or sections.

Concepts   phrase

phrase arrangement (repetition and contrast; unary, binary, and ternary song forms)

sequence

tonal patterns and their alterations

Subgeneralization: Devices: Melodies can be manipulated. (Children might say, "Melodies can be changed in different ways.")

Concepts   transposition

diminution

augmentation

inversion

retrograde

melodic variation

rhythmic variation

harmonic variation

Subgeneralization: Melodies may reflect national or cultural styles.

Subgeneralization: Some melodies are functional in that they tend to communicate ideas and moods.

Harmony, Polyphony, and Texture

Generalization: Harmony pertains to the vertical aspect of music, the successions of chords and the relationships among them. (Children might say, "Harmony means chords and their changes.")

Generalization: Texture, a term derived from weaving, pertains to vertical and horizontal elements ("threads") in music which produce such effects as light, heavy, thick and thin, and which include styles of composition such as homophonic and polyphonic.

Subgeneralization: Homophonic music consists primarily of one melody with an accompaniment.

Concepts accompanied song
accompanied instrumental solo
music of the nineteenth century
harmony suggested by chord tones in melodies

Subgeneralization: Polyphonic music has two or more melodic lines sounding at the same time; these melodic lines are connected in tonal music by harmonic relationships.

Concepts round, canon
counterpoint
contrary motion
fugue
fugal entry
music of Palestrina and J. S. Bach
harmony suggested by chord tones in melodies
descriptive terms: contrapuntal, imitative, canonic, fugal, atonal polyphony

Subgeneralization: A chord is any simultaneous combination of three or more pitches; some may be more agreeable to the ear than others. (Children might say, "A chord is three or more notes sounded together.")

Concepts Chord construction—3rds, 4ths, 5ths, clusters, contrived chords
inversions
relation to key centers
  triad
  scale
  major
  minor
  question and answer (V_7—I)
  cadence: full, half, plagal
relation to melody
  harmonizing a tune
  chord tones
  passing tones
  consonance
  dissonance
  primary and secondary chords
  chording

chords relating to no tonal center
atonality
chords as conjunctions of melodic lines
parallel chords

Subgeneralization: Identical harmonies can be sounded at different pitch levels.

Concepts transposition
key signatures

Subgeneralization: Harmonies can be combined.

Concepts bitonality
polytonality

Form

Generalization: Musical forms are similar to plans of construction made by architects.

Form in Music

Subgeneralization: Melodies may be divided into parts.

Concepts phrase
period
sequence

Subgeneralization: Melodies can be extended and altered.

Concepts introduction   diminution
coda   inversion
interlude   retrograde
sequence   thematic development
repetition   augmentation
section

Forms of Music

Subgeneralization: Most musical form is based on the principle of repetition-contrast (same-different, unity-variety).

Concepts a a
a b
a b a
A B A sections
rondo (A B A C A; A B A C A B A)
variation

Subgeneralization: Some forms can be classified as contrapuntal.

Concepts   round
             canon
             fugue

Subgeneralization: A compound form comes into being when several movements are combined to form a complete musical composition.

Concepts   movement (of a larger work)
             instrumental compound forms
               sonata-allegro
               concerto
               suite
                 classical dance
                 ballet
                 other
               symphony
               overture

When children explore music within the framework of such an outline as that presented above, they should be able to think musically. The good teacher remembers that children do not learn concepts by memorizing definitions. Instead, the learner develops the meanings of concepts through many and varied experiences and by selecting and using pertinent facts. This has an inductive nature about it. *Most generalizations are tentative;* they will be tested, refined, and explored further. The same "big idea" or generalization is frequently studied at all levels of instruction but at different depths of conceptualization. Bruner writes, "A curriculum, as it develops, should revisit these basic ideas repeatedly, building upon them. . . . "[3] Young children learn that "Sound and silence have duration," but such a generalization will be expanded, refined, and made more specific as these children study it again and again as they proceed through the elementary school years.

Children should be helped to formulate a definition of music. They should know that it is sound which is intended to be music taking place in time, and that it may be very simple or very complex. In its more simple forms music will contain only some type of sound in some type of pattern; in its more complex forms it may involve all of the elements of music.

[3] Jerome Bruner, *The Process of Education* (Cambridge, Mass.: Harvard University Press, 1963), p. 53.

COGNITIVE PROCESS SKILLS

Cognitive process skills include the following:

1. Collecting and organizing data—listing, grouping, and labeling.

2. Generalizing and making inferences from the data—comparing and contrasting (differentiating); interpreting data; making inferences; developing generalizations.

3. Application of knowledge—using what has been learned in new and different ways.

Essential to the development of cognitive process skills is the use of questions. According to research, teachers often fail to do more than ask questions at the data level—those that demand only memory-recall. If a teacher is to be able to guide the development of a child's ability to think critically he must be able to ask different levels and types of questions at the appropriate times.

Presented below is a chart adapted from Jarolimek and Bacon[4] which illustrates the use of questioning strategies in developing cognitive process skills.

QUESTIONING STRATEGIES
INVOLVING COGNITIVE PROCESS SKILLS

Task	Procedures	Illustrative Questions
Concept Attainment and Augmentation	Teachers can help children learn to form or augment concepts through asking questions which require children to: (a) summarize their observations; (b) help identify common properties (attributes) for grouping; and (c) label or define the grouping.	(a) *Observation* 1. What did you hear? See? Feel? Find? (b) *Grouping or Classifying* 1. What belongs together? On what criterion? (c) *Labeling or Defining* 1. What would you call these groups? 2. What belongs under what heading? 3. How would you name or label this?

[4]John Jarolimek and Philip Bacon, codirectors, *A Behavioral Approach to the Teaching of Social Studies.* Monograph, Tri-University Project in Elementary Education, Social Studies-Science (Seattle: University of Washington Press, May, 1968).

Task	*Procedures*	*Illustrative Questions*
Generalizing and Making Inferences from Data	Teachers can help children in forming generalizations and making inferences from data by asking questions which require children to: (a) compare and contrast data from different samples (differentation); (b) interpret the meaning of certain data; (c) make reasonable inferences based on the data itself; and (d) develop a generalization.	(a) *Comparing and Contrasting (Differentiating)* 1. What did you hear? See? Feel? Find? 2. What things are the same? Different? 3. How can you distinguish among things partly the same and partly different? (b) *Interpreting Data* 1. What does this mean? 2. How does it relate to other things? (c) *Making Inferences* 1. What can you infer from this? Imply? 2. What does the data suggest? (d) *Developing Generalizations* 1. What can you conclude?
Application of Knowledge	Teachers can help children in learning to apply knowledge by asking questions which require them to make application of facts and generalizations by: (a) exploring (b) focusing (c) interpreting data (extending ideas and perceiving relationships) (d) summarizing, concluding, or generalizing (e) verifying (verifying predictions, hypotheses, and inferences)	(a) *Exploring* 1. What will happen if we omit all rests when we perform this music? (b) *Focusing* 1. Why do you think that the first hypothesis could or would happen? (c) *Interpreting* 1. How could this change the _____? 2. What would be the consequences? (d) *Summarizing, Concluding, or Generalizing* 1. What can we say in general about our hypothesis (guess prediction)? (e) *Verifying* 1. Let's test (try out, perform) to find if it is possible that this will really happen.

The following lesson plan illustrates the use of various cognitive process skills. The teacher should not attempt to pattern all of his lesson plans after every step listed here, for some goals do not lend themselves to all of the processes. He should, however, include all that are applicable to his goals. The following plan is probably for eight- or nine-year-olds, depending upon their musical maturity. This plan can also be used as an example of how to organize a lesson based upon performance objectives. It incorporates the three essential parts of a correctly stated performance objective; it establishes the condition or situation for the behavior; it contains specific performance terms; and it indicates the criteria or degree of performance. To learn to state performance objectives in this plan, see p. 39.

LESSON PLAN

Content Goal: To teach the generalization that "regular accent determines meter."
Concepts to support the generalization: beat, accent, meter, meter signature (or time signature).

Situation: Asking the class to listen and observe, the teacher plays a drum or claps her hands with steady beat, sounding no accent.

Observing: "How would you describe what you heard?"
"Could you tell what the meter (time signature) might be?"
"Why not?"

Comparing: The teacher now repeats her performance except that she accents every other beat.
"How would you compare what you just heard with what you first heard?"
"What is the musical term for the stress I placed on some of the beats?"
Answer: Accent. "How often did I accent the beats?" (every other beat.)
The teacher repeats her performance, but accents every third beat. "Compare what I did this time with what you heard the other times." (We have now heard no accent, an accent on every other beat, and an accent on every third beat.)

The teacher writes what she did the first time on the chalkboard:

A child is asked to draw a short line either above or below the note stem as the teacher plays the example again, stressing every other beat:

The teacher again writes the series of note stems on the chalkboard and asks another child to come forward to notate accents. She now plays an accent every third note.

Classifying: How many classifications of accents do we now have? (three: no accent, an accent every other beat, and an accent every third beat.)

The teacher now asks a child to draw a barline before each accented note.

What meter signatures can we place in front of these examples?

(none for the first, ²⁄₄ [or ²⁄₂ or ²⁄₈] for second and ³⁄₄ [or ³⁄₂ or ³⁄₈] for the third.)

What names can we say that conform to these two-beat and three-beat meters?

Ma-ry, John-ny, Jack-son, Ok-la-hom-a

Mel-o-dy, Ros-a-lie, Jon-a-than

The class repeats each name a number of times while claping or stamping the accent. (Children suggest and experiment with others.)

Collecting and Organizing Data: The children open their music books and search for meters with two and three beats to the measure. These are listed on the chalkboard under each category.

Summarizing Statement: When a meter contains two beats, the two appears high in the meter signature; when a meter contains three beats, the three appears high in the meter signature. (An exception is fast $\frac{6}{8}$, which will be dealt with later.)

Recognizing Assumptions: The teacher says, "Some people say that all music 'swings' in two's or three's." "How can this be when some of the meter signatures you saw in your books were $\frac{4}{4}$ and $\frac{6}{8}$ and perhaps others?"

At this point, the books are opened again, and the children are helped to find that $\frac{4}{4}$ can be considered to be $2 + 2$, and $\frac{6}{8}$ to be $3 + 3$. The latter meter should be closely examined in the music, for $\frac{6}{8}$ meter is practically always written in such a manner that the measure can be divided to illustrate that $3 + 3$ characteristic (rather than a mathematically possible $2 + 2 + 2$). Meters such as $\frac{5}{4}$ and $\frac{7}{8}$ should probably be reserved for study at a future date when this information becomes necessary.

Creative Thinking: The teacher suggests that the class invent meters up to six beats in a measure.

The class invents and labels a number of meters by placing regular accents at different intervals by clapping, stamping, or using percussion instruments.

Inferring from the Data: Students state in their own words: accent determines meter; regular accents result in meter; there are many meters.

Analyzing: The teacher plays recordings of short selections that clearly denote $\frac{2}{4}$ and $\frac{3}{4}$ meters. The children are asked to "feel" the beats and accents, and determine the meter of the selections.

Application: The children find songs they like in their books and sing them with a "feel" for the meter; they might also conduct the meters. This will lead them to discover that some songs are more heavily accented than others, and that the strength of the accent is sometimes a matter of musical taste rather than a matter of musical mechanics.

MUSIC SKILLS OBJECTIVES

If students are to engage successfully in music learning activities they will need to learn a variety of music skills that will asist them in their growing understanding of music. Appropriate objectives should be developed in the following areas of music skills:

LISTENING   Listening is the basic music skill because learning the skills of singing, playing, and moving to music are dependent on the learner's ability to listen to, analyze, and appreciate music.

MOVING TO MUSIC   Young children learn music by moving their bodies to its salient characteristics as they listen to it. They need to experiment with free interpretation, characterization, dramatization, fundamental movements, singing games, and dances.

SINGING   Singing is one of the most satisfying of human activities. Children need to be able to sing on pitch with a tone quality suitable to the meaning of the words they sing. By the time they leave the elementary school they should possess the ability to sing independent parts of songs such as parts of a round, chants, and descants, and those necessary for harmonic part singing.

PLAYING INSTRUMENTS   The desire to manipulate musical instruments seems to be in all children; they ordinarily find great pleasure in playing instruments. Through performing on percussion instruments, bells, xylophone, and recorder, they can contribute to their understanding of rhythm, pitch, form, dynamics, tempo, and melody. By chording on the Autoharp and piano they can learn much about harmony and chord construction.

READING MUSIC   This skill relates to all the other skills in that music notation symbolizes what is heard and what is performed. There are music symbols for pitch, duration, meter, tempo, dynamics, and harmonization.

CREATIVE SKILLS   Children can create their own music in the same spirit that they create their own stories, poems, paintings, and dances. They can create a melody; they can make a song from a poem, add percussion parts as accompaniments and create percussion compositions; improvise vocally and instrumentally; and assist in group projects such as creating an operetta.

Following is a suggested outline of a plan for teaching skills.

LESSON PLAN FOR TEACHING SKILLS

The specific skill to be developed: _____

Performance objective(s) to be realized: _____

1. Description and Demonstration
   The skill is demonstrated or otherwise made known to the learners.
   a. The specific skill action is described.
   b. The skill may be demonstrated by a performer (such as the teacher or a skilled student) or by audio-visual means.

2. Trial to Assess Degree of Skill and Need for Improvement
   The learners are led to try out their present degree of skill in order that the teacher or the learners identify common errors or the general need for improvement.

3. Practice for Mastery
   The practice of the skill, how this is arranged for, and a listing of the drill activities. Remember that these are sometimes in the form of games.

4. Application or Assignment
   The use of the new skill in other settings, for variety, practical application, and for measurement of the degree of mastery of the skill by the learners.

OBJECTIVES IN MUSIC ATTITUDES, VALUES, BEHAVIORS

An attitude may be defined as a predisposition to react in a certain way to objects, ideas, or subjects. It may be rational or irrational.[5] Attitudes and values result from an individual's total experience. They are flexible, and change as the learner's experiences in living are expanded. They are therefore extremely personal.

When teachers plan for this kind of learning, Raths, Harmin, and Simon[6] suggest that teachers design objectives in this area that:

Encourage children to make choices and to make them freely.

Help them discover and examine available alternatives when faced with choices.

Help children discover what it is they prize and cherish.

Give them opportunities to make public affirmation of their choices.

---

[5]John Jarolimek, *Social Studies in the Elementary School*, 3rd ed. (New York: The Macmillan Co., 1967), p. 59.

[6]Louis E. Raths, Merrill Marmin, and Sidney B. Simon, *Values and Teaching: Working with Values in the Classroom* (Columbus, Ohio: Charles E. Merrill Books, Inc., 1966), pp. 38–39.

Encourage them to act, behave, and live in accordance with their choices. Help them to examine repeated behaviors or patterns in their own lives.

Research indicates that children's attitudes and values regarding music may reflect the attitudes of both the peer group and those of high-status adults. Thus it is possible that a child's music attitudes and values can be affected by contradictory musical influences emanating from adults and peers, and from radio, television, and recordings. At the same time, music teachers should not strive for nor expect that all children acquire the same set of musical values.

The attitudes and values of teachers are highly important in the instructional process. The chance remark of a teacher might have a lasting influence on a child. The teacher's personal attitudes toward music will usually affect children's valuing more than formal class presentations on learning to value.

Teachers should work toward a classroom environment in which the varied opinions of children toward the many different types of music are listened to with interest and defended with musical knowledge when necessary. (Why did you like or dislike this music?) Such an environment permits disagreements that can be expressed in ways that permit personal differences while arguing intellectual points in support of positions taken. Musical values and attitudes toward music cannot be separated entirely from respect, concern for the feelings of others, and the acknowledgment that people can hold differing views—especially in a classroom situation in which there is neither hostility nor aggression. An intellectually sound position for a teacher to take is one that attempts to judge "good" music in accordance with how well it performs its function, and to operate in a climate of openness that admits the exploration of every type of music to attempt to find out what it is used for, how it is constructed, what values are reflected in it, and how good it is in its category.

The students' feelings about and interest in a learning experience determine to a significant degree what they learn about a subject cognitively. What a person learns cognitively and affectively *cannot be separated.* The affective domain influences every part of the learning and evaluation process.

Finally, all sensitive teachers want children to enjoy and appreciate music. They know that when children like music, music takes on a personal meaning for them. Teachers also are aware that when children are involved personally with composing, conducting, experimenting with and interpreting music that they learn more readily and that they are inclined to appreciate and value music.

Even though the development and evaluation of objectives in the affective domain are somewhat more difficult to design, they should be included in planning for music instruction.

Designing Plans for Teaching and Evaluating

Thinking in terms of the four areas of objectives described above, the teacher plans the music program for the entire year. He studies state and local music guides; obtains information from the principal and fellow teachers; studies appropriate records of each child to find out his musical background and level of competency. Then he formulates the major goals to be developed in the year immediately ahead. He considers local, state, and national events, seasons, holidays and special days to determine to what extent content related to these special events can be included in the year's program. He will locate all available music materials and examine them to see which of these he will use. He will incorporate flexibility into the details of his planning so that the children can make some decisions and choices. He will also realize that there should be continuous planning progressing from week to week and from one day to the next, within the framework of his formulated plan for the year.

In order to make plans, it is necessary to know the amount of time allocated to teaching music. Minimum time allotments for music vary among states and among school districts. It is obviously difficult to designate specific time allotments in self-contained classrooms where the teacher, in addition to scheduled time for music, integrates it when appropriate into all areas of the curriculum throughout the school day. This is especially true in nursery school, kindergarten, and first grade.

The types of plans also vary in accordance with the objectives, the type of school, and type of classroom organization. The use of objectives as a basis for sound planning for the teaching of music is expained below.

OBJECTIVES AS A BASIS FOR PLANNING

Traditionally teachers have considered the teaching of music as a series of specific activities such as keeping time with the music, singing, and playing instruments, with too little thought as to the objectives or purposes for these activities. Therefore music has tended to remain a vaguely defined and poorly evaluated discipline. The teaching of music can be greatly enhanced by stating objectives in performance (or behavioral) terms which indicate precisely ends toward which both teacher and student are moving. Included below are explanations of performance objectives, a guide to writing them, and examples of them.

PERFORMANCE OBJECTIVES

It is common practice to state objectives in behavioral terms. Teachers who state objectives behaviorally think of them in terms of the learner's performance; thus one might consider them to be performance objectives. An example might be, "After examining, discussing, and listening to different types of instruments, the children will be able to identify all common reed instruments both by their appearance and by their tone qualities." This is much more precise than if it were written as: "The reed instruments will be studied at the fifth grade level," because it is stated in language that enables the teacher to measure in observable terms whether or not, or to what extent, the objective has been achieved. The performance objective incorporates a means of evaluation by indicating specifically what a child will be able to do as a result of his learning experience and to what degree of mastery. A practical way to identify such an objective is to ask, "Specifically, what and how much will the children be able to do under the stated conditions?"

GUIDE TO FORMULATING PERFORMANCE OBJECTIVES

All correctly stated performance objectives contain three essential factors which can be used in formulating and evaluating them. They are as follows:

1. Designate in performance terms *what the learner will do.*

2. Include stated *conditions* under which the desired behavior will take place.

3. Indicate the *criterion or standard of accomplishment* for acceptable performance.

The three factors are included in this example:

After listening several times to a tape that presents the sounds of the common orchestra string instruments and their names (*setting conditions*), the learner will arrange pictures (*what the learner will do*) of all of these instruments in correct order (*standard of accomplishment*).

Evaluate the following objectives, identifying the three factors. If one of them is missing, supply it.

Tone Quality.

Identify 80 percent of the various instruments by name as a recorded selection is played; tell whether one or more instruments are sounding.

Dynamics.

Listen to a tape and recognize loudness and softness in music by clapping or stamping feet in similar volume.

Rhythm.

The children will clap, beat time, rock body to different tempos as they are played on selected recordings. As the class sings familiar songs, create rhythm patterns with percussion instruments or clapping.

First draw attention of the pupils to rhythmic sounds heard in their environment; then they will identify the sources (ambulance, siren, clock striking, pneumatic drill). From a chart containing several representative quarter and eighth note patterns, the children will clap the rhythm patterns correctly.

Melody.

As the teacher hums several songs or themes the children will identify the songs by name.

While listening to selected recordings the children will indicate by dramatizing with body responses that melodies differ from one another (high, low, happy , sad, etc.)

The children will compose their own melodies and sing or play them.

Harmony.

Signal chord changes while listening to melodies accompanied by the I and V_7 chords.

Listen to a selection and tell whether it consists of only a melody or a melody with accompaniment.

Form.

Signal awareness of contrast and repetition of melody or rhythm pattern by holding arms together for repetition and holding arms outstretched for contrast.
The class will identify the forms as either ABA or rondo when they hear them in unfamiliar recorded compositions.

Reading.

Given a four-measure phrase of notation which consists of note patterns previously studied, the children will sight-sing the phrase.

Attitudes and Values.

Describe verbally or demonstrate physically:
1. Which musical selection the learner likes best. Why?
2. Explain what part of a musical selection he likes best.
3. Tell which music moves slower. Do you like this kind of slow music? Why or why not?
4. Which music is softer? Why do you think the composer wanted it to be soft? Would you rather that it would have been loud? Why?

If after doing this drill you yet have difficulty with performance objectives, refer to the Mager reference at the end of this chapter.

It should be obvious, however, that all a child has learned in any given lesson will not be demonstrated immediately in performance terms. When he has had other experiences to combine with the ones he has in the lesson, perhaps during the next day or week there may appear observable performance evidence of the things explored in the lesson. This is one of the criticisms aimed at the "immediate feedback" claim of those who champion the performance objective. Futhermore, some critics believe that individual initiative and creative learning are sacrificed through a too-strict application of these objectives. However, this should not happen if a well-designed lesson plan based upon performance objectives provides freedom and flexibility to use a variety of resources, both planned and spontaneous. Having specifically designed plans should in no way prevent children from enjoyment and spontaneity in their music learning. A teacher remains free to sense and use possibilities arising in incidental ways for the developing of childen's capacities. Plans can be designed that involve children in creative inquiry and self-discoveries. There is no doubt that lesson plans containing specifically stated objectives can give direction and purpose to learning.

FUNCTION OF WEEKLY PLANS

In designing weekly plans the teacher formulates or selects general objectives which guide the learning of musical concepts, skills, thought processes, and attitudes and values. He indicates in outline form types of teaching procedures and learning experiences appropriate for realizing the stated objectives. He also outlines possible ways of involving individuals and in providing a balance among the types of music learning experiences. He selects music materials and media most appropriate for the realization of the chosen objectives. He then assembles the materials and media he will need for the week.

Weekly plans serve as a framework and guide to the development of specific lesson plans. Learnings mastered in any lesson are related to the solution of problems and objectives in the subsequent ones, thus providing meaning, sequence, and continuity to learning. The weekly plan is divided into a series of lesson plans which include more specifically stated objectives (usually performance objectives), teaching procedures, pupil learning experiences, materials and media, and ways to evaluate and/or measure pupil progress.

DESIGNING LESSON PLANS

The most effective plans are designed to free the teacher to establish a learning situation in which the children can become involved in the exploration of music and in autonomous learning. Teachers sometimes become slaves of rigid plans which emphasize musical content and musical skills as ends within themselves. Overly rigid lesson plans can be a major cause of a pupil's lack of interest and consequently in his limited learning of musical concepts. It is impossible to present a specific model of a lesson plan to be used in all music classes because a lesson plan must be tailor-made for a specific group of children in terms of their maturity, background, interest, and capability. Nevertheless, essentials of any sound lesson plan can be specified and they should be incorporated in creative and pertinent ways in most organized plans. These essential parts are indicated below:

1. *Performance (Behavioral) Objectives.* These are drawn from the four areas of instruction: music content, cognitive process skills, music skills, and attitudes and values, and state *what* is to be learned and under what conditions. They also identify in performance terms when possible what the learners are to do and designate the criteria or standards by which their performances are evaluated.

2. *Methods and Materials.* This step is concerned with *how* to teach the lesson and with what materials and equipment will be needed to develop the lesson. It includes procedures—the use of questions to guide inquiry, activities to initiate the lesson and to develop it, individual and/or group activities, and materials and media to be used to realize the stated objectives.

3. *Summary and Evaluation.* In this final step the lesson is assessed as to the extent the stated objectives have been attained. Those not realized may be included in subsequent lessons.

Extensive introductions to lessons should be avoided. Children want to be actively involved in making music; they tend to lose interest in a lesson in which verbal introductions are lengthy. Proper timing is essential to capture maximum interest.

The first lessons of the year for ages 8–12 are usually informal, being centered around pleasurable singing and getting-acquainted experiences. They might include something like the following:

First Day.   Sing familiar songs.
What did you learn to sing at camp last summer? Can you teach it to us?
What are your favorite songs from last year?
Common repertoire songs.

Second Day.   Review familiar songs; try to add something new to them. Discover or invent a rhythm pattern to be used with percussion instruments with a song.
Learn a new song.
Begin to utilize songs or parts of songs for individual and group tone matching.

Third Day.   Sing familiar songs.
Make up a tune for a short poem.
Introduce a new recording for listening purposes; create some appropriate
physical responses.

The following *Suggested Form for a Lesson Plan* is one designed to emphasize concept development. (Also see the example of a plan to teach concepts, p. 36.)

Suggested Form for a Lesson Plan for Teaching Concepts

Date _____

Name _____

State the Generalization or Main Idea to which the concepts to be taught

in the lesson relate: _____

Musical Content— *Concepts and* *Related Data*	*Performance* *Objectives*	*Teaching Strategies* *(Learning Experiences* *and Teacher's Questions)*	*Materials*

		A. Introduction
		  1. Question(s)
		  2. Activities
		B. Development of work-study activities and pertinent questions
		C. Questions and activities for concluding or formulating generalizations from the lesson.	

OTHER PLANS

Lesson plans vary in complexity from the extremely simple to the highly intricate. However, the entire subject of lesson plans is complex because plans that are simple in design can be intricate in their development. A plan in which one song, one recording, or one rhythmic response appears is usually too brief or too monotonous (because of the many repetitions of the single musical experience that takes place). It is also likely that individual differences cannot be well accommodated in such a plan. Experienced teachers have learned that it is essential to a good plan that more than one music activity be employed in order for children to respond to and analyze music in different ways. Many college teachers refuse to accept a one-idea plan, although some do when they are the initial attempt of a student. However, it is understood that as later plans are designed, they will reveal the student's ability to organize more complex plans in which several of the music skills appear.

A good source of materials of instruction for lesson plans is the "Music Examples" section of a book edited by Charles Gary.[7] Specific songs with their sources, specific recordings and other examples are stated in relation to concepts being developed. The simple one-song or one-recording plan is exemplified by some of the suggestions offered by Bergethon and Boardman;[8] however, these are intended to be incorporated into more complex plans. Wheeler and Raebeck[9] present suggestions for plans of different levels of complexity. The student can profit from examining such plans and applying the following criteria when revising them for their own purposes.

CRITERIA FOR LESSON PLANS

While there are always some exceptions, most lesson plans can be evaluated by applying the following criteria:

1. The teacher has definite objectives that are clearly stated. These come from one or more of the *four areas* of music instruction: music subject matter, cognitive process skills, music skills, and attitudes-appreciations-values.

2. The teacher's objectives are, as far as possible, stated in performance terms in order that evaluation is built directly into the plan.

3. There is a variety of activities presented in logical sequence that employ all appropriate senses—the ear, eye, and muscular response.

4. Activities are balanced in terms of intake types (such as listening, viewing, and reading), and expressive types (such as performing and creating).

[7]Charles L. Gray, ed., *The Study of Music in the Elementary School—A Conceptual Approach* (Washington, D.C.: Music Educators National Conference, 1967.)

[8]Bjornar Bergethon, and Eunice Boardman, *Musical Growth in the Elementary School*, 2nd ed. (New York: Holt, Rinehart and Winston, Inc., 1970.)

[9]Lois Raebeck, and Lawrence Wheeler, *New Approaches to Music in the Elementary School*, 2nd ed. (Dubuque, Ia.: Wm. C. Brown Company Publishers, 1969.)

5. Individual differences are accommodated.

6. The teacher's key questions are stated.

7. The students will be kept active mentally and/or physically during the entire lesson.

8. Each activity has been selected to assist in the realization of a specific objective.

9. The plan contains routine procedures such as what all participants are to do when the children or teacher enter and leave the classroom. Distributing books, finding pages in books, getting instruments ready to play, and sounding the first pitch are some of the aspects to be planned. For example, if song titles and page numbers are on the chalkboard, both time and the teacher's voice can be saved.

10. The plan lists all necessary materials of instruction needed for its implementation.

Evaluation

The purpose of evaluation is to appraise both children's musical growth and the teacher's success. Appropriate means for evaluating all aspects of musical growth—knowledges, skills, cognitive processes, and attitudes and values—should be utilized. The objectives to be realized become the basis for and the guide to evaluation.

Musical understanding can be revealed behaviorally by students' ability to manipulate the elements of music in creative work: making up songs, instrumental pieces, codas, introductions, interludes, descants, harmony parts, and variations. Ability to improvise can be a means of assessing musical sensitivity and taste. Musical knowledge is frequently demonstrated through written tests on factual items such as terms, symbols, forms, notation, and information about composers. Tests of more complex types measure both knowledge and understanding. In such tests, children prove their understanding by using facts and concepts to solve musical problems. The level of attainment in music performance abilities can be observed, as can skill in moving to music. Note reading skills are observed when children sight sing or sight read music, and when they write notation in response to pitch dictation, which is also a listening skill. Students' ability to analyze music aurally is a measure of their skill in listening, while their ability to analyze music from the printed page is a measure of their understanding of notation. Attitudes and habits are reflected by degrees (tastes and amounts) of liking music, participating in it, reading about it, and in musical activities outside of school. Habits are revealed through singing, playing instruments, writing music creatively as a hobby, improvising music, listening to recordings and worthwhile radio programs, viewing worthwhile television programs, and attending concerts.

By stating the objectives behaviorally and by evaluating the child's ability to behave and perform in certain ways, there is immediate "feedback" to the teacher and to the learner of his accomplishments in music knowledge, skills, cognitive thought processes, and habits, attitudes and values. Obviously the child's goals are in a state of constant adjustment as he matures and advances in musical growth.

In order to evaluate learning in the four areas of objectives it is necessary to use a variety of evaluative means. Some possible means of evaluation are as follows:

observations	discussions
check lists	charts
samples of creative work	performance activities
aural analysis	visual analysis
dramatizations	role playing
attitude scales	teacher-made tests
questions	standardized tests
recorded performances	

Everyone who is involved with the learning of music should have a part in evaluating it. Administrators, parents, other adults in the community, teachers, and pupils should work together in this process. The teacher has the leading role, serving as a guide in this cooperative endeavor. Children learn best when they are given opportunities to identify what they are to learn, plan how they are going to learn it, and appraise how well they have succeeded.

IN CONCLUSION

When the teacher begins planning, it is wise for him to ponder the warning of Charles Leonhard not to overemphasize the intellectual aspects:

> We should exercise caution in abandoning the goals we have worked toward under the often vague term appreciation. One danger that I see in the current emphasis on concepts and structured learning is that we may

become so involved in the specifics and minutiae of music that we forget that the musical experience is basically an affective experience. Whatever else it may achieve, music loses its value when it fails to touch the hearts and stir the feelings of people.[10]

The above words urge the teacher to consider children's appreciative responses to music and to realize that they are often of non-verbal character. This is part of affective learning—the feelings and emotions aspect. Music is always a reflection of humanity; its technical aspects should assist this means of communication. It is necessary to be reminded of this in a day when stress is being placed on concept development and the structure of disciplines. *Music is an aesthetic experience and a social language as well as an intellectual experience,* and the good music teacher never forgets this when he plans the music lesson.

Summary

In this chapter, the authors identify and explain the four major areas of objectives. The teacher is advised to include objectives from all four areas in organizing a balanced and effective music program. There is also included a list of concepts and generalizations to assist in teaching music knowledges; a model illustrating questioning strategies in the development of cognitive process skills; and a guide presented in outline form to be used in designing lesson plans for teaching music skills. How to design plans for teaching and evaluating is discussed, with objectives as a primary basis for planning. The performance (behavioral) objective is defined and a guide is presented to assist the teacher in formulating them. Various designs of lesson plans are described, with a list of criteria for their evaluation. Finally, evaluation in general is discussed.

REFERENCES

BERGETHON, BJORNAR, and EUNICE BOARDMAN, *Musical Growth in the Elementary School.* 2nd ed. New York: Holt, Rinehart and Winston, 1970. Contains lesson plans.

[10]Excerpt from an address by Dr. Charles Leonhard at the Conference to Improve the Effectiveness of Music Education in Oregon Elementary Schools, Gearheart, Oregon, April 27–28, 1967. State Department of Education, Salem, Oregon.

CARIN, ARTHUR A., and ROBERT B. SUND, *Developing Questioning Techniques.* Columbus, Ohio: Charles E. Merrill Books, Inc., 1971.

COLWELL, RICHARD, *The Evaluation of Music Teaching and Learning.* Englewood Cliffs, N.J.: Prentice-Hall, Inc., 1973.

FRAENKEL, JACK R., *Helping Students Think and Value.* Englewood Cliffs, N.J.: Prentice-Hall, Inc., 1973.

GORDON, EDWIN, *The Musical Aptitude Profile.* Boston: Houghton Mifflin Co., 1965. Designed to assess musical aptitude in grades 4–12.

GARY, CHARLES L., ed., *The Study of Music in the Elementary School: A Conceptual Approach.* Washington, D.C.: Music Educators National Conference, 1967.

HUNKINS, FRANCIS P., *Questioning Strategies and Techniques.* Boston: Allyn & Bacon, Inc., 1973.

KIBER, ROBERT, *Behavioral Objectives and Instruction.* Boston: Allyn & Bacon, Inc., 1970.

LEONHARD, CHARLES, and ROBERT W. HOUSE, *Foundations and Principles of Music Education.* 2nd ed. Chap. 6. New York: McGraw-Hill Book Co., 1972.

MAGER, ROBERT F., *Preparing Instructional Objectives.* Belmont, Calif.: Fearon Publishers, 1962.

NYE, ROBERT E., and VERNICE T. NYE, *Music in the Elementary School.* 3rd ed. Chaps. 4, 5, 6, 19. Englewood Cliffs, N.J.: Prentice-Hall, Inc. 1970.

RAEBECK, LOIS, and LAWRENCE WHEELER, *New Approaches to Music in the Elementary School.* 2nd ed. Dubuque, Ia.: William C. Brown Company Publishers, 1969. Contains sample lesson plans.

RATHS, LOUIS E., et al., *Values and Teaching: Working with Values in the Classroom.* Columbus, Ohio: Charles E. Merrill Books, Inc., 1966.

SIDNELL, ROBERT, *Building Instructional Programs in Music Education.* Englewood Cliffs, N.J.: Prentice-Hall, Inc., 1973.

WILHELMS, FRED T., ed., *Evaluation as Feedback and Guide.* Washington, D.C.: Association for Supervision and Curriculum Development, 1967.

part two

Part One was devoted to organizing the classroom for learning, the objectives of music teaching, and planning and evaluating music instruction. Part Two will present many learning experiences for inclusion in lesson plans, most of them devoted to ways to approach the elements of music and music skills.

If the college teacher wishes to follow the chapter organization, he will find all of the elements of music dealt with in Chapter Three in ways that do not require the use of books or recordings, in Chapter Four in ways that emphasize the use of songs and pitched instruments, and in Chapter Five in ways that reveal the uses of recordings and films. This organization is a reflection of a spiral curriculum in which the same subjects are studied repeatedly in new ways in order to expand the understanding and knowledge of the concepts under consideration.

If the college teacher prefers to organize his instruction in a manner that deals with the elements of music separately, he can utilize the sections of each of the three chapters that deal with tone quality, dynamics, tempo, rhythm, melody, harmony, and form. In this instance the index is helpful in providing the page numbers of these sections. The index is helpful in other ways also. For example, although the music of other cultures is stressed in Chapter Five, some aspects of this subject are found in the other two chapters; the index will guide the reader to these pages. This will be true of other items.

3

an introduction to
teaching strategies

This chapter is concerned with teaching strategies that usually require no books or recordings in the hands of the learner or the teacher. This approach is generally rather easy to develop. It provides for individual initiative, imagination, creativity, and flexibility, and is designed to instill confidence in the prospective teacher of music. Later chapters will examine strategies that require songs, pitched instruments, and recordings. However, no matter what the classroom activity is, the college student is never to lose sight of the reasons for employing it. The teaching strategy will always relate to the content of the four areas of learning described in Chapter Two.

The college student is asked to keep in mind that there is no *one* way to teach music; there is no simple recipe that applies universally. The mainstream of United States music education has always been eclectic—that is, it views the teaching of music as being made up of an amalgam of strategies selected by the teacher from many different sources. At the conclusion of the methods course the college student should possess knowledge of a variety of methods and activities to select from and to adapt to the particular student or group of students the student teacher or the professional teacher will guide.

Beginning with easy things to do in studying sounds and tone qualities, this chapter will proceed with suggestions for working actively with tempo, dynamics, duration (rhythm), pitch, harmony, and polyphony. The college teacher and his or her students can select from the suggestions to follow those that are the most profitable for their purposes; teachers in service may find ideas new to them. *All can add their own invented strategies* as their experience grows in finding better ways to help children learn music.

The order of difficulty in the lists of activities is ordinarily from easy to increasing difficulty. In most instances they are listed beginning with those for young children and proceeding to those for older children. When it is not possible for the college student to help elementary school children with the activities, the college class can be a substitute for the children. The college student who takes the teacher's role should plan for the learners' success when he guides them in music learning experiences. The degree of success should be evaluated in terms of the specific overt behaviors of the learners. Did they perform the activity successfully? To what extent did they master it successfully? If success was not attained, the class can analyze what occurred and suggest ways to make success possible.

The first activities are those developed by the Manhattanville Music Curriculum Program. They encompass one type of approach to music teaching—that of musical discovery, invention, and composition. It is an approach that is easy to initiate and can be adapted to any age group. Like all methods, it requires some years to develop its full potential. Aspects of it should be experimented with in the methods class in order that the college student understands how musical learning takes place when the learner is actively involved in making his own music. For a complete explanation of this approach to music teaching of young children aged 3 through 8 read *MMCP Interaction: Early Childhood Music Curriculum*, Media Materials, Inc., P.O. Box 533, Bardonia, New York 10954.

Sounds and Tone Qualities

Conceptual Idea	Learning Experiences For Young Children 3–8
Sounds are everywhere.	While in the classroom or on a short field trip have children listen to and describe sounds of the environment. "Are they high, low, soft, loud, dull, short, steady, rumbling?, etc." Vocabulary is needed in order to express sound and tone qualities.

Our bodies can be used to make sounds. Have children explore the many sounds that can be made with the body. These will include clapping hands, slapping thighs, snapping fingers, rubbing palms, stamping feet, clicking tongue, hissing, "shh," and others. Ask that several of these be organized into a short composition. When it has been practiced it can be tape recorded and played for the children's evaluation.

Imitating sounds. Children can imitate sounds better than many adults. Have them imitate sounds from their environment such as fire sirens, police cars, birds, garbage trucks, and jet planes. Develop a repertory of sounds to draw upon later. Try to avoid the stereotyped sounds adults have built into the child's world such as "oink, oink" and cock-a-doodle-doo" because these are not authentic imitations of animal sounds. Let the children create their own.

Objects can produce different kinds of sounds or tone qualities. In order to increase sensitivity to tone qualities, ask young children to identify sources of sounds in listening games. The teacher might use a cardboard screen to hide the sound source. Suggestions of such sources might include those such as an egg beater, air escaping from a balloon, pouring water, crinkling paper, as well as more conventional sounds.

After children know the game, they can be assigned in pairs to develop sounds they can challenge the class to identify. Later on the teacher can make the game more complex by producing somewhat different sounds from the *Vibration.* same object. Children might discover that some percussion instruments should normally be held in a way in which they are free to vibrate.

Analyzing instrument sounds. With young children select for example a tambourine and make sounds with it. Ask questions such as "Can it sing a song?" (no) "Can it play softly?" (yes) "Can it play loudly?" (yes) "Does it make jingling sounds?" "Can it make a short sound?" "Can it make a long sound?" After this, find uses for the tambourine in a song or as a sound effect in a story. Do the same with other instruments.

Percussion instruments can be classified in many ways.

Young children can classify percussion instruments in accordance with the type of sound. Which instruments click? ring? jingle? swish? rattle? boom? Which instruments have sounds that are light? heavy? medium? This activity can relate to the functions of instrument tone qualities in accompanying songs and recordings. Older children might use adult classifications and decide to group percussion instruments under headings such as membrane, hollow, solid, and keyboard. Let children suggest other possible classifications; there are many more.

Sounds can be the same or different.

The teacher prepares a number of sound producers *in pairs* to assist young children to recognize similarities and differences in sounds. There may be identical-sized jars or cans or plastic containers with the same and different numbers of peas or beans in them. Some could contain pebbles or marbles or beads. The task is to shake them, listen to them, and classify the pairs that sound alike.

Tone qualities relate to sound effects.

Young children can decide upon the suitability of specific instruments or other sound sources for sound effects. They can select them to correspond with characters in stories such as The Three Bears, Three Billy Goats Gruff, and Three Little Pigs. (Older children can create stories in sound such as "My Day," "A Storm in the Mountains," "A Day at the Seashore," "A Haunted House," "Halloween Night,"

"Space Journey," and "Little Red Riding Hood.")

Every voice sounds different.

Plan for young children to listen to different speaking voices in the class. With eyes closed, can these voices be identified? Plan such listening games, emphasizing the uniqueness in the vocal sounds of each person. Encourage children to classify the speaking voices in terms of low, medium, and high. Children can relate these to choric reading that emphasizes differences in the tone qualities of the speaking voice.

MMCP Interaction.

The material to follow explains in brief the strategies involved in the Manhattan Music Curriculum Program for children aged 3 through 8.

Music consists of sounds and silences presented in some organized manner.

The *free exploration* of sound sources (paper, metal, body, rubber, plastic, glass, and materials from nature) is recommended. This comprises the first of a series of steps that lead to experiences with every component of music. The second step is *guided exploration*, in which the teacher encourages the children to find additional

There are many kinds of sounds. Sounds can be classified.

sounds, to find more ways to produce sounds (this involves skills), to label new sounds (this involves vocabulary), to classify new sounds in various ways, to listen and react to sounds produced by other children and by the teacher, and to learn to respect the efforts of others. The purpose of evaluation is not to point out failure, but to clarify and extend children's ideas and judgments. The teacher assists the children's learning by such actions as presenting clues and examples, presenting words, asking questions, showing pictures and other types of illustrative material, and presenting musical examples. Contrasting words (walking-running, crawling-skipping) suggest different movements in time; those such as whispering and shouting suggest different dynamic levels and different ways of producing sounds.

Sounds can be organized and related.

Step three is *exploratory improvisation.* The child is encouraged to repeat sounds he enjoys and to relate them to other sounds. This relationship might be contrasting sounds, through which the child may learn that contrast can heighten the expressive implications of sounds, or it might be that by combining two or more sounds a new and different effect can be achieved.

Two or three people may produce more varied music than only one person.

Step four is *planned improvisation.* In this phase children are to be gaining performance and memory skills necessary to produce compositions that are aesthetically satisfying. They are guided by the teacher to organize groups of sounds into meaningful musical ideas, to identify the ways these sounds are arranged, to criticize constructively the arrangement of the sounds, and to use this experience to suggest other ways of improvising their own music.

We can compose music as individuals or in small groups.

The teacher accepts and works with whatever the child produces, regardless of its quality, remembering that these exploratory experiences are important and real to the child, and that the type of learning is basically intrinsic, not dictated by the teacher. After a trial run of a student composition, teachers might ask questions such as: "How do you know when to start and stop?" (This helps them to discover the need for a conductor if they do not have one.) "Do you have a leader?" "Did you hear a change of tempo?" "What kinds of sounds did you hear?" "Did it sound the way you wanted it to sound?" "Would you want to change this piece if you had a chance to do it over?" "Are you satisfied with it?" The composing and performing of a composition can bring into focus problems in duration, pitch, tone quality, dynamics, and tempo, and teach compositional techniques such as the *ostinato* in a practical setting that is honest and logical to the child.

The fifth step is *reapplication.* As the child continues to compose his own music, he will discover and find need for all the component elements of music as well as skills in musical notation. First he will find a need to save his composition, and he will invent his own notation for this purpose. Eventually standard notation will be necessary for him to do what he wants to do with his musical ideas. When children are trying to invent their own notation, teachers ask questions such as: "What if you wanted to show a thin texture in your music?" (Use a thin symbol.) "What if you wanted to show a thick texture?" (Use a thick symbol.) "What if you wanted to show low?" (Use the bottom of the page.) "High?" (Use the top of the page.) "Short?" (Use a short symbol.) "Long?" (Use a long symbol.) "Rising pitch?" (Use a rising symbol.) "Silence?" (Use a blank space, a circle, or?) "Falling pitch?" (Use a descending symbol.)

This same type of beginning in musical learning can be used by the older children also. Even the junior high school student can enjoy the thrill of experimenting freely with music.

There are immediate problems with this approach, one of which is the noise factor. MMCP calls this "creative fallout." As the group work expands, there must be space for the children to work, and in many schools this is not easily found. However, many teachers have discovered that children are able to concentrate in group composition while all groups are in the same classroom, one group in each of the four corners while others occupy the center area. The size of the group will vary in accordance with the assigned task. It can be from two to six, with four and five commonplace.

MMCP Interaction suggests that the teacher can organize the activity so that at a given time the class will explore sounds coming from paper, metal, or the voice. Other possibilities include those made by rubber, glass, plastic, outdoor materials, and other sound sources. It states possible questions the teacher might ask to stimulate interest and creativity.

The following example is reproduced from *MMCP Interaction*.

ALTERNATE SERIES: Metal Encounters

Phase I—Free Exploration

Instructional Objective: To explore a wide variety of sounds using metal sound sources.

Procedure: 1. Place a variety of metal objects, such as old kitchen utensils, large nails, horseshoes, pipes of varying sizes and lengths, metal bars, keys on a key ring, pans, pan lids, tea trays, empty coffee cans, etc., in a place designated as the sound materials center.

2. Encourage pupils to select and explore the objects for sounds. This may be done on an individual basis during the course of the school day, or pupils may select metal objects and share sounds in groups.

3. After adequate time for initial sound explorations, the following questions may serve to stimulate discussions of the sounds:

Were any sounds alike? If so, how were they alike?

Why were some sounds different? Could the differences be described?

Pupils will identify the differences and similarities in sounds in many different ways, including the physical techniques involved in performing them, relating sounds to personal experiences, and their acoustical characteristics, i.e., timbre, pitch, duration, volume.

4. Suggest that pupils find other metal objects, metal toys, pie plates, paint cans, etc., to add to the sound materials center.

5. All new objects should be explored for the variety of sounds they can produce.

Phase II—Guided Exploration

Instructional Objective: To explore a wide variety of metallic sounds and sound-producing techniques.

Procedure: 1. Invite pupils, as a class or in small groups, to find two very different or contrasting sounds with the metal objects they have selected from the sound materials center.

2. Allow an appropriate amount of time for exploration.

3. After individual pupils perform their sounds, other group members or the entire class should attempt to imitate the two contrasting sounds on other metal objects.

4. Discussion during and after performance and imitations may deal with the following:

How was the sound made? Did the beater make a difference?

Can the sound be made in any other way? Are any imitations exactly the same?

Note: A few minutes of exploration may be desirable before volunteers are ready to imitate a performed sound.

5. Pupils should be given two or three minutes of exploration time to investigate each of the following questions posed by the teacher:
What kind of sounds can you find that remind you of a clock ticking; water dripping; a baby walking; a father's heavy footsteps; a ball bouncing; teeth clattering; a horse galloping; a snake crawling?
6. After each question and a period (two or three minutes) of pupil exploration, volunteers can be invited to perform their sounds.
7. After all sounds have been performed and taped, listen to the tape and try to identify the sounds, i.e. clock ticking, snake crawling, etc.

Phase III—Exploratory Improvisation

Instructional Objective: To explore a variety of ways of producing and combining repeated patterns.

Procedure: 1. Pupils should select three sounds which they can play over and over again in the same manner with metal objects.
2. Allow an appropriate amount of time for selection of sound sources and sounds, and for rehearsals of the desired patterns.
3. As a class, or in small groups, listen to the repeated patterns performed by individual pupils.
4. Discussion can be centered on the following: Were any of the sound patterns difficult to repeat? Why?
If some were difficult to repeat, can you suggest an easier way of playing them?
Which two patterns do you think would sound well together (one after the other)?
5. Experiment with combinations of sound patterns as suggested by the pupils.
6. Tape combined performances of repeated patterns for immediate playback and discussions.
7. Play for the students some recording contain-

ing a repeated pattern of metallic sounds, such as the *Symphony of Machines—Steel Foundry* by Alexander Mosslov.

8. Discussion of the listening example can be focused with the following questions:

What did you hear? Did you hear any repeated patterns?

How could we build a sound machine?

Phase IV—Planned Improvisation

Instructional Objective: To arrange repeated patterns in ways which are expressive and meaningful.

Procedure: 1. Build a sound machine. A sound machine is a game in which a number of sound patterns, organized in various sequential combinations, aurally represent the moving parts of an imaginary machine. The patterns developed in the previous encounters may be used, or new patterns may be investigated.

2. Pupils may work in groups of three, four or five, or the teacher or volunteer pupils may construct a sound machine by conducting members of the class in a sequential performance of their patterns. Students may wish to physically display the motions of the machine as well as their sounds.

3. Tape all the performances for listening and comparison of the differences and similarities.

Were the sound machines different? If so, how were they different? If not, what could we do to make the sound machines sound different from one another?

Were the sound machines the same in any way? If so, how were they the same?

4. When appropriate extend the discussion with the following:

Were the conductors satisfied with their results?

Did performers do what was expected of them?

If not, discuss how better results might be achieved. Pupils should lead these discussions as much as possible.

Note: In order to successfully control entrances and exits of groups of performers, pupil conductors may have to develop simple gestures for starting and stopping performers.

5. The following questions posed individually during follow-up encounters may stimulate further thought and experimentation:

What would happen if,

some patterns or sounds were played at the same time?

all metal objects were silent some of the time?

the sound machine slowly broke down rather than suddenly stopped?

we had two sound machines—a big one and a little one?

MMCP Synthesis.

For students aged 9 and older, the Manhattanville Music Curriculum Program has resulted in another publication, *MMCP Synthesis.* This consists of a spiral-type curriculum that considers the elements of music on gradually advanced levels called "cycles." As in *MMCP Interaction* composing of music on the child's level is the major activity. The students compose, conduct, perform, and evaluate music. Sample strategies are suggested for teaching music at 12 levels (cycles). These begin with the same type of sound exploration described earlier, but move quickly into compositions that are taped in order that the composers and the class can hear them and evaluate them.

In cycle 1 the student begins with activities such as finding sounds made from objects in the classroom, performing different sounds from the same object, and experimenting with dynamics (degrees of loud and soft) and with combinations of sounds, adding a steady beat to ordered combinations of sounds. In each of the suggested activities, the book suggests questions to ask the students and recordings of music of all types and times that are intended to stimulate interest and furnish information needed by the student composers.

It is of importance that the college class experiment with some of the sample lessons provided in *MMCP Synthesis* in order that the prospective teacher understands this type of approach to learning music. It stresses children's understandings of the following aspects of music: timbre (tone quality), dynamics (degrees of loud-soft), duration (degrees of long-short and rhythmic elements), pitch (including melody, harmony, and polyphony), and form. The teacher is assigned the task of being a guide, a creator of problems to be solved by the children, and a resource person. He is to stimulate rather than dominate, and to encourage rather than to control. He is to question more than answer, and he is to be sensitive both to children and to the art of music. His classroom is to be a laboratory in which children act as musicians who have a world of sound to explore.

Examples from *MMCP Synthesis* follow.

SAMPLE STRATEGY

Cycle 1. The quality or color of sound, the timbre, is a major factor in the expressiveness of music.

Each student selects an item or object in the room with which he can produce a sound. Preferably, the item or object will be something other than a musical instrument.

After sufficient time has been allowed for students to experiment with sounds or selected objects, each student may perform his sound at the location of the item in the room.

Focus on "listening" to the distinctive qualities of sounds performed. Encourage students to explore other sound possibilities with the item of their choice.

Discuss any points of interest raised by the students. Extend the discussion by including the following questions: How many different kinds of sounds were discovered?
Could the sounds be put into categories of description, i.e. shrill, dull, bright, intense, etc.?
After categories of sound have been established, experiment with combinations of sounds.

Is there any difference between sounds performed singly and sounds performed in combination?

In listening to the recorded examples focus on the use of timbre.

How many different kinds of sounds were used?
Could we put any of the sounds in this composition into the categories we established earlier, i.e. bright, dull, shrill, etc.?
Were there any new categories of sounds?
Could we duplicate these?

ASSIGNMENT: Each student should bring one small object from home on which he can produce three distinctly different sounds. The object may be a brush, a bottle, a trinket or anything made of wood, metal, plastic, etc.

Suggested Listening Examples:
Steel Drums—Wond Steel Band; Folk 8367.
Prelude and Fugue for Percussion—Wuorinen, Charles; GC 4004.
Ballet Mécanique—Antheil, George; Urania (5) 134.

SAMPLE STRATEGY

Cycle 1. The pulse is the underlying beat that may help to create a feeling of motion in music.

Allow 30 seconds for each class member to think of an unusual vocal sound. The sound can be made with the throat, voice, lips, breath or tongue. Each student may perform his sound for the class. Focus "listening" on the distinctive qualities of the vocal sounds performed.

Discuss any points of interest raised by the students. Extend the discussion by including some of the following questions:
Did anyone perform his sound long enough to communicate a feeling of motion?
How would you describe the motion?

Divide the class into groups consisting of 4 or 5 students. One person in each of the groups should be a conductor. Each group will concentrate on producing their individual sounds to the motion of an item of their choice or one which has been suggested to them, i.e., the steady motion of a carpenter hammering a nail, the steady motion of a worm crawling, the steady motion of a person jogging, the steady motion of a horse galloping, etc.

Allow approximately 10 minutes for groups to plan and practice their improvisations. At the end of the designated time each group will perform.

Tape each improvisation for immediate playback and analysis. Discuss any comments made by the students. Extend the discussion by including the following questions:
How would you describe the motion, slow, medium, fast?
Did it have a steady beat or pulse?

Summarize the discussion by introducing tempo as the characteristic which refers to the speed of music and pulse which is the underlying beat (sometimes not heard but only sensed).

In listening to the recorded examples focus attention on the use of tempo.
How would you describe the tempo—slow, medium, or fast?
Did the pulse or underlying beat change before the end of the composition? What was the effect?

Suggested Listening Examples:
Flight of the Bumblebee—Rimsky-Korsakov, Nicolai; Epic LC 3759.
String Quartets Op. 76, No. 5, No. 79—Haydn, Joseph; Turnabout TV 34012S.

Music can be improvised by a conductor.

The teacher distributes from 4 to 6 percussion instruments having contrasting types of tone qualities. A student conductor will establish a steady beat, then will point to those children who are to play, cueing the players in and out, having them play alone or in combination. From this experiment should come interesting sound sequences and an attempt to organize a composition. This can be done with an entire class by assigning specific instruments to groups.

New or unusual sounds can be produced when tone qualities are combined.

The teacher selects four sound producers, either invented ones, simple instruments, or a combination of these. Each sound producer will have a distinctively different tone quality. Assign groups of children to combine them in a musical score, experimenting with the sounds singly and in combination. It may be necessary to devise notation to "preserve" the composition.

Acoustics.

Some advanced older children may wish to explore acoustics. Relating music and science, the teacher helps them study resonance, harmonics, the overtone series, partials, and vibrato.

Percussion score.

Assign children the task of filling in a blank score as a musical composition.

Percussion Score in 5/4 Meter

	1 2 3 4 5	1 2 3 4 5	1 2 3 4 5	etc.
Triangle				
Tambourine				
Wood block				
Bongo drums (or small drum)				
Conga drum (or large drum)				

Rhythm

There is no definition of rhythm that can describe all of its aspects. However, rhythm can be said to be everything pertaining to the duration of musical sound. This would automatically involve such concepts as duration, beat, accent, articulation, meter, divisions of the beat, and, when written, note values.

A Swiss musician, Emil Jacques-Dalcroze, found in the early part of this century that unless rhythm is first felt by the entire body, the would-be musician might produce music mechanically, without feeling, thus never develop the responsiveness essential to genuine musicianship. By moving to music, children can learn to hear music with perception, to respond to it with imagination, and to explore the expressive ideas it contains. Teachers should keep in mind that it is *unnatural* for children to sit quietly for long periods of time. They need to move, and this need can be fulfilled in relation to music.

Fast-slow (tempo) and soft-loud (dynamics) are among the first music-related concepts young children are helped to learn. The teacher can help each child discover his natural tempo by playing a drum or piano, or clapping in time with his steps as he walks across the room, or as part of a game. After the relation between his step and the sound the teacher makes has been learned, the child will be able to govern his steps in accordance with the tempo the teacher performs, and can then walk slower or faster as the beat dictates. Body movement, percussion instruments, and clapping are used to develop the concepts *accelerando* (gradually faster), and *rallentando* and *ritardando* (gradually slower), with English words taught first, then the internationally-used Italian terms.

Loud and soft are easily-learned concepts, and from them are gradually acquired concepts of relative degrees of loud and soft. Percussion instruments and hand clapping can assist in learning about *crescendo* ——— (gradually louder) and *decrescendo* or *diminuendo* ——— (gradually softer).

DYNAMICS AND TEMPO

(Refer to these headings in the Musical Knowledge or Content of Music listing in Chapter Two).

Soft, loud.

The teacher plans simple activities with clapping, stamping, and listening that exemplify degrees of soft and loud, beginning with those that are unmistakable and progressing to lesser degrees of difference. Among the almost infinite possibilities are body movements such as soft and loud walking, and soft and loud hand clapping.

Slow, fast.

Many teachers use imitations of animals to teach these concepts. For example, the teacher claps or plays on a percussion instrument a slow rabbit hop and the children hop in time with the sound. Then the teacher claps or plays faster to describe the rabbit running away; the children imitate. A

Heavy-slow.
light-fast.

slow elephant walk might be played for the children to imitate. Then an imitation of a bird walking might be played. All of this leads to more animal rhythms and eventually to animal songs that continue the study of fast-slow and heavy-light. (A snail was selected by some young children as the slowest animal to imitate.)

BEAT, DIVISIONS OF THE BEAT, RHYTHM PATTERNS

Beat (pulse).

The teacher adapts clapping, a drum beat, or piano improvisation to the natural rhythm of the learner's walk.

Beat.

After children have learned to respond physically to a steady beat, they are asked to dramatize an activity that is done to a steady beat, such as chopping wood, shoveling snow, hammering, sawing, and rowing. They will do dif-

Fast, slow.

ferent dramatizations in appropriately different tempos, adding to their concepts of fast and slow.

Heart beat.

Find, feel, and imitate the heart beat. Have children find out when the heart beats slow or fast.

Beat.

Discussion. Adults are apt to overlook or underestimate the need children have for a great deal of experience with the regular and continuous beat that is characteristic of most music. To the adult this regular beat may seem too simple for much consideration, thus some teachers tend to give it too little attention. The result of this becomes obvious when children have difficulty in marching, keeping in step, or walking in a natural rhythmic manner. Physical growth, personality development, and musical growth are interrelated here.

The ear, the eye, and the body are employed in building the concept of the beat. As the child sees, hears, and feels responses to the beat, he learns little by little to be "in time." He feels the beat through body responses and by playing percussion instruments. He feels it with his whole body by walking, marching, swaying, hopping, clapping, slapping thighs, and by making other hand, arm, and foot movements. He also feels it by speaking words that reflect the beat and its divisions. He sees others respond to the beat and he sees it pictured in simple forms of notation such as:

| | | ⊓ | |

Beat.

Dramatize the beat by walking, "How many different ways can you walk?" (tired, slow, lightly, fast, heavily, like a toy soldier, like a rag doll.)

Notating the beat.

After young children have learned to walk in time with the beat, ask them to draw their original pictures or notations of the beat.

Beat.

Utilize rhythmic speech with rhymes such as "Hickory Dickory, Dock," and "Sing a Song of Sixpence," speaking the words and clapping and/or walking the beat on the word syllable accents.

Eighth notes.

Dramatize running. "How many ways can you run?" (as if in a race—fast, as if you are tired—slow, jogging, quietly so no one will hear you, etc.)

2-to-1 relationship.

Select children's names that have one and two syllables. Have children speak the names while drumming or clapping on the first syllable:

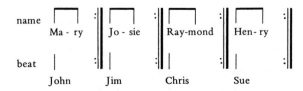

Drum talk.

The child plays his name on a drum as he speaks it. Other children answer, speaking and playing their names. The experience is heightened by using two drums, one of high pitch and the other of low pitch available to each child as he speaks and plays. Example:

After this experience has been absorbed, the child can begin to use drum talk to say things such as:

Two such statements can be combined as an experiment in sound.

Fundamental movements[1]

The teacher improvises with drum or piano; the children respond with the appropriate motion: walking, running, skipping, galloping, hopping, swaying, rowing, as they are able. When the piano is used, the black keys provide an easy way for the nonpiano player to improvise acceptably. Galloping is done with one foot kept ahead of the other, the back foot being brought up to meet it. Children pretend they are ponies or horses. See pp. 241–245 for a brief discussion of fundamental movements and a list of related recordings.

Divisions of the beat.

The teacher writes a simple quarter note or quarter-and-eighth note pattern. Children first act it out in their own original ways. Then they write it on paper either with the *ti-ti ta*

---

[1]Robert E. Nye and Vernice T. Nye, *Music in the Elementary School*, 3rd ed. (Englewood Cliffs, N.J.: Prentice-Hall, Inc., 1970), pp. 183–85. Contains a more detailed explanation of the fundamental movements.

notation or with invented symbols such as large and small circles:

Notation.

| | | ⊓ | ◯ ◯ o o ◯
ta   ta   ti - ti   ta

Beat.

Have the class speak the words of "Hickory Dickory Dock" in a steady, slow tempo. After the class knows the words well, ask half the class to be the clock, speaking "tick, tock" steadily on the beat while the rest of the class speaks the words of the nursery rhyme. Convert these parts into clapping in which half the class claps the "tick tock" beat while the other claps the rhythm of the words. Try this with other rhythmic nursery rhymes. Limericks can be fun, too.

Divisions of the beat.
(eighth notes)

Teacher and children can make up patterns for the class to read with the *ti-ti ta's* and with percussion instruments. Example:

Triplet (tri-ple-it).

| | | | |⊓ | ⊓ | || | | | | |⊓⊓| ⊓⊓| || | ⊓ | ⅔ ||

Find many interesting words to write in this simple notation. Examples:

⊓ | ⊓ ◻ | ⊓ ◻ ⊓
Mich - i - gan   State   Al - a - bam - a

⊓ ◻ ⊓ ◻ ⊓ ◻ ⊓
Choc - o - late   Val - en - tine   Ko - ko - mo

Rest.

Young children can be helped to understand *rest* by the use of sheets of colored paper.

■ ■ ■ ■   (Red)

◻ ◻ ◻ ◻   (Pink)

Learn about rests by removing a sheet or sheets of paper.

Accent.

Learn about accent by the use of two shades of any one color.

Then go into any meter the teacher wishes.

Divisions of the beat.

Use paper cutouts for note values.

then and so on

Children play games by arranging these note values and performing them. However, the note groupings cannot be larger than the whole sheet as illustrated by the whole note.

Beat.

The class beats a slow steady beat with clapping, pounding lightly on desks, or with percussion instruments while each child says his name twice in time with the beat. Next, the class translates the rhythm of some of the names into the *ti-ti-ta's* and the *tri-ple-ti's.* The teacher selects some of these to be written in quarter and eighth note abbreviated notation (without note heads). This last step requires that names be screened by the teacher because some demand a complexity beyond the present ability of the children to notate them. In such cases a nickname might be substituted, or only a first or a last name would be used. The class could chant the complex names but not notate them at this time.

Quarter rest.

The quarter rest can be introduced by challenging the children to invent a motion to do when there is no sound on the beat:

| | | | |

| | |

| | | |

| | |

Rhythm pattern.
Percussion score.

Young children can invent percussion scores through use of word rhythms such as:

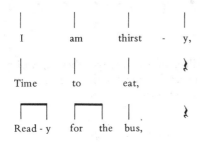

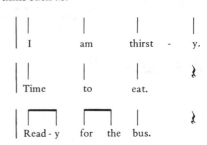

Such patterns can be transferred to percussion instruments, hand clapping, thigh slapping, etc.

Rhythm pattern.

One child creates a rhythm pattern within limits set by the teacher, such as using only *ta* and *ti-ti*. A second child creates a different one that "fits with" the first one. The two patterns may be written on the chalkboard; the students and/or the class plays or claps them in sequence, then in combination. Percussion instruments of contrasting tone qualities may be selected to play them.

Improvising patterns.

Game: Establish a steady beat in a specific meter. Give each child in turn an opportunity to clap a pattern to "fit with" the beat. Each pattern must be different from that anyone else has clapped. ¼ meter would probably be an easy one to start with. Each child continues clapping his pattern until the result equals the amount of complexity the class can absorb, then the game begins again. The teacher may wish some of the improvised patterns notated. They can be transferred to percussion instruments for further exploration of pattern, combinations of patterns, and their instrumentation.

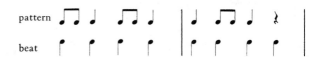

pattern

beat

Rhythm pattern.

Utilize words whenever they can assist children's comprehension of the pattern. Examples:

violet, daffodil, peppermint, bumblebee

marigold

water-lily

"Sit in a circle and clap your hands"

wisteria

Divisions of the beat.

Let children manipulate colored sticks or colored sheets of paper cut in sizes to represent the relative values of whole, half, quarter, and eighth notes. Students are to arrange sticks or paper into various combinations with the stipulation that no combination can be of larger size than the largest stick or sheet. Students can place these on the floor and walk or step them as they count the beats of the measure. More advanced students can chart short songs in this manner.

Divisions of the beat.

Use *Threshold to Music* Experience Charts, First Year, charts I-XI. These assist the understanding of the beat, and quarter note, eighth note, and quarter rest values. The teacher plays a series of measures by beating a drum. The children respond by translating these into the *ti-ti ta's.*

"Which one did I clap?" The teacher asks children to identify the measure he claps:

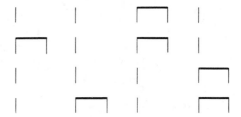

Note values and note reading.

"Which one did I play?" The children select the correct rhythmic grouping or pattern from six different small cards or small charts at their desks or from six large charts on the wall. This can be done in traditional notation.

Rhythm pattern and note memory.

Use flashcards with simple rhythm patterns. The teacher shows a card, then conceals it. He then asks the class to clap it, thus promoting note memory.

Note reading.

The teacher writes a test for the class to clap. The notation he has written has two objectives, note reading and irregular meter, the latter a characteristic of some contemporary music. Older children are to establish the beat, then clap. The teacher invents others of this type, and the class continues to meet the challenge of reading them and clapping them.

Words, rhythm, and notation.

"Rain, rain, go-away," is *ta ta ti-ti ta*, or

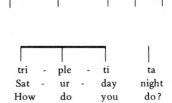

Triplet.

tri	-	ple	-	ti	ta
Sat	-	ur	-	day	night
How		do		you	do?

4 to 1 relationship.

From this beginning the learner can eventually use and understand the concept of four-to-one or

Sixteenth note.

ti	-	di	-	ti	-	di	ta
huc	-	kle	-	ber	-	ry	pie

and its variants:

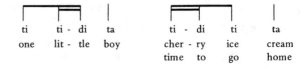

ti	ti - di	ta		ti - di	ti	ta
one	lit - tle	boy		cher - ry	ice	cream
				time	to	go	home

Rhythmic verse can be notated.

Percussion instruments, clapping, and the use of feet can be added to enhance the rhythm and add to the interest—for names can be "said" with feet and instruments. The teacher should be alert to the fact that most of these word-rhythms can be altered according to different ways of accenting words. Several different rhythms can be correct for one word. Rhythms of some radio and television commercials are interesting to work with; they have the advantage of being well-known by the children.

Divisions of the beat.

Experiment with clapping one note value while stepping another note value with the feet.

Rhythm patterns.

Experiment with clapping a simple rhythm pattern while doing another one with the feet.

Echo clapping.

Echo-clapping is one appropriate introduction to rhythmic instruction because normal children of school age have the physical coordination to do it with ease (although a few six-year-olds need to be taught how). If children can imitate the teacher's clapping perfectly, the teacher knows that they are comprehending the rhythms he claps and that they possess the physical coordination to respond. Children of all ages are interested when the teacher suddenly says, "Listen to what I clap; then you clap it." First establish the beat, then:

Soon children will be able to clap improvised patterns to be echoed by the class.

Question-and-answer clapping.

Another interesting type of echo-clapping is the question-and-answer, in which the teacher or a child claps a rhythmic question to be answered creatively, such as:

Clapping in canon.

This activity leads to discovering and creating questions and answers in melody, and to increasing comprehension of the phrase.

Later on, echo-clapping in canon form can develop rhythmic memory. In this activity the class echoes perhaps one measure behind the leader and in so doing must (1) remember what was clapped and repeat it later *while at the same time* (2) hearing and remembering what the leader is doing at the moment. For example:

Leader

Class

Children can take the part of the leader, and percussion instruments can be used instead of the clapping or along with it.

Responses to note values.

After children have learned to respond to note values in the above ways, they can analyze the notation of simple songs by clapping, speaking, and stepping. Songs such as "Hot Cross Buns" can be studied in this way by young children.

walk   walk   step-bend   walk   walk   step-bend

run-run   run - run   run-run   run - run   walk   walk   step-bend

ACCENT AND METER

Accent.

Use selected words to discover accent. Examples:
    mu-sic   a-rith-me-tic   ge-og-ra-phy

Regular accents result in meters.

Try accenting beats grouped in two's and three's:

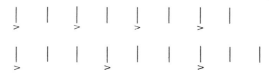

(This can be related at once to familiar songs.)

Words can help too:

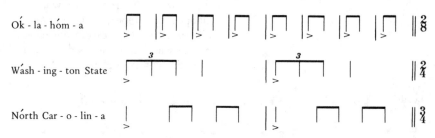

Ok - la - hóm - a

Wásh - ing - ton State

Nórth Car - o - lin - a

Such examples can introduce children to the concept that in normally accented music, the bar line is placed *before* the heavily-accented beat, and that variety in rhythm can be accomplished in any meter by changing the accents to accommodate a different meter for a time. For older children:

There are many meters.

Invent a number of meters by placing regular accents at different intervals by clapping, stamping, or using percussion instruments.

$| \, | \, | \, | \, | \, | \, | \, | = \frac{1}{4}$

$| \, | \, | \, | \, | \, | \, | \, | = \frac{2}{4}$

$| \, | \, | \, | \, | \, | \, | \, | \, | = \frac{3}{4}$

$| \, | \, | \, | \, | \, | \, | \, | = \frac{4}{4}$

$| \, | \, | \, | \, | \, | \, | \, | \, | \, | = \frac{5}{4}$

$| \, | \, | \, | \, | \, | \, | \, | \, | \, | \, | \, | = \frac{6}{4} \text{ or } \frac{6}{8}$

Inventing responses to meter.

Ask children to invent ways to respond to the beats and accents in various meters. Possibilities:

²⁄₄ touch knees, then head

¾ touch knees, hip, forehead

⁴⁄₄ clap above head for the first beat, clap normally (opposite chest) for the second beat, slap thighs for the third beat, and touch knees for the fourth beat.

For all meters: push both hands high into the air for the first beat and pull back for the other beats.

Changing meters.

Assign children the task of composing a percussion score with an unusual meter pattern such as one measure each of ¾ and ⁴⁄₄ in succession throughout. Try other "different" meter combinations.

Meters can be conducted.

This activity is done in relation to familiar songs.

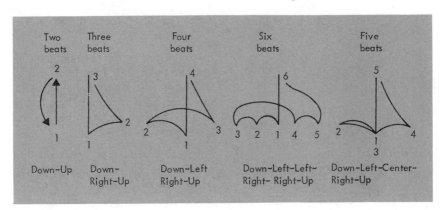

One of the Dalcroze exercises consists of children's conducting different meters while marching. Although marching is ordinarily done to duple meter, it can be done to triple meter, as testified by some Spanish marches in ¾ time.

Syncopation.

Syncopation can be introduced and explained by using a song the children know, such as "Li'l 'Liza Jane."

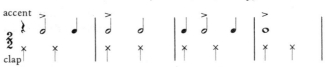

The children should be able to deduce with the aid of the teacher's questioning that while the clapping is regular because it is on the beat, the accents are not. They may be able to discover that syncopation takes place when the accent falls on a part of the measure not usually accented. Some people call this a *displaced* accent. After this, the children may wish to employ syncopation in their percussion compositions. They can experiment with syncopation in several ways:

Writing accent marks on beats not normally accented. Beginning a measure with an eighth note followed by a quarter note.

Using a tie to connect a weak beat with a strong one:

Placing a rest at the beginning of the measure as in "Li'l 'Liza Jane."

Ordinarily, the longer the note value, the more stress it receives (the louder it is in relation to the other shorter note values).

Polyrhythms.

Polyrhythms result from unlike rhythms sounding at the same time. They can be introduced by word rhythms.

Children can write simple polyrhythmic scores to play, tape record, and evaluate in class.

Accent, meter, patterns, form.

Utilize dance. Children can create dances based upon specific accents, meters, rhythm patterns, and forms.

Some dance improvisations based on these elements can be done by couples with hands on each other's shoulders. Traditional dances can be learned, and their notated rhythm patterns can be observed and related to body movement. See pp. 120–121.

Composers' devices.

In today's music education older children have an interest in and a need for some of the devices utilized by the adult composer. The terminology may seem complex at first, but it is all rather simple when explained. Consider the terms *augmentation* and *diminution*. To augment something, one makes it bigger; to diminish something, one makes it smaller. This is what happens in rhythm. If a young composer is writing a score for percussion instruments and selects the pattern

to begin with, he finds that he can, if he chooses, apply diminution by making this pattern one half its original value and repeating it. Writing this down, it looks like this:

The extension of the original pattern adds to the feeling of tension he wants to create. He might follow this with an application of augmentation by making the original twice its size in time. He then would have constructed a four-measure composition from one pattern, a composition which built up to a climax, then produced a feeling of release. Next he utilizes a canon treatment of his pattern to add more to his composition, and assigns this to the woodblock. He decides that a continuous eighth-note pattern played by maracas would add a certain stability and help unify his piece further. He then chooses to be daring enough to experiment with polyrhythms by adding a hand drum playing quarter note beats in ¾ meter. Now his composition is complete. He has done as many adult composers would do—used diminution, augmentation, canon, and polyrhythms. All he needs now is a group of his classmates to read, perform, and evaluate it. Learning *can* be exciting, creative, experimental, and intellectual—all at one time.

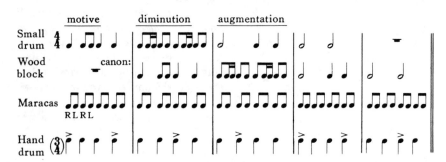

The above ¾ is written in ¼ meter by using the bar lines of the other parts. The accent dictates the true meter.

A rhythmic idea can be altered in a number of ways:
Play it louder or softer (changes in dynamics).
Play it faster or slower (changes in tempi).

Augmentation.   Use augmentation (make note values proportionately longer).

Diminution.   Use diminution (make note values proportionately shorter).

Instrumentation.   Use other instruments to change the tone quality or sound effect.

Syncopation.   Place accents in different places than they usually occur.

Rest.   Omit some notes; substitute rests.

Composing with a tape recorder. Let older children record a variety of sounds and rhythm patterns. These might include singing, playing instruments of various types, percussion sounds, and sounds of the environment. Then let them splice the tape to result in unexpected changes of sounds. Finally, let them change the speed of playing the tape to further alter the sounds. This activity should be related to recordings of electronic music such as *Dripsody* by LeCaine and other compositions on the Folkways record *Electronic Music* (FM 3436). The tape loop can be experimented with also. The activity described here would take place over a rather long period of time in most instances.

Melody

PITCH AND SINGING

Most teachers think of teaching pitch in terms of children's ability to match pitch with their singing voices. Actually, inability to sing a prescribed pitch does not prove that a child cannot hear pitch differences. It probably means that the child has not yet learned *what it feels like* to sound his voice in unison with a given pitch. Thus, one of the teacher's objectives in helping a child to match pitches with his voice is to provide the child with this kind of experience. The most common vocal problem teachers are confronted with is that of the child's low-pitched speaking voice coupled with his temporary inability to sing comfortably at the pitch range in which the teacher wants the class to sing, usually "too high" for the child. Research has revealed that for many children a generally lower pitch is more conducive to pleasurable and successful singing than is a generally higher pitch.[2] It has revealed further that successful singing with a wider range of pitches develops from permitting the child to sing in his own natural range, and working with his voice to gradually expand that range— usually upward. The important principle to remember is that there exists great individual differences in the vocal ranges of children. The task of the teacher is to recognize and know the different ranges of voices present and to ac-

[2]Dorothy Wilson, "A Study of the Child Voice from Six to Twelve" (Unpublished dissertation, University of Oregon, 1970).

commodate them in plans for singing. Fortunately this can be done without too much difficulty. It does, however, do away with the idea that all young children can sing in the same vocal range. Let the class sing the song at times in the natural range of one of the "low" singers. Let the low singers sing a chant (vocal ostinato) along with a song—a chant that is in their lower range. Much difficulty can be avoided at the beginning of the school year if the selected songs are within the range of middle C to the G or A above, or from B flat below middle C to G. Most children can sing easily in those ranges. After successful singing in these beginning ranges has been accomplished, the teacher then places familiar songs in gradually higher keys to increase the common range until most children can sing to at least the D or E flat near the top of the treble staff.[3]

There will be a few children who have natural high voices. These children will enjoy singing high parts, and can be assigned high descants or group solos to show the other children that (1) every child has his own natural range, and (2) it is possible to sing high pitches easily. In whatever range the child sings, it should be one that does not cause strain. The teacher can observe this in facial expression and neck muscles. When strain occurs, she will know that further analysis of that child's range must be made, with a resulting change in his assigned part.

For children of nursery school age (3 to 5), the first vocal range used for unison singing is usually that of the five scale tones within the interval of a fifth such as from middle C up to G. Kodály wrote a book of songs for young children in this restricted range beginning with the D above middle C up to A.[4] The next step is to expand this to a sixth. There are many well-known songs within that range, which could be from C up to A, or B flat up to G. It behooves teachers of any level in the elementary school to use such songs on the first days of unison singing in a school year.

To help children we must find ways for them to *listen* for pitch and pitch changes. The following activities are presented here to assist teachers with things to do other than with song books or recordings. The teaching

---

[3]A study by Adock found that "the composite unison boys' vocal range" is from B below Middle C to C sharp a ninth above. Eva J. Adock, *A Comparative Analysis of Vocal Range in the Middle School General Music Curriculum*, (The Florida State University, Ph.D., dissertation 1970). University Microfilm #71–6925. The boys tested were from grades 5–8.

[4]Zoltán Kodály, *Fifty Nursery Songs*, trans. Percy M. Young (New York and Toronto: Boosey & Hawkes Publishers Ltd.) See also Denise Bacon, *Let's Sing Together!* (Wellesley Hills, Mass: Kodály Musical Training Institute, Inc.).

of songs and their utilization in learning music will be stressed in Chapter Four.

Tone qualities and pitch.

To progress toward control of the singing voices, teach for tonal perception. Review activities in the "Sounds and Tone Qualities" · section of this chapter that pertain to differentiating between sounds, identifying and classifying sounds. Game: Children turn their backs to the teacher, identify the sound producer, and tell which pitch of two sounded is high or low. Later, ask them to match the pitch with their voices *if the pitch is in their normal singing range.*

Vocal imitation.

Ask children to imitate vocally by singing, whistling, or other mouth sounds, the sounds of birds, animals, musical instruments, train whistles, auto horns, and other environmental sounds.

High, low.

Game: The teacher of young children groups simple instruments or other pitch producers according to high and low in pitch. The children (one, two, or three at a time) experiment with them and compare their high and low sounds. Later the teacher mixes the sound producers and the children are asked to group them into those that produce high pitches and those that produce low pitches.

High, low.

Have children relate high and low in pitch to relative high-low positions of the body and of objects. Reach high and low in relation to obvious high and low pitches. Use body movements, marks on a chalkboard, a glockenturm (a German bell-type instrument that is played vertically and shows visually the relationship of keyboard and staff), step bells, standard bell sets placed in vertical position with large bars down. Find or discover high-low in speaking voices, bars on resonator bells, and different sized drums. Work toward such generalizations as "the larger the sound producer, the lower the pitch."

High, low.

Game: Use three pitches, middle C, the octave above, and the G in between. When the children hear the highest pitch, they place their hands over their heads; when they hear the middle pitch, they place their hands in front of them; when they hear middle C, they place their hands on their thighs (or hips, if standing). Having eyes closed at times will permit the teacher to find out if some are imitating others or if they are hearing the pitches. Another approach is to let the children freely dramatize the pitches to reflect high and low physically.

High, low.

The teacher produces a pitched sound (on anything) in medium range, and repeats it at intervals so the children can remember it. They then explore the room to find objects that will produce (1) a lower sound, then (2) a higher sound. After this, "What can you do to change the kind of sound you made?"

Rhythm of words related to the minor third interval.

Establish the rhythm of selected words. Then relate these to the minor third in a vocal range comfortable for the child.

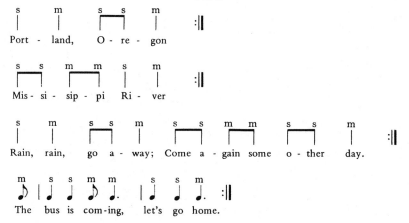

HAND SIGNS

The low *do* is formed at waist level. The signs move upwards step by step in the illustrations below. *So* is made approximately even with the mouth. High *do* is made even with the forehead.

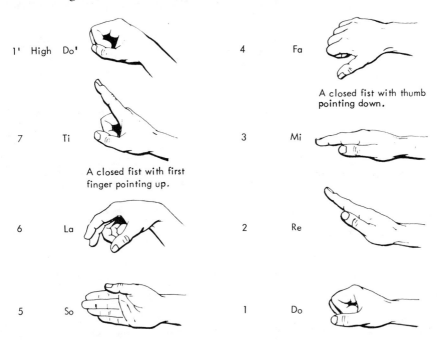

1' High Do'

7 Ti

A closed fist with first finger pointing up.

6 La

5 So

4 Fa

A closed fist with thumb pointing down.

3 Mi

2 Re

1 Do

Improvised question-and-answer.

Utilize tonal conversations in which the teacher sings questions, comments, or directions to which the children improvise singing replies. They may use any pitch they like. Examples:

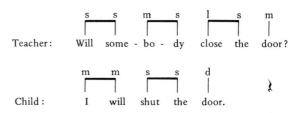

Teacher: s s m s l s m
Will some - bo - dy close the door?

Child: m m s s d
I will shut the door.

Hand signs for so, mi.

Have children first clap hands on hearing *so* (5), and slap thighs upon hearing *mi* (3). The teacher sings various combinations of the two pitches; the children listen, then respond by singing and the above body responses. Later, have them simply hold palms together for *so* and hold palms down for *mi* (no clapping or slapping). Later, relate the tonal patterns sung to the *ti-ti tahs* and to the abbreviated notation:

```
s          m          s    s          m
|          |         ⌐‾‾‾⌐              |
```

"Children's chant" 5–3–6–5–3.

Use this tone pattern in many creative combinations. Show it on the staff as a picture of what is sung. Expand the activities used with *so-mi* to include *la* (6).

```
s              l          s    s    m
Port    -    land,        O -  re -  gon
```

```
s      s     ·s    l       s      m
Mis -  si -  sip - pi      Ri -    ver
```

```
s      l       s    s     m      s    s     l     l     s    s     m
Rain,  rain,   go   a  -  way,   come a  -  gain  some  o  - ther  day.
```

```
m      s     l      s       m       l     s      m
The    bus   is     com  -  ing,    let's go    home.
```

```
s      s     l      s      s      m     s     s     l     s
Moth - er    is     wait - ing,   and   she's all   a  - lone.
```

Hand sign for la.

Teach the hand sign for *la* and ask the children to sing with the three signs they now know (*so, mi,* and *la*). Game: The teacher makes hand signs for some sequence of the three pitches. The children watch, think silently what the pitches will sound like, then at the teacher's signal, sing what signs they observed, first in syllables, then with the *ti-ti ta's*.

Name songs.

Using bars CDE GA from a set of resonator bells, have each child play a tune representing the rhythm of his name.

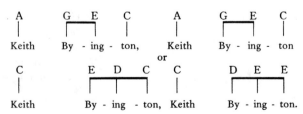

```
A        G    E      C          A        G    E      C
|       ⌐‾‾‾⌐         |          |       ⌐‾‾‾⌐         |
Keith   By - ing - ton,         Keith   By - ing - ton
                              or
C        E    D    C    C          D    E    E
|       ⌐‾‾⌐‾‾⌐    |    |         ⌐‾‾⌐‾‾⌐
Keith   By - ing - ton, Keith     By - ing - ton.
```

Home tone.

Then sing the name with the words, syllables, letter names, and the *ti-ti ta's*.

The teacher sounds the chord sequence that centers the children's hearing on the home tone: I V₇ I, using Autoharp, guitar, or piano. The class may also sing the scale demanded by these chords, and the teacher will again center attention on the home tone (*do* or *1*). Next the teacher plays on piano, bells, small wind instrument, or sings well-known melodies such as "Mary Had a Little Lamb," omitting *do* each time it appears. The class is to sing every *do* omitted by the teacher. Next, the teacher will sound the tune in a different key so that the class will have the experience of identifying and singing the home tone in other keys.

Ear training.

The teacher sings the child's name in pitches of the common pentatonic scale. The child answers by singing the same pitches in syllables or numbers.

Improvisation.

The teacher plays a repeated drone interval of a perfect fifth on the piano or low-pitched xylophone, metalophone, or cello. After listening to the drone, a child or small group experiments vocally, relating their improvised pitches to the drone. The mood may vary from an Indian dance to a lullaby.

So, mi, la.

The following excerpts are reproduced here from *Twenty-Two Music Lessons* by permission of the Nova Scotia Department of Education.

LESSON 15

Using Roll-Call To Reinforce So-Mi and Arm Signals

Teacher says: "I will clap the Rhythm Pattern of someone's name. I would like that person to (stand and) answer by saying and clapping it." (There may be several people whose names have the same Rhythm Pattern—let them all respond at once). Then the whole class responds by clapping and saying the rhythm syllables (ta & ti-ti)

LESSON 15 (*cont.*)
Examples:

| Teacher claps: (John Anderson) | Pupil responds saying name and clapping: | Class claps & says: |

(Elizabeth MacDonald)

perhaps:

(Rosemary Stewart)

or it might be considered:

2. Using *so* and *mi*, the teacher calls each child by name (full name preferably), and each child echoes, as in the examples below:

John-ny Jones   John-ny Jones

Dan-ny Mac-Au-lay   Dan-ny Mac-Au-lay

Gail Bruce Gail Bruce

Vir-gin-i-a Mac-Far-lane Vir-gin-i-a Mac-Far-lane

LESSON 15 (*cont.*)

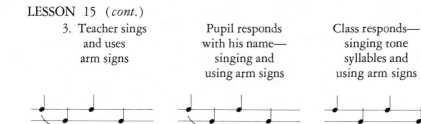

3. Teacher sings and uses arm signs	Pupil responds with his name— singing and using arm signs	Class responds— singing tone syllables and using arm signs

| Wayne   Rob - erts | Wayne   Rob - erts | so   mi   so   mi |
| A-dri - enne Mil - ler | A-dri-enne Mil - ler | so so mi   so   mi |

4. Teacher sings as before, but now instead of the echo, the child responds to the teacher's question, singing and using arm signs. The class responds, as in (3):

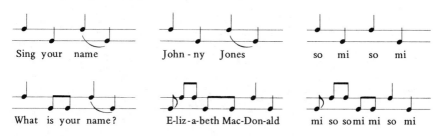

| Sing your   name | John - ny   Jones | so   mi   so   mi |
| What is your name? | E-liz-a-beth Mac-Don-ald | mi so so mi mi so mi |

PART OF LESSON 19

Added suggestions: using recorder, melody bells, piano, or "loo":

1. Give a four-beat rhythmic pattern using *so* and *la*.
*indicates *so:*

| so   la   so   la | so so so so la   so | so   la la so   la |

2. Now try the roll-call patterns, employing *mi, so,* and *la,* as outlined in Lesson 15. Here are some examples:

Teacher:	Pupil:	Class:
Ka - ren Mur - phy	Ka - ren Mur - phy	so la so mi
Sing your name	Don - ald Wat - er - man	so la so so mi

LESSON 19 (*cont.*)

 Teacher: You will find that the children will usually echo your tonal
 pattern. You will have to do the arm signals with them, at
 least at the beginning.

Teacher:	Pupil:	Class:
Sing me your name	Sus - an Dav - is	so mi la so mi
What is your name?	Mar - i - lyn O'-Bri - en	so so mi la so mi
Are you pres - ent?	Dav-id Pat-rick Mur -ray	so so la la so mi
Can you sing your name to me?	E - van-gel-ine Mac-Lel- lan	mi so la so mi so mi

Tonal memory.

The children know a familiar song.
They sing it. The game takes place
when the teacher gives a prearranged
signal during the singing. When the
teacher does this, the class does not
sing, but continues to *think* the melody
silently as it continues in their minds.
When another signal is given, the children resume singing. Words, syllables,
or numbers can be used. The teacher
or a child hums a melody, or sings it
with a neutral syllable such as "la" or
"loo." The children then try to identify
the melody. When it is identified, the
entire class may sing it with the
leader.

Hand signs for re and do.

Teach these signs; then use scale tones
1,2,3, 5,6 for song-like drills and for
the creation of tunes and songs by the
children. Eventually show the pitches
on the staff to explain, "This is what
it looks like when it sounds that way."

Tonal memory.

After giving the pitch of *1* or *do* the teacher makes hand signs in silence. The children remember the signs and sing the signaled pitches. At first the teacher repeats the signs as the children sing; later he does not. (They are to develop memory of pitches without this repetition of signs.)

Improvising endings.

The teacher provides the first two measures of a four-measure phrase. Individual children improvise vocally the final two measures to complete it. Example:

So, mi, do.

Game: The teacher sings at random the pitches of scale tones 5, 3, 1 (*so, mi, do*). Children use hand signs to identify which of the three pitches is sung.

Fa.

The hand sign for scale tone 4 (*fa*) is taught. The teacher sings in syllables or numbers the pitches 1,2,3,4,5,6 in song-like drills. Children make hand signs to match the pitches sung. Later the teacher sings these pitches with *loo* or *la* (neutral syllables) and the children continue to identify the pitches by hand signs.

Pitches.

The children invent body movements to dramatize the direction of the pitches in tone patterns, scale lines, and skips heard in selected songs or in teacher-invented tone patterns. Such body movement is applicable to many of the activities mentioned earlier.

Tone patterns.

Game-drill: Children sing selected common tone patterns from chalkboard, magnetic board, or flash card, responding with numbers, syllables, or note names as the teacher requires.

Tone matching.

Game: The class is divided into two teams. Each has an interesting name the children invent. Corners of the room are the four bases of a baseball diamond. A score-keeper is appointed. At first the teacher uses scale tones 1–2–3–4–5 and later increases these to the complete major scale. He plays on an instrument short tone patterns that always begin on 1. At first there are no skips, only scale lines and repeated tones. After careful listening, the one "at bat" reproduces what was played by singing each pitch accurately. If he does this successfully, he advances to the next base. After three players strike out, the other team goes to bat. Score is kept on the chalkboard. The difficulty is increased as the players' skill grows. A variant of the game adds a flannel or magnetic board on which what was played is notated. Another variant asks that the children respond with syllables or numerals. Still another asks them to respond with hand signs.

Pitches.

Employ the following scale patterns in improvised drills, using a pointer, or hand signs, or notation. The children are to sing in response to the teacher's directions. The major objective is to become familiar with common scale patterns.

$$5 \ 4 \ 3 \ 2 \ 1$$
$$3 \ 2 \ 1 \ 7_1 \ 6_1$$
$$6 \ 5 \ 4 \ 3 \ 2 \ 1 \ 7_1 \ 6_1$$
$$1^1 \ 7 \ 6 \ 5 \ 4 \ 3 \ 2 \ 1$$

Pentatonic scale.

Create song-like drills with scale tones $5_1 \ 6_1 \ 1 \ 2 \ 3 \ 5 \ 6$. The children can respond with syllables, hand signs, numbers, and the *ti-ti ta's*. The pitches can be related to bars on resonator bells. The children can use these to create tunes and songs.

Tonal memory.

Write a scale on the chalkboard that is in easy singing range for the children. Have them sing it; then have them sing it with the elimination of one note, which they must think silently. Continue this procedure, eliminating more pitches until most or all of the pitches are heard inwardly, not sounded vocally.

NOTATION OF PITCH

Staff.

Relate high-low concepts to the treble staff. Use the glockenturm or standard bell set placed on end with large bars lowest. Relate the pitches of these instruments horizontally to the lines and spaces of the staff written on chalkboard, magnetic board, or flannel board. Parts of well-known songs can be used.

Melodic contour on the staff.

Relate melodic contour to notation. Use known songs. Make charts of complete simple songs in two-measure sections. Mix these so that they are out of order. The children then arrange them on a chalk rack in proper order and then sing the song from the notation they arranged.

Note names.

Bells and other melody instruments can be used to relate pitch notation to note names. Sing familiar songs in numbers, syllables, and note names.

Note values.

Game: Manipulate a melody rhythmically. The teacher writes a short melody on the chalkboard or transparency in which all or most of the notes are quarter notes. The children are to make the tune more interesting by using eighth notes and half notes when they feel they would be appropriate. Later, with other melodies, they will use dotted notes and other note values in increasing complexity and with growing musical judgment. The class sings the tune in the various versions produced by the children and evaluates their effectiveness.

Note values and composing.

Select a simple poem of four phrases to be set to music. Give the children the first phrase with the pitches written in even note values (as in the preceding activity). The words are placed under the staff. The class changes note values to add rhythmic interest to this first phrase. Then the teacher assigns groups to compose the melody for the other three phrases. The class evaluates the results and suggests changes if these seem necessary.

Modulating melodies.

Challenge the class to learn to read examples of modulating melodies with syllables, numbers, and hand signs. Example:

d r m f s l s d t l t d d s f m r d r d

Atonal melodies.

The teacher writes an example of an atonal melody on chalkboard or transparency. The class is challenged to sing it, using the *fixed do* system in which middle C is always *do*. This study relates to aspects of some contemporary music. Relate to recorded examples; see Chapter 5.

SCALES AND THE TONAL CENTER

Scale.

Write the major scale vertically on the chalkboard in numbers or syllables. Game: The class or child sings the pitches to which the teacher points. Make it very easy at first, then increase the difficulty as the children master the relation of the pitches to their position within the scale.

Home tone.

In emphasizing the tonal center or home tone, the teacher sings or plays a melody, but stops before it is complete. The children are to sing the the home tone or make up an ending that concludes with the home tone, depending upon at what point in the melody the teacher ceases singing or playing.

Key signatures.

Explore the reasons for key signatures. Play familiar songs with arbitrarily changed key signatures. What is the result? Why are key signatures used by composers? This study can relate to scale patterns.

Pentatonic scale.

Relate the common pentatonic scale to the black keys of keyboard instruments. Then transpose this scale pattern of whole steps and minor thirds to keys that we think of as the keys of C, F, and G. Compare the pentatonic scale pattern to the major scale pattern in those keys. After this, find the form of pentatonic scale that reminds us of the natural minor: major scale steps 6–1–2–3–5–6. Use these scales to compose pentatonic songs and tunes. Listen to a recording of pentatonic music such as Bartók's *An Evening in the Village* (Adventures in Music 5, v. 2).

Natural minor.

Find the natural minor scale pattern by beginning the scale on *la* or 6 of the major scale in any given key signature. Draw its pattern to show where the whole and half steps are. Relate the scale to songs in this tonality—the Aeolian mode.[5] Compare the natural minor scale pattern with the major scale pattern. Have children play the two scales on the bells or small wind instruments. Have them compose melodies in this minor tonality.

[5] The modes are discussed on pp. 130–132.

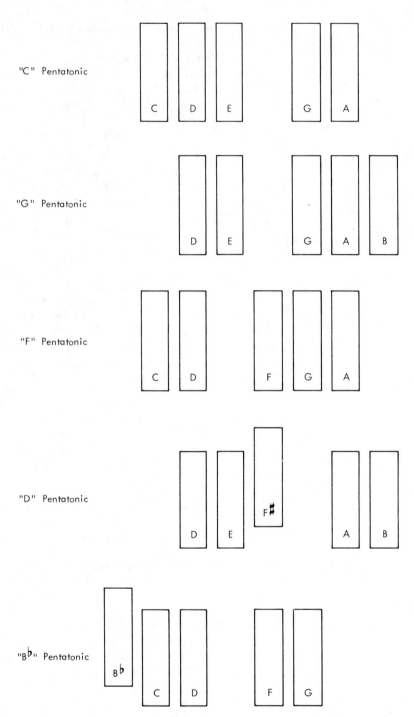

Pentatonic Scales on the Keyboard Instruments

Tone row.

Construct a tone row from the pitches of the chromatic scale. The 12 resonator bells within the scale of C can be used; however, the teacher can choose to use less than 12 if he wishes. To add interest, a child who is blindfolded can mix up the bars and arrange them in a row. Then, without the blindfold, he can play the resulting sequence of tones. If three or more pitches remind the listeners of a melody moving toward a tonal center, these must be changed so that no key feeling is suggested. A child can now play the row in two ways, from left to right, and from right to left (retrograde). Next, the class can select the rhythm in which these pitches are to be sounded in a composition. Write the tone row on the staff. Then the class or each child in the class can take this row and write a composition. They can use such techniques as diminution, augmentation, inversion, retrograde, retrograde inversion, and canon. (See p. 85.) Repetition of pitches can be done also, but no tone in the row can be repeated otherwise until all others have been sounded in row order. *Making Music Your Own*, Book Six, p. 202, is an example of how a series book introduces the tone row. The teacher should permit the children to use the row in a free rather than in a totally restricted way. The rhythm is added in the form of note values and meter to make a tune from the row. Sometimes this rhythm can be the same as that of a familiar tune; this can be fun.

Improvisation on a tone row.

Several children can improvise on a written tone row.[6] One might begin

---

[6]For a report of a sixth grade's experience with the tone row, see Mary Val Marsh, *Explore and Discover Music* (New York: Macmillan, Inc., 1970), pp. 131–38

by playing a recorder or other small wind instrument. He could be joined by another playing the row on the bells. Later, a third could join them, playing a xylophone. (Piano might substitute for the xylophone.) The class should evaluate the experiment. How might the effect be improved or changed?

Ethnic scales.

Study and compare ethnic scales. One source is Gertrude P. Wollner's *Improvisation in Music*, Doubleday, 1963, Chapter Five. Children can use these scales to compose songs and instrumental pieces, some in relation to social studies.

Invented scales.

Have the children invent their own original scales. These might have as few as four steps or as many as twelve. Ask them to write melodies based on these scales. Use them with familiar songs to discover what happens when a song is played in a new scale setting.

MELODY AND HARMONY

Hearing two pitches at once.

One half of the class sustains one pitch, *do* or *1*, while the other half sings other pitches as indicated by the teacher's pointing to scale degrees written in numbers or syllables on the chalkboard, or by the teacher's use of hand signs. Later, both *do* and *so*, and *la* and *mi* can be used as alternating sustained pitches.

Write the major scale vertically in numbers or syllables. Divide the class into two groups, left hand and right hand. Each group sings to the corresponding hand of the teacher as he points with it. The teacher points to scale degrees that will produce interesting two-pitch combinations. It is good to start with a unison and experiment from there. Later on, do the same with scales other than the major. For older, experienced children, this activity can progress until both groups are singing moving parts indicated by two-hand signs given by the teacher or an advanced student. From this they can proceed to a chart or chalkboard with notation.

Improvising two-voiced pentatonic melodies.

Small groups can improvise in the pentatonic idiom. For example, with five children, three might play contrasting-toned percussion instruments while one might play the bells and the other a small wind instrument to create two-voiced polyphony. Of course the specific pentatonic scale must be identified and used by both players of melody instruments.

Canon.

The teacher creates simple canons and writes them in numbers or syllables for the class to sing. There will be two parts. Later, some of these should be notated and sung from notation. Examples:

1 1 2 3 4 5 — 5 4 3 2 1 —
    1 1 2 3 4 5 — 5 4 3 2 1 —

Composition over a bourdon.

A young child strokes an open fifth on a guitar that is tuned for this purpose. Other children listen to this repeated bourdon and make up a tune based upon it, using the "children's chant" pitches as a beginning (*so mi la so mi*). The tune may develop into a lullaby. The bourdon could also be played on a bell set or xylophone.

Composition over an ostinato.

Create a simple ostinato, then have individuals or small groups compose a melody over it. Teachers usually plan a pentatonic ostinato to begin with.

However, the following example is not pentatonic, this is *diatonic.*

I, V₇, IV chords.

These chords are the *tonic, dominant seventh,* and *subdominant,* respectively. The teacher plays the chords slowly and repetitively on the Autoharp, piano, or guitar. The children are asked to describe, identify, and compare the chords in some inventive way. When this has been done, an identification game can be played. For example, some children have identified the I-chord as the "at home chord," and the V_7-chord as the "away from home chord." They sometimes identify the IV-chord as the "leaning chord" or the "yearning for home chord." The chords can be identified by arm motions. V_7 may be arms up; I may be arms down; IV may be arms at an angle or out in front.

Major, minor chords.
Improvising harmony.

Adding to the above activity, children can identify major and minor chords by palms up for major and palms down for minor. The teacher plays on the piano, or loudly on an Autoharp, a slowly changing succession of chords. The class will listen carefully to the chords and hum pitches to "fit" the harmony the teacher is playing.

Relating chords to scales.

Dramatize the relation of chords to scales by forming a major scale of eight children standing before the class, each with a resonator bar representing the correctly-ordered notes of that scale from 1 through 8 (or 1'). The teacher asks children holding bars 1, 3, and 5 to step out in front of the scale and to play their tones together in tremulo style so that the chord can be sustained. "How can we make a minor chord?" "Can we make a minor chord based on scale step 2?" "How can we find the V_7 chord?" "Where are the notes belonging to the V_7 chord when we have only these eight pitches to work with?" "What does this look like in notation?" When notes are needed that are not in the eight scale tones, others from the class can be called upon, given his tone bar, and placed in keyboard position with the others. For example, a problem may be to act out the whole-tone scale. "What other bars will be necessary?" "What does it sound like?" "How can it be notated?"

Melodic improvisation based on chords. Use written chord sequences as the basis for melodic improvisation. Begin with I IV I V_7 I sequence in familiar keys. One child can play the chords on Autoharp or piano while another improvises over the chords on bells, a small wind instrument, or with his singing voice.

$$\frac{4}{4} \quad F \ | \ B\flat \ | \ F \ | \ C_7 \ | \ F$$

Tone clusters. Another technique in contemporary composition is use of the tone cluster, a multiple pitch sound used by composers such as Charles Ives and Henry Cowell. To make a tone cluster, place the entire palm or forearm on the piano keys. (They can be made in other ways, too.) Young children use tone clusters to imitate the sound of a large animal walking.

Form

Phrase. Help children to discover phrases as identifiable sections of familiar songs. Lead the children to generalize in their own words that music is written in sections called phrases. Children often believe that phrases are two measures in length when in reality they may be four measures long. This is not important at the elementary level; what matters is that children learn to identify sections that to them can reasonably be called phrases.

Child concept of phrases:

1. Row, row, row your boat
2. Gently down the stream
3. Merrily, merrily, merrily, merrily
4. Life is but a dream

Adult concept of phrases:

1. Row, row, row your boat, gently down the stream.
2. Merrily, merrily, merrily, merrily, life is but a dream.

It is better to accept the children's definition of the above phrase than to go into an exploration of why they may not be correct. The main idea is for them to discern logical sections, and the elementary teacher should be rather flexible about such things. Regularity in phrase length is no longer considered the rule; phrases can be any length as long as the musical line is logical in its natural divisions.

Phrase improvisation.

The words of a clearly phrasewise poem are taken from literature or from an unfamiliar song and placed on chalkboard or transparency. Individual children improvise musical phrases to suit the words and to complete the melody. The music can be written so that they can see what they created, if the teacher so desires.

Repetition and contrast.

Groups of children can be assigned the task of developing a percussion composition in simple ABA form, illustrating the repetition (A–A) and contrast (B) of musical ideas. This can eventually be extended into a rondo form such as ABACABA or some variant of this.

Rondo.

Children may notate their own scores of compositions they wish to keep. The

Composition.
  Beginning with a phrase.

tape recorder should be used to assist the children in evaluating their efforts and to find if they wish to make changes in the score.

The teacher writes the first phrase of a composition-to-be on the chalkboard, and the children complete the composition from there. Some teachers prefer to use this activity before the one immediately above.

Note values.
  (rhythm variation)

The teacher writes a self-contained phrase (one that sounds like a complete song) on the chalkboard; it is of four or five measures. All measures but the last are filled with quarter notes; the last measure contains but one long note. The task of the children is to vary this phrase with different patterns of note values and rhythmic alteration of the phrase. The class selects the most interesting variations to play or sing and record. (Teachers can easily make manuscript paper for the older children by typing the staff with the underline key on a master copy for duplication.)

Variations.

The teacher writes a four or five measure self-contained melody on the chalkboard. The children's task is to vary it in terms of melody, rhythm, and meter. The variations are then performed and evaluated by the class.

Summary

This chapter was concerned with teaching strategies that usually require no books nor recordings in the hands of the learner or the teacher. Its purpose was to assist the teacher to be able to work directly with children and music in independent and flexible ways. Teaching strategies were listed in order that the teacher could select those that best developed the chosen objectives in a teaching situation, and those that were most appropriate to the teacher's personality and musical capacities. These strategies were classified conceptually in ways relating to the Music Concepts and Generalizations outline on pages 21–29.

In the chapter to follow, more teaching strategies will be listed under the same classifications; however, performance of songs and performance on pitched instruments will be emphasized as means by which children learn music knowledges and skills. The teacher will add to his objectives from these areas other objectives from the cognitive skills and attitudes-values areas.

REFERENCES

ADAM, JENO, *Growing in Music with Moveable Do.* New York: Pannonius Central Service, P.O. Box 2028, Grand Central Station 10017.

ARBUTHNOT, MAY HILL, *Time For Poetry.* Chicago: Scott, Foresman and Company, 1952.

Dalcroze School of Music, 161 E. 73rd St., New York, N.Y. 10021

DARAZS, ARPAD, and STEPHEN KAY, *Sight and Sound.* New York: Boosey & Hawkes, Inc., 1965. Student Book and Teachers Manual.

DE ANGELI, MARGUERITE, *Book of Nursery and Mother Goose Rhymes.* New York: Doubleday & Co., Inc. 1954.

DE LA MARE, WALTER, *Rhymes and Verses.* New York: Holt, Rinehart and Winston, 1947.

DWYER, TERRENCE, *Composing With Tape Recorder.* New York: Oxford University Press, 1971.

FINDLEY, ELSA, *Rhythm and Movement: Application of Dalcroze Eurythmics.* Evanston, Ill.: Summy-Birchard Company.

GOULD, A. OREN, "Developing Specialized Programs for Singers in the Elementary School." In Council for Research in Music Education *Bulletin No. 17,* n.d., 9–22.

HUBER, MIRIAM BLANTON, *Story and Verse for Children,* 3rd ed. New York: The Macmillan Company, 1965.

KERSEY, ROBERT E., *Just Five.* Melville, N.Y.: 11746: Belwin Mills. A collection of 84 pentatonic songs.

LANDIS, BETH, and POLLY CARDER, *The Eclectic Curriculum in American Music Education: Contributions of Dalcroze, Kodaly, and Orff.* Washington, D.C.: Music Educators National Conference, 1972.

LEAR, EDWARD, *Nonsense Verse.* Boston: Little, Brown and Company, 1950.

Manhattanville Music Curriculum Project, *Interaction* (ages 3–8), and *MMCP Synthesis.* Bardonia, New York, P.O. Box 533: Media Materials, Inc., 10954.

MARSH, MARY VAL, *Explore and Discover Music,* New York: Macmillan Inc., 1970.

MILNE, A. A., *When We Were Very Young.* New York: E. P. Dutton & Co., Inc., 1961.

NICHOLS, ELIZABETH, *Orff Source Book,* vol. 1 and 2. Morristown, N.J.: Silver Burdett Co., 1970.

NYE, ROBERT E., and VERNICE T. NYE, *Music in the Elementary School*, 3rd ed. Englewood Cliffs, N.J.: Prentice-Hall, Inc., 1970. Chap. 8.

ORFF, CARL, and GUNILD KEETMAN, *Music for Children, I-Pentatonic*, English adaptation by Doreen Hall and Arnold Walter. New York: Associated Music Publishers, 1956.

SMITH, ROBERT B., *Music in the Child's Education*. New York: The Ronald Press Company, 1970, chap. 2, "The Early Childhood Vocal Program."

STECKER, MIRIAM B., et. al., *Music and Movement Improvisation*. New York: The Macmillan Company, 1972.

WEIDEMANN, CHARLES C., *Music in Sticks and Stones; How to Construct and Play Simple Instruments*. New York: Exposition Press, 1967.

WHEELER, LAWRENCE, and LOIS RAEBECK, *Orff and Kodály Adapted for the Elementary School*. Dubuque, Ia.: Wm. C. Brown Company Publishers, 1972. Part 1.

4

learning music
with songs and instruments

Songs have always been one of the most attractive vehicles for learning music. Perhaps this is because song is such a very human phenomenon. Singing brings out heightened feelings. The words of songs are important; someone is trying to say something to us and that person may be a contemporary or he may be a voice from distant centuries. Humanity has recorded its history in song and has reflected every human feeling in song. And melody is integrally related with rhythm, tone quality, tempo, and dynamics.

Children have a natural affinity for the mechanical. This may be the reason why musical instruments have universal appeal to them. Percussion instruments were stressed in Chapter Three. In this chapter melody and harmony instruments are dealt with in more detail. One of the surest paths to learning note reading is that of playing melody instruments by note. However, this should be tied to sight singing in that most of what is performed on these simple instruments should first be sung. When the instrument is being learned, the child should sing the tune or exercise before it is sounded on the instrument for two reasons: (1) to help establish accurate pitch, and (2) to learn sight singing along with learning to play.[1]

In Chapter Three it was stated that songs of limited range were the best to use for beginning experiences in singing, and that the pitch range of these songs for most children should be between the B-flat below middle C to the A above.

The following list of songs is helpful to the teacher who seeks songs of limited range.

3-*note range*:	Hot Cross Buns Merrily We Roll Along Good News (refrain) Trampin' (refrain) Fais do do (Go To Sleep) (first part)
4-*note range*:	Sally Go Round A-Hunting We Will Go (one version) Hokey Pokey
5-*note range*:	Go Tell Aunt Rhody Cradle Song (Rousseau) Lightly Row Sleep, Baby, Sleep Mary Had a Little Lamb Oats Peas Beans and Barley Flowing River Green Gravel Whistle, Daughter, Whistle Grandma Grunts Old Woman (some versions) When the Saints Come Marching In Jingle Bells (refrain)
6-*note range*:	This Old Man Baa Baa Black Sheep Old MacDonald London Bridge

[1]For a detailed account of this method see Robert Nye and Vernice Nye, *Music in the Elementary School*, 3rd ed., (Englewood Cliffs, N.J.: Prentice-Hall, Inc., 1970), pp. 266–67.

Lovely Evening
Hey Betty Martin
Skip To My Lou
Goodbye, My Lover, Goodbye
O Susanna
Old Brass Wagon
Pop! Goes the Weasel
Hickory Dickory Dock
Looby Lou
Caisson Song
Jolly Old St. Nicholas
Up On the Housetop
Au Clair de la Lune
Susy, Little Susy
Cindy
The Mocking Bird

Something to consider when teaching young children is that they often confuse *high* with *loud* and *fast*, and *low* with *soft* and *slow*. When we analyze this, we find that high and low in pitch are abstractions; the association of high and low pitch with high and low physical levels is artificial, however necessary for building understanding of these concepts. To make them concrete for children it is essential that they be made real in terms of high and low physical positions both with the body and with objects, in terms of pictures, and by relating to things in the child's world such as airplanes, trees, and stars (all high), and floor, rug, and grass (all low). There are songs that help teach high and low. Teachers often make up their own for this purpose.

The out-of-tune singer was discussed in Chapter Three. Repetitious songs and echo-type songs help children to first listen, then try to imitate the pitches of the melody.

The following examples are to be found in *Singing With Children.*[2]

Repetitious songs helpful in tone-matching:

Are You Sleeping?
Grandma Grunts
Hole in the Bucket
Clickety-Clack
Hush Little Baby
Angel Band
Whistle, Daughter, Whistle

[2]*Singing With Children*, 2nd ed., Robert Nye, Vernice Nye, Neva Aubin, and George Kyme (Wadsworth Publishing Company, Belmont, Calif., 1970).

Examples of echo-type songs:

How Do You Do?
If I Ask You
Getting Acquainted
What Did You Do Last Summer?
John the Rabbit
The Sparrows' School (Chichipapa)
Hoo Hoo!
Follow On
Ol' Texas

Tone Quality

THE CHILD VOICE

The child voice is often described as light in quality as well as in volume. It is also an extremely flexible mechanism, as illustrated by the strident cries of the playground. The teacher is confronted with a voice that is capable of expressing many moods in song. Since there are many moods to express, this child voice can be sweetly soft and ethereal as it sings "Lullaby and good night" and can be momentarily harsh as it sings "David *killed* Goliath!" A logical way of deciding upon the voice quality desired in any song is for the teacher and children to determine what manner of voice should be used to express the meaning of the words effectively and to evaluate this continually when they sing. Although the child voice is light in quality, it should not sound weak or overly soft.

Many of the problems related to vocal quality can be solved when one adds to the above idea the following:

1. To make a generally pleasing sound (simple, natural, and clear).

2. To sing in a manner that avoids strain and tenseness.

3. To take breaths where one does when speaking the words (usually as the punctuation indicates); do not interrupt the phrase by breathing in unnatural places.

4. To enunciate clearly, but pronounce r's as Southerners do (ah(r)), and sound final consonants distinctly and in unison.

After the children learn that each child has a unique voice, it is a challenge for them to work to blend their voices—to try to sound together more like one voice than many. They can select a child whose voice is pleasing to them and one which they agree is a type of tone quality worthy for the entire class to imitate. Then this child will sing a tone or a few tones alone. After this, one child joins the first, and the game is to make the two voices sound as much as possible like one voice. Then another child joins the first two, and this continues until all the class is trying to blend in an attempt to unify the tone quality.

Dynamics

As children work to improve their performance of songs, the vocabulary peculiar to dynamics becomes useful to them. It is also useful in their own compositions. There should be increasing ability to enter into the analysis of songs they are singing with respect to dynamics. Accent, crescendo (cresc.), decrescendo (descresc.), mezzo piano (mp), pianissimo (pp), mezzo forte (mf), fortissimo (ff) are commonly used terms. The children will suggest the dynamics needed for their compositions, and they will experiment with dynamic levels for the purpose of communicating ideas by means of musical sound. The song "Clickety-Clack" in *Singing With Children* is an example of the use of dynamics.

Tempo

Songs can be sung that suggest appropriate rhythms for the movements of animals, nature, machines, and man. The child should see and be able to identify tempo designations in such songs and show that he understands their usage. The teacher will select songs that encourage such identification. Eventually the child will be able to provide useful tempo terms for songs in which these are lacking, and he may wish to change the tempo in songs that have these terms. "What would happen if the tempo of this song is made slower?" "Let's try it." "Is the result better or worse?" "Why do you think so?" "Can you think of ways to change the tempo that might improve this song?" "What terminology can you use to describe the changes in tempo that you have made?" Sometimes tempo can help describe characters, as in "The Quaker's Courtship," *This Is Music*, Book 5 (Allyn and Bacon).

Rhythm-related Experiences

Tonal memory.

To develop tonal memory in the "inner ear," the teacher or a child claps hands or plays a percussion instrument in the melody rhythm of a song that is familiar to the class. The game is to identify the song from hearing its rhythm. With very young children, ask them to choose between two or three known songs. Older children can vary the game by having each child in turn perform a different melody rhythm for the class to identify.

Appropriate sounds.
Beat.
Pattern.

Have children select the most appropriate percussion instruments to use for accompanying songs and to provide suitable sound effects to emphasize descriptive words or actions, to stress the beat, and to emphasize important rhythm patterns. The trend today is to avoid the mass use of percussion instruments for these purposes. Help the children to be selective and to evaluate the suitability of their choices when they listen to the results of their selections. It is a part of genuine showmanship as well as aesthetic sensitivity to find the right balance between the percussion instruments and the singing. In some songs only one instrument might be "just right." In other songs, ten or twelve carefully selected instruments might produce the desired result. Use songs such as the following from *Singing With Children:*

Balance.

My Tambourine
Zuni Sunrise Song
Free America
Tangalayo
Clickety-Clack
Over the River and Through the Wood
When Johnny Comes Marching Home
Calypso Band (Mary Anne)

Meter, metrical rhythm, melody
rhythm.

Have children conduct the meter while singing a song to discover that two concepts are operating together, the metrical rhythm (meter) and the melody rhythm.

Combining melody rhythms.

Experiment with combining the melody rhythms of two songs. Example: "Are You Sleeping?" and "Row Your Boat," even though they are in different meters, ²⁄₄ and ⁶⁄₈. Clap or play the rhythm of one melody at the same time as ı that of the other. At first the teacher selects well-known melodies having the same meters or combinable ones such as the above. Later she will select songs of different meters having the same tempo for experimentation with polyrhythms.

Tonal memory.
Rhythmic notation.

Game: The children tap a steady beat while the teacher plays or sings a short tune to the beat. The tune can be one the children know, or it can be improvised by the teacher. The game is for the children to remember the tune and write it in rhythmic notation. A third grade wrote this teacher-improvised melody rhythm correctly:

Rhythm pattern.
Ostinato.

Ask children to devise a notated rhythm pattern to use as an ostinato throughout a familiar song. Let them evaluate its degree of success as they listen to a few perform it with appropriate percussion instruments. Then ask them to clap it while they sing the song. (They will be performing two rhythms at one time.) Two or three suggested ostinati might be combined and the result evaluated by the class. The teacher should use a tape recorder whenever this assists the evaluation.

Changing meter.

Experiment with well-known songs to find answers to questions such as "What would it sound like if ⁴⁄₄ became ¢ in this song?" "If slow ⁶⁄₈ became fast ⁶⁄₈?" "If ³⁄₄ became ³⁄₈?" "Can we change this song from ⁴⁄₄ meter to ³⁄₄?" "How?"

Changing meter.

Experiment with writing a familiar song in a number of different meters, including some less common ones such as $\frac{5}{4}$ and $\frac{7}{8}$.

Changing note values and meters.

Ask children to alter familiar songs of their choice by changing note values and meters. Then have the class sing these, perhaps by putting them on a screen through an opaque projector, as a fun experience in note reading.

ABA form.
Improvising a dance.

This experience with form is for the primary level. The song "Shoo Fly," commonly found in music textbooks, is a good one to improvise a dance for, and in doing so to enact ABA form. It might go like this:

Shoo, fly, don't bother me,
Shoo, fly, don't bother me,
Shoo, fly, don't bother me,
For I belong to nobody.

(Walk in a circle to the right as the class sings.)

I feel, I feel, I feel,
I feel like a morning star,
I feel, I feel, I feel,
I feel like a morning star.

(Walk to the center of the circle)
(Walk backwards from the center to form the circle again.)

Shoo, fly, don't bother me,
Shoo, fly, don't bother me,
Shoo, fly, don't bother me,
For I belong to nobody.

(Walk in a circle to the right as the singing continues.)

The above dance is perhaps one of the most simple possible for the song. The teacher will ask questions that lead to the children's generalization, "When the music sounds the same again, we make the same motion," and the observations, "The song is different in the middle," and "If the song were drawn on the chalkboard, it might look like this."

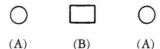

(A)   (B)   (A)

There are many other ways to emphasize ABA form such as this. For example, children could slap thighs for A and clap for B; they might draw something to represent A, and something different to represent B. The "game" is to show the difference between A and B in some interesting way. (There are many similar songs.)

Traditional dances.

Songs for specific dances can be useful when teaching those dances. Examples: "Weggis Song" for the schottische; "Buffalo Gals" for the polka, "Sweet Nightingale" (in *Singing With Children*) for the mazurka. The indexes of the music text books, books concerning dance, and some song collections will guide the teacher to song-dance relationships and the dance directions. These dances are generally for older children.

The rhythm patterns of Latin-American dances stimulate the creating of percussion accompaniments.

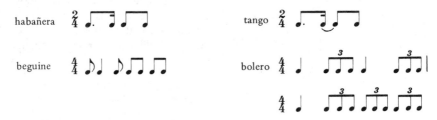

The standard maracas rhythm is a steady eighth note pattern, played with arms moving back and forth and stiff wrists. For a soft effect they can be tapped by the fingers rather than shaken. The bongo drum often has an identical pattern:

The conga drum often has this pattern:

Ethnic dances.

Many songs and dances are closely related as they are taught and performed in conjunction with each other. Here is an example from the Maori people of New Zealand, "Me He Manu Rere."

ME HE MANU RERE

Contributed by Cheryl Lau Oi

VERSE 1

4 times

Me he manu rere ahau e, 1-4

3 Times

Kua rere ki to moenga, 5-8

Turn a full clockwise circle in 6 steps

Ki te awhi to tinana, 9-12

E te tau tahuri mai. 13-16

VERSE 2

Kei te moe to tinana, 1-4

Fists move back and forth 6 times in time to music

right left
right left
right left

Kei te oho te wairua, 5-8

Kei te hotu te manawa, 9-12

E te tau tahuri mai. 13-16

Me he manu rere ahau e,	*Had I the wings of a bird,*
Kua rere ki to moenga,	*To your side I would fly,*
Ki te awhi to tinana,	*To hold you there and see you,*
E te tau tahuri mai.	*Please turn to me.*
Kei te moe to tinana,	*Though you are enchained,*
Kei te oho te wairua	*Yet my spirit is free to roam,*
Kei te hotu te manawa,	*My heart yearns for you,*
E te tau tahuri mai.	*Please turn to me.*

Action songs or chanted songs accompanied by simple steps and gestures are developed from the Maori term *waiata kori,* or dance song. The actions, which are completely complementary to the words and music, mirror and often intensify the meaning conveyed by the song. The enjoyment of the *kori* was the music, art, drama, and dance for the village maidens and young lads in New Zealand. Not only a pleasing style of entertainment, the action song merits serious study, for it is a reflection of the modern Maori culture. It typifies the harmonious blending of the old and new; it embodies the music and poetry which is the soul of the race, and it expresses pride and hope for the Maori future.

LESS COMMON METER ORGANIZATION

Music of our day reflects a desire for some contrasts to the more commonplace meters and rhythms. Thus there is a new emphasis on exploring less familiar meters once the common ones have been mastered. Some examples are found by looking under "meter" in music textbook indexes.

Alla breve meter (¢) is really 2/2 meter. It could also be considered as 2/4 written in 4/4 so as to be more easily read, the notation being "less black" in that it has fewer eighths and sixteenth notes to decipher. 3/2 is not uncommon; songs such as "Kum Ba Ya" are written in that meter, and 9/8 is the meter for "Down in the Valley." Familiar songs can and do change meter, as testified by "Goodbye, My Lover, Goodbye." and "We Three Kings of Orient Are." The indexes of some of the music textbooks will guide the teacher to songs of different meters. The most common meters in use in the elementary school are as follows:

Number of *Beats*	*Duple* *Meter*	*Triple* *Meter*
1		3/8 3/4 (tempo di valse)
2	2/4 2/2	6/8 6/4
3		3/8 3/4 9/8
4	4/8 4/4 4/2	12/8

Combinations of 2's and 3's

5	5/4 (3+2 or 2+3)
6	6/8 6/4 (3+3 or the less common 2+2+2)
7	7/8 7/4 (2+2+3, 2+3+2, 3+2+2)

What do meter signatures mean? They tell us only how many of a certain kind of note or its equivalent can be found in one measure. If the signature is 3/4, there are three quarter notes or their equivalent value in the measure. Whether each receives one beat or not is usually not revealed by the meter signature alone. Most of the time they will receive one beat, but when the tempo is very rapid the entire measure would receive only one beat. If the meter is 6/8, we know that there are six eighth notes or their equivalent in each measure, but we do not know from the meter signature whether there are two or six beats in those measures—whether each eighth note receives one beat or one third of beat. Thus, the upper figure does not always tell us the number of beats in a measure, and the lower figure does not always tell us the kind of note that receives one beat. Meter signatures tell us only the number of a certain kind of note or its equivalent that can be written into one measure.

There is a possibility that in stressing meter accent teachers limit the capacity of children to think beyond its regularity. One way to begin to overcome this is to have them listen for accent in an excellent rendition of "America" from a recording or played on the piano by the teacher. The correct performance will reveal little or no meter accent. To add a definite accent to the first beat of each measure would destroy the solemnity and dignity of this melody. Hearing recordings of Gregorian chant will reveal no regular recurring beat or accent. Aspects of music which tend to make rhythm more free—less bound to the rigidity of regular beats and accents —include *rallentando* and *ritardando* (gradually slower) and *accelerando* (gradually faster). *Rubato* is a term which implies that the performer treats the tempo and note values very flexibly, employing many slight accelerandos and ritardandos. This may be done in two ways, either by applying this freedom to the melody while the beat remains stable, or by applying it to the music as a whole. Syncopation upsets the normal meter and accent by deviating from a regular recurring accent; it shifts accents to normally weak beats. The familiar "Hokey-Pokey," "Dry Bones," and "Rock Island Line" are among the many songs from which children can learn about syncopation. Some Negro spirituals are excellent for this purpose. An important point about performing syncopated music is that the performer relax and permit himself to be a natural medium for transmitting the rhythm. The more one tenses himself and "tries very hard," the less success he is apt to have.

METER AND MUSIC OF THE WORLD

There is a new emphasis on the music of the world that calls for some knowledge of meters used by peoples of the Middle East, Eastern Europe, Africa, and Asia.

While this can become a highly complex study, an easy introduction can begin with 5/4 meter, one that is used to some extent in the folk music of the West. Children accept this meter readily. While a few songs in 5/4 meter are found in the music textbooks, a creative approach can be made by students composing their own percussion scores and songs in that rhythm. *The important principle is that the beats in this and the meters to follow are organized in groups of two's and three's.*

⁵⁄₄ = 3 plus 2   *or*   2 plus 3

EXAMPLES:

In Latin-American music we find occasional measures in fast 6/8 meter that are performed differently than those in traditional North American music. Traditional American music always has this meter divided into two-beat measures. South of the border one finds a three-beat measure among the predominant two-beat measures.

In Eastern Europe, the Middle East, and Asia are found 7/8, 8/8, 9/8 and other meters. Measures in those meters can be divided by beat-count as follows:

$$7/8, 7/4 = \quad 3 \text{ plus } 2 \text{ plus } 2$$
$$2 \text{ plus } 2 \text{ plus } 3$$
$$2 \text{ plus } 3 \text{ plus } 2$$
$$8/8, 8/4 = \quad 2 \text{ plus } 2 \text{ plus } 2 \text{ plus } 2$$
$$3 \text{ plus } 3 \text{ plus } 2$$
$$9/8, 9/4 = \quad 2 \text{ plus } 2 \text{ plus } 2 \text{ plus } 3$$
$$3 \text{ plus } 3 \text{ plus } 3$$

Writing music that shows these groupings can be a fascinating task.

Learning the following Greek folk song will help one to become oriented to a less common meter. The tempo is fairly fast. When the song is learned, it will be found that counts 1, 4, and 6 mark the beats.

GERAKINA

Words adapted by H. V. N.   Greek Folksong

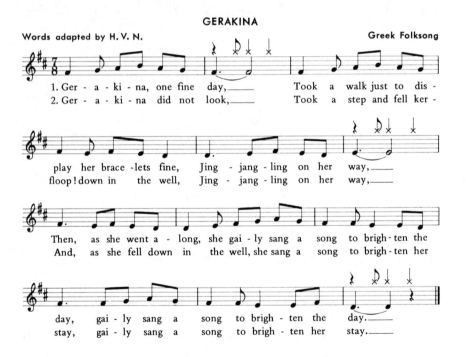

1. Ger - a - ki - na, one fine day,_____ Took a walk just to dis -
2. Ger - a - ki - na did not look,_____ Took a step and fell ker -

play her brace -lets fine, Jing - jang - ling on her way,_____
floop! down in the well, Jing - jang - ling on her way,_____

Then, as she went a - long, she gai - ly sang a song to brigh-ten the
And, as she fell down in the well, she sang a song to brigh-ten her

day, gai - ly sang a song to brigh - ten the day._____
stay, gai - ly sang a song to brigh - ten her stay._____

3 Gerakina gave a shout, Soon a young lad pulled her out for all to greet,
Jing-jangling on her way.
Then, as she thanked the lad, she gaily sang a song to brighten his day,
gaily sang a song to brighten his day.

4. *Gerakina took a look, Looked and felt her heart go floop! then very soon,*
Jing-jangling, they were wed,
So, all through life, they say, they gaily sang a song to brighten
each day, gaily sang a song to brighten each day.[3]

The original Greek song ends less happily. Gerakina (pronounced "Yehr-ah-kee-nah") went to the well to bring fresh water, with her bracelets resounding. When she fell, shouting, into the open well, young and old ran to the rescue, and the singer, who felt miserable because he was in love with her and she had ignored him, ran with them to help her but never succeeded in attracting her attention.

Music Fundamentals

Tonal memory.

Tonal memory is essential for the singer. Teachers can assist the development of tonal memory by the following activities, some of which have been mentioned earlier.

1. Hum a familiar tune and ask children to identify it; then ask children to hum it back to the teacher.
2. Arrange a signal whereby children stop singing during the performance of a song, but continue to *think* the tune for a phrase or two. Then the teacher signals them to change from thinking the tune to singing it, and so on.
3. Play a game in which individual children hum a tune for the class to identify.
4. Have the class sing songs with neutral syllables (*la, loo*) rather than the words so that the singers can concentrate on the melody.
5. Challenge the class to sing familiar songs with Latin syllables or numbers.
6. Challenge individual children to explore the black keys of the piano, working alone to find the melodies

[3]From Vernice T. Nye, Robert E. Nye, and H. Virginia Nye, *Toward World Understanding With Song*, © 1967.

of pentatonic songs they know such as "Old MacDonald," "All Night, All Day," "Get on Board," "Auld Lang Syne," "Land of the Silver Birch," "The Campbells Are Coming," and "Swing Low, Sweet Chariot."

7. Ask children to notate parts of well-known songs from memory when they are sufficiently advanced for this activity.

Scale:
major, minor.

If learning about a scale is a teacher's purpose, "Experience first; explanation later," is a good motto to consider. First select and teach interesting songs that are constructed on or in the particular scale; then explain the relationship.

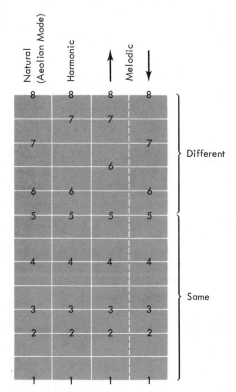

Find these minor scales on the bells and play them.

MINOR SCALES

Compare this scale chart with the others. Which suits you best? Why?

		do	re	mi	fa	so	la	ti	do
MAJOR		do	re	mi	fa	so	la	ti	do
PENTATONIC		do	re	mi		so	la		do
MINOR la natural	la	ti	do	re	mi	fa	so	la	
MINOR la harmonic	la	ti	do	re	mi	fa		si	la
MINOR la melodic	la	ti	do	re	mi	fi		si	la

How are minor scales alike? How are they different?
How would you sing them with numbers?

Most music textbooks for primary-age children contain some scale-line songs based on the major scale. Examples: "Department Store Elevator," "Taffy," and "St. Paul's Steeple" are in *Singing With Children.* Contributing concepts are up and down (high and low), whole step, half step, and for other children, the augmented second in the harmonic minor scale. Children may be assigned the task of composing songs or instrumental melodies in a particular scale; this may give the scale some utility in the mind of the learner.

Examples of songs in *Singing With Children* that illustrate minor scales include: natural minor—Wraggle Taggle Gypsies" and "On My Journey Home;" harmonic minor—"Joshua Fought the Battle of Jericho" and "Coventry Carol." There are few examples of the melodic minor in songs. One is "Charlie is My Darling."

Pentatonic scales.

Sing songs and create songs and instrumental melodies that are based upon the most common (to us) forms of the pentatonic scale and guide children to hear the difference between them. The first scale implies major tonality; the second implies minor. Pentatonic songs can be found listed in indexes of music textbooks. Some of them have chord-change harmonizations that can be reduced by the teacher to I-chord accompaniments. The songs listed below are in *Singing With Children*.

1.

Examples: "Auld Lang Syne," "Swing Low, Sweet Chariot," "Sparrow's School," "Campbells Are Coming," "Night Herding Song," "Nobody Knows the Trouble I've Seen."

2.

Examples: "Dakota Indian Song," "Trot, Pony, Trot." "Wayfaring Stranger" is in this book, p. 188.

3.

Examples: "The Riddle Song" and "Zuñi Sunrise Song."

Modes.

Some scales were used more frequently in earlier centuries than recently. Today both contemporary composers and folk singers have brought them to a more prominent position in the music that surrounds us. They can be utilized to compose songs and instrumental pieces with a "different" flavor and to reflect older periods. For example, a troubadour song could be written with both words and melody that communicate feelings from that time in world history. Indexes in series books guide teachers to modal songs. The Ionian mode is the major scale pattern; the Aeolian is the pure minor scale pattern. Less common modes are the following scales:

Dorian	Phrygian	Lydian	Mixolydian
8	8	8	8
			7
7	7		7
6		6	6
	6		
5	5	5	5
		4	
4	4		4
		3	3
3	3		
2		2	2
	2		
1	1	1	1

For a different "flavor", compose in the old modes.

Some examples of songs written in less common modes are "Every Night When the Sun Goes In," which is Mixolydian, "The Shanty Boys in the Pine," which is Dorian, and "I Wonder as I Wander," "Days of '49," and "Ground Hog." Refer to indexes of music textbooks for modal songs. Plain chants from church sources which exemplify earlier use of the modes are found in some of the books. For more examples of modal songs, see the Haynes and Coolidge reference at the end of this chapter.

Dorian mode.

Many songs in the Dorian mode are accompanied by a simple chord progression: I IV with a raised third. This occurs naturally in the Dorian mode and would be D MIN and G MAJ on the Autoharp. Children can compose charming songs or melodies over these two alternating chords.

Plainsong.

Teach a plainsong melody. They are often based upon the less common modes. Try singing it in parallel fourths, then in fifths. To do this, the teacher divides the class into two groups and pitches the beginning of the melody a fourth or fifth apart. Tape record the results when the groups are able to hold the interval throughout the song and let the class evaluate the result. This can be related to religious sources, primarily Hebrew and Catholic. Examples: "On This Day," (Dorian) *This Is Music*, Book 6, published by Allyn and Bacon.

Tone patterns.

Knowledge of common tone patterns (common note groups) is an essential aspect of sight singing skill. Such patterns found in songs can be taught as parts of those songs. Among the many patterns are:

1.

the minor third

"So Long"
"Brahms Lullaby"
"The Blacksmith"

2.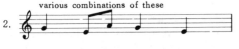

the "children's chant"

"The Caisson Song"
"A-Tisket, A-Tasket"
"Camptown Races"

3.

"Hot Cross Buns"
"Are You Sleeping?"
"Polly Wolly Doodle"
"Golden Slippers"
"Shortnin' Bread"

4.

"Star Spangled Banner"
"Blue Danube"
"Dixie"
"Goin' to Boston"
"Bow, Belinda"

5.

"There Was a Little
  Woman"
"Dixie"
"The First Noel!"

When the children have identified these and other tone patterns and can find them in songs and hear them from recordings, the next step is to identify variant uses of the patterns. For example, with reference to pattern number 5 above, the teacher may ask, "**Find** out how this scale-line pattern is used differently in 'Twinkle, Twinkle, Little Star,'" and "Look for it in 'Joshua Fought the Battle of Jericho'; how is it different in that minor song?"

Sequence.

A sequence is the same tone pattern repeated at a higher or lower pitch. This concept can be readily taught by using songs containing sequences. Some good ones are "Bingo," "I Love the Mountains," "The Bear Went Over the Mountain," and the following from *Singing With Children:* "The Donkey," "Angels We Have Heard on High," and "We Wish You a Merry Christmas."

Interval.

Knowledge of intervals by ear and by sight is as essential aspect of sight singing.

In order of using and learning melodic intervals, the young learner usually begins with the descending minor third. The second is part of any scale-line pattern; the octave, the fouth, and the fifth are commonly used in children's songs. The sixth, then the seventh, would probably come next in order of usage. They are learned through associations with their use in familiar songs, followed by "guessing" games of interval identification. To be certain they have identified the interval correctly, children can test their decision by beginning with 1 or *do* and "singing the scale tones up to it."

The minor third is exemplified in "Brahms' Lullaby," "The Caisson Song," and "Lightly Row"; the major third in "Mary and Martha," "Little David," and "Swing Low, Sweet Chariot"; the fourth in "Taps," "I've Been Working on the Railroad," "Auld Lang Syne," and "Hark! the Herald Angels Sing"; the fifth in "Twinkle, Twinkle, Little Star," and "Baa, Baa, Black Sheep"; the sixth in "My Bonnie," "Bendemeer's Stream," and "It Came Upon the Midnight Clear"; and the octave with "Annie Laurie," and "Wait for the Wagon." The minor sixth is often identified by thinking the major sixth first, then comparing it with the half-step smaller interval. The minor and major sevenths are often identified by comparing them with the octave.

Ability to read music through knowledge of intervals becomes essential in the instance of contemporary melodies that do not move in the scalewise and chordwise manner of traditional melodies.[4] If syllables are used with this music, the teacher should consider using the *fixed do* system in which C is always *do*.

The usefulness of tone patterns and intervals in reading music can be understood when songs are analyzed with

[4]That is, music with no tonal center.

these aspects in mind. For example, "Love Somebody" contains tone patterns one, three, and four, the interval of a perfect fourth numerous times, and the interval of a perfect fifth once. Anyone knowing these and the rhythm patterns discussed in the previous chapter can sight-sing the song. How many times do each of the tone patterns occur? How many times is the interval of the fourth used?

LOVE SOMEBODY

Intervals and chords.

Have older children determine the relationship of intervals and common chords. How many intervals can one find in a chord? Why is a seventh chord called a seventh chord? (Examine one in root position to answer this.) Use songs that relate to chord tones. Examples include "Dixie" and "The Star Spangled Banner." Many familiar songs that have chord-line patterns in their melodies are listed in *Singing With Children*, p. 86. The reader can analyze melodies in any songbook and find good examples.

Chord inversions.

Guide children to discover chord inversions by extracting vertical chords from chord-line sections of selected melodies. (Refer to the previous activity.)

Key signatures.

Children who have explored the scales and understand their organization will have no difficulty in determining why key signatures are necessary. When they fit the major scale pattern to different places on the keyboard they find black keys essential. From these, key signatures can be derived. Unless children find uses for scales and key signatures, they will soon forget them. One logical use is in their own compositions. Another is in the performance of instrumental music; one must use the key signature in order to know what note to play and what fingering to use. Children who play the bells and small wind instruments learn practical applications for key signatures. Vocal music does not demand the same analysis of key signatures that instrumental music does; all the singer needs to know is the beginning pitch and where that pitch is in the scale. However, in order to know where the pitch of a new song is in the scale, one needs to know the key signature in order to locate the home tone (*1* or *do*). If the teacher knows this, the children hardly need to, for the teacher can then give them the pitch and tell them where it is in the scale by having them sing first 1–3–5–3–1, then sing up or down the scale to the beginning note as is found necessary. Thus, in a purely vocal approach the teacher must invent situations in which this signature is of use to the learner. One is to select a student to be the teacher of a new song and ask the class to help the teacher plan what to do. Usually the need to know where the beginning note is in

Modulation.

relation to the scale will appear early in this exploratory process. It is best to use two or more songs, each beginning on a different scale tone. For how to identify the key from the signature, see "Learning Notation," #13, p. 209, near the end of this chapter.

Arrange for the children to discover modulation in songs such as "The Erie Canal," and "We Three Kings of Orient Are," both in *Singing With Children*. Have them find the modulating chord and analyze its function.

Some Activities With Songs in Primary Grades

There are numerous activities possible with songs. Among them are:

1. Move in time with the beat by motions such as clapping, swinging, tapping, rocking, skipping, and jumping.

2. Walk on the beat while standing in place or moving in a circle formation.

3. Walk to the beat anywhere in the room, but with directions given such as "Do not touch or bump anyone," and "Walk in the same general direction."

4. While walking to the beat of the song, do things such as clapping, slowing down, and speeding up.

5. Clap the rhythm of the melody.

6. Clap the rhythm of the melody while walking the beat.

7. Clap the beat while stepping the melody. (The song should be very slow and simple.)

8. Think the melody and clap it while stepping the beat.

9. Sing the first phrase; do "inner hearing" with phrase two; sing phrase three; do "inner hearing" with phrase four, except for singing the last pitch of the song. Try this while walking the beat.

10. Establish the pitch and tempo. Clap the beat, think the song with "inner hearing," then sing only the final word.

11. The teacher or student leaders turn the singing on and off; the children try to keep the rhythm steady so that they can come in at the same place in the song.

12. The children stand in a circle. As they sing an object is passed from hand to hand on the beat. Next, it is passed on the first word of each phrase. (Maybe two objects can be used, one for the beat and one for the phrase.)

13. A one-measure rhythm pattern can be selected from the song, or created, to be sounded throughout the song as an ostinato while the children sing that song.

14. If the song is pentatonic, select a phrase from the song which a group can sing repeatedly while the rest of the class sings the song.

15. If the song is pentatonic, try it as a round.

16. If any two pentatonic songs are in the same meter and have the same number of measures, they can be sung at one time as "partner songs."

17. Have the children conduct the song by using the appropriate metrical beat pattern.

18. Act out pitch levels and/or the melodic contour with hands and arms.

19. Have the class analyze the melody in terms of scalewise and skipwise pitch movements.

20. Have the class identify any outstanding rhythm patterns and tonal patterns.

21. Determine whether the music swings in two's or three's.

Teaching Rote Songs

When one tries to describe the teaching of rote songs he is tempted to say that there are almost as many approaches as there are songs. Many short songs can be taught as complete songs rather than in sections. However, one of the easiest types to begin with is the song which calls for an answer. "John the Rabbit" is one in which children reply, singing the words "Yes, ma'am". "Old MacDonald" is another. Children want to sing "Ee-i-ee-i-o" while the teacher sings the rest of it.

The echo-type song is one in which children sing parts which repeat pitch for pitch what the teacher has sung. "Are You Sleeping?" is one of this type. Every measure of this song is followed by an exact repetition. Thus the teacher presents it as a complete song first, then eventually asks the class to sing each part after her. A signal is developed such as the teacher's pointing to herself when it is her turn to sing, and to the children when it is their turn. "Follow On" is another echo song. Later on some of the children will sing with the teacher in "Follow On," and ultimately the class can be divided into two groups, one of which will sing the teacher's part. "Old Texas" can be sung in the same general way; six-year-olds who can sing on pitch will sing it well.

FOLLOW ON!

Repetitious songs are easily taught by rote. "A-Tisket, A-Tasket" is a young children's song centered about the 5–3–6–5 tone pattern. Its sing-song repetitiveness makes it easy for children to learn. Other songs of this type include "Tideo," "Rig-A-Jig-Jig," "Pick a Bale of Cotton," "Hole in the Bucket," and "Standin' in the Need of Prayer." "Trampin" is also an example.

After the teacher introduces "Trampin" by singing it all the way through, the children may begin entering on the chorus part, "Tryin' to make heaven my home." In reviewing the words and meaning of the song the teacher may ask, "What is the singer doing?" (trampin') "What does that mean?" "What is he trying to do?" "Has he ever been to heaven?" "What has he been told about it?" Later on, a child or group of children will sing the teacher's solo part, with everyone singing the chorus.

TRAMPIN'

Songs such as "O Tannenbaum" and "Lightly Row" which have a phrase organization of *a a b a*, and other songs of longer length than these, are commonly taught by phrase-echoing. The teacher sings the song or plays a recording of it, then discusses its meaning with the children, endeavoring to increase comprehension and interest. He then sings the first phrase; the children echo this. Then he sings the second phrase; the children repeat this phrase also. He then asks them to sing both phrases and they do. The teacher next sings the *b* phrase, which seems more difficult because it is different; the children echo this. The process continues, phrase by phrase until the song is learned. More complex songs may require a combination of these different approaches. Teachers need to study each song, analyze each thoroughly, then plan the best strategy for learning the particular melody.

Music Concepts and Rote Teaching

While rote singing is a necessary step in musical growth—and it is an honored procedure from the standpoint of the history of man—if teachers go no farther than this type of teaching, the result can be only a form of music illiteracy. Phyllis E. Dorman writes, "There is a certain dignity and logic in the simplest song. A song, any song, makes use of the same tools present in the most complicated of the musical classics. Songs should be used to teach musical concepts."[5] She recommends that *music* be taught instead of only songs.

Although singing of rote songs may take place at any level and at any age, more of this type of learning is necessarily used with young children who can do little or no reading of notation. However, every song contains elements of music the teacher can use in some way to prepare for or begin work with understanding music and learning about notation. The following can be considered steps in teaching young children rote songs, keeping music concepts in mind while doing so.

ESTABLISHING THE PITCH

Because the range of any song is a crucial matter, the teacher *must* establish the key and the beginning pitch accurately. This means using pitchpipe, bells, Autoharp (in tune), piano, or some other reliable instrument. At any level of instruction the teacher should hum the tonic chord ($1-3-5-3-1$; *do mi so mi do*) or play it on the bells. In keys such as D, E♭, E, F, G, and A♭ the low 5 (5_1) can be sung or played to further reinforce the key feeling ($1-3-5-3-1-5_1-1$; *do mi so mi do so do.*) In minor keys this process begins on *la*, the sixth step of the major scale according to the key signature. Older children should be able to do this after the teacher gives them the key note; it is an ear training experience and it is good to involve the class in establishing the pitch. In this process concepts of pitch, tone pattern, and key feeling are being nurtured. Furthermore, this care in establishing key and the beginning pitch (for the next step is to sing up or down the scale to the beginning note of the song if it does not begin on the key note) marks the difference between success or failure in some of the children's singing on pitch.

[5]Phyllis E. Dorman, "A Protest Against Musical Illiteracy," *Music Educators Journal*, November, 1967, p. 99.

MOTIVATING INTEREST

There are many possible ways to motivate songs. Sometimes the teacher announces the title and tells briefly with what it is concerned. Sometimes it is all a surprise—the children listen to find out what it is about. It is wise to take very little time for this because the school day is too short, and every minute counts; no time should be wasted. Pictures may help. After the teacher sings the song he should ask the children what its story or message is in a series of questions illustrated earlier in this section of the chapter.

BEAT AND METER

As the teacher sings the song again he might walk quietly in place to the beat while the children do likewise or imitate his walk with creative adaptations, such as walking with the hands in the air, with fingers on desks, or with silently clapping hands. Accents may call attention to the meter, whether or not children understand what meter is at the earliest levels.

PHRASE

As the teacher sings the song again, the phrase order can be stressed. For young children, the teacher may ask them to stand and imitate what he does—move arms to depict a phrase ⌒ , step the beat while turning the body, reversing directions for a contrasting phrase, holding up a finger for phrase one, adding a finger for each subsequent phrase, and so on. Some of this can be done with older children; however, those with good music backgrounds can sense the phrase order by listening, using their better-developed tonal memory. Logical questions to ask include, "How many phrases did you hear?" "Are there any that are the same?" "Similar?" "Different?" "Which ones?"

MELODIC DIRECTION: CONTOUR

The teacher can ask the children to show by their hand positions what they think is the up and down direction of the melody. In a later lesson their analysis can give them answers to questions regarding steps and skips in the melody line and if certain phrases conclude up or down.

INDEPENDENT SINGING

After the children have heard a song several times with this kind of analytical guidance, they should sing it without the teacher's voice. The teacher can assist by high and low hand positions, but he will join in singing only if necessary. A goal is to assure the children's independence of both the teacher's voice and the piano. Also, teachers cannot listen to children's singing if they too are singing. The children may then repeat the song, sometimes using the hand positions with the teacher.

TEXTURE

The next time the children sing the song, the teacher may use accompanying instruments to provide different textures. If the piano sounds the same as the melody the children sing, it is sounding only the melody in unison with their voices. It is an example of monophony. If the Autoharp or guitar sounds a chordal accompaniment which supports the melody, there is homophony, a quite different texture. "Did it sound the same or different this time?" "What made it sound different?" comprise a way to begin a discussion of texture even though the children may not know the adult terminology. Different types of accompaniments can be discussed, described, analyzed, and evaluated for their suitability for the melody. The accompaniments of recorded songs can contribute to the study of texture.

TONE QUALITY

Tone qualities of voices and of accompanying instruments can be evaluated in terms of their suitability to express the meaning of the song or in terms of beauty.

DYNAMICS

The children can be encouraged to try to sing the song at different dynamic levels—loud, soft, crescendo, decrescendo, with accents, and so on. They should determine the dynamics most suited to the song, thus learning about interpretation and aesthetic discrimination.

Thus the teaching of rote songs can become "rote-note" teaching because it can expand children's music concepts to the place when what they already have sensed and worked with is described in notation which, after all, is only a kind of picture-description of the melody.

General Directions

FINDING THE KEYNOTE IN MAJOR TONALITIES

This is necessary to enable the teacher and children to establish the pitch and key feeling (tonality) of a song. In review, the ways to find the keynote (home tone) from key signatures are:

1. The sharp farthest to the right is scale tone 7 or *ti*. Count up to 8 or *do*, or down to 1 or *do*. The letter name of 8 or 1 is the name of the key.

2. The flat farthest to the right is scale tone 4 or *fa*. Count down to 1 or up to 8; the letter name of 8 or 1 is the name of the key. A quicker way for key signatures containing two or more flats is: the next-to-the-last flat on the right is the keynote.

Songs in major tonalities ordinarily end on 1, 3, or 5.

FINDING THE KEY IN MINOR TONALITIES

1. Find the major tonality indicated by the key signature.

2. Find the sixth degree of the major scale (6 or *la*). This note is the keynote of the relative minor tonality.

Songs in minor usually end on *la*, and rarely on *do* or *mi*.

OTHER SUGGESTIONS

Learn the song thoroughly before attempting to teach it.

Have the children participate actively in some way as soon as possible.

Don't plan too much to do with the same song on the same day; this can become boring.

Playing the I V₇ I chord sequence on Autoharp, guitar, or piano is one good way to establish key feeling. Then ask the children to sing the home tone.

Take breaths generally at the end of phrases. People do not "break a phrase" by taking a breath during it when speaking; neither should this be done when singing. Periods, commas, and semicolons often point out the proper places to breathe.

Encourage children to suggest ways for better interpretation of the song.

A worthwhile college class activity is to answer the question, "How many different ways are there for a teacher to succeed at having a room full of children begin singing a known song *together?*" The problem is to find ways of signalling the children to begin singing on pitch and at the same time. To solve the problem, the class can follow these three steps:

1. Establish the pitch, meaning the beginning pitch of the song, and possibly establish also the key feeling.

2. Establish the tempo, and possibly a feeling for the meter.

3. Find a way to convey to the class when everyone should begin to sing the song.

To work with this problem the college student needs to have known songs to use, and to employ these in experimental attempts to find ways to help his classmates begin singing. The class should be helpful in making suggestions and in evaluating each attempt to judge whether or not it was successful, and why it was or was not. Different songs may suggest different approaches. Among them may be those employing clapping, finger snapping, counting, formal conducting, and others that will be suggested by the class.

POLYPHONY

Round.

Write all or part of a traditional round with all parts fully notated on the chalkboard, or prepare this on a transparency. Children are asked to sing rounds and to listen to them, but they seldom see them notated in complete form so that they can obtain a visual image of what a round is. First, the class should learn to sing the round. This one can be sung in from two to four parts; a new group enters two measures after the preceeding group. Then after studying the score, questions such as the following can be asked. "What is the harmonic plan of this round?" (a two-measure phrase in which C and G_7 share the first measure with two beats each, while C harmonizes the second measure.) "Analyze this round vertically to be sure that this harmonic plan is really in operation." (The notes, viewed vertically, can be made into chords and played on bells or piano to show that the harmonic plan is consistent—that the C and G_7

chords are really there.) Older children can be given manuscript paper and asked to write a round, using this same plan. Next, other rounds are studied and their harmonic plans revealed. Then rounds with other specified harmonic plans can be written by the children.

JUNE, LOVELY JUNE

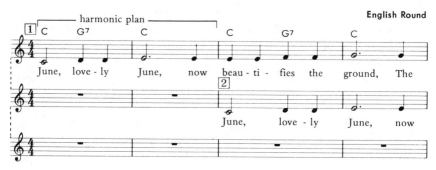

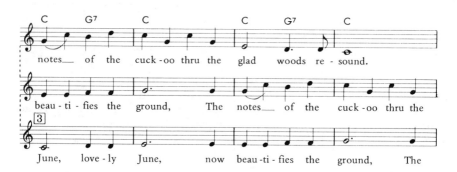

Descant, counter-melody, and round. Sing and play songs that have descants and counter-melodies. Ask the children to describe the difference between rounds and added parts of these types. Page 229 in *Singing With Children* lists songs with descants; also see indexes of music textbooks. A counter-melody is a melody composed to be sung or played with another melody. Of the songs listed in *Singing With Children*, the following contain what could be termed counter-melodies:

"Mystic Number" (first half), "Streets of Laredo," "Ash Grove," and "O Give Me the Hills."

HARMONY

Dissonance.

Experiment with singing as a round a known song that is not a round, having active harmonic changes of irregular nature. It should be a song that when sung this way will result in obvious dissonances (disagreeable sounds). Perform it this way, tape it, and let the class hear it. Ask the children to analyze the reasons for the dissonances, to try to define dissonance, and to evaluate their performance that exemplified it. Since dissonance is one of the characteristics of contemporary music, children should have some experience with it and know what it is.

Nonharmonic music.

Before asking young children to comprehend chord changes that are characteristic of harmonic music, they should have experienced a great deal of music in which there are no chord changes. This includes short tonal fragments and calls, pentatonic music, I-chord songs, and unaccompanied melodies that do not suggest harmonic changes. One chord played on the Autoharp suffices to accompany such music. Examples include "Old Mac-Donald" and "The Farmer in the Dell." More I-chord songs are listed in the Autoharp Accompaniments Index the heading "Exemplary Songs," *Singing With Children*, p. 228. The teacher can finger the Autoharp while young children stroke the strings.

Major and minor.

Arrange that children experience major and minor tonalities through familiar songs. For example, first sing "Merrily We Roll Along" in a major key, with a chorded accompaniment. Then sing it in minor, again with a chorded accompaniment. Ask the class to describe the differences, and ask them which suits the spirit of the song best. Do the same with "Old Aunt Rhodie" ("The Old Grey Goose").

Chord.

Many children think of a chord as a triad of three notes, and they are correct. However, their concept of chord can be expanded by asking them to write on the grand staff the pitches of the C major chord as they are shown and sounded on the Autoharp. Ask them which chord tones are repeated at octave intervals, how this might affect their definition of "chord," and how this might relate to their future compositions. Have them try to play the Autoharp chord on the piano. How many hands will it require? Can the chord be extended to more pitches than are on the Autoharp?

Chording accompaniments.

Arrange for children to create their own Autoharp, piano, or ukulele accompaniments for easy two and three-chord songs. The songs are to have no chord designations to help the learners. The problem is to decide which chords to use. The solution can be done in groups, with reports being made back to the total group. The eye must be used to study the melody line for chord clues, and the ear must be used to test whether or not the chord "sounds right." The class may discover that some songs can be harmonized in several different ways.

Bitonality.

The class sings a familiar song such as "Twinkle, Twinkle, Little Star" while the teacher plays the accompaniment on the piano in another key. This could be done on the Autoharp if the instrument is amplified. In any event, the result should be taped and played back to the class for evaluation. Relation should be made to contemporary recorded music that clearly exemplifies *bitonality*—two keys used at once. (Refer to Index.)

Quintal and quartal chords.

Traditional chords are constructed of thirds when in root position. Some chords used in contemporary music are constructed as a succession of perfect fourths—*quartal* chords, while others are constructed as a succession of perfect fifths—*quintal* chords. Have several children perform such chords at the piano. Discuss how they might be used in compositions and for sound effects.

HARMONIC PART SINGING

Partner songs.

"Songs having identical harmonization in identical harmonic rhythm can be sung simultaneously" is a generalization that older children can discover when they experiment with singing two such songs at once. "Three Blind Mice," "Row Your Boat," and "Are You Sleeping?" can be combined with each other in performance. Other combinable songs are "Ten Little Indians" and "Skip to My Lou;" "Solomon Levi" and "A Spanish Cavalier;" "Goodnight Ladies" and "When the Saints Go Marching In;" "Keep the Home Fires Burning" and "There's a Long, Long Trail;" "Humoresque" and "Old Folks at Home;" "Ring the Banjo" and "The Girls I Left Behind Me;" and the choruses of "Blue Tail Fly" and "Shoo Fly." Frederick Beckman has developed this idea in his two collections, *Partner Songs* and *More Partner Songs*, published by Ginn and Company. Be sure to sing the songs in a manner in which the children can hear both of them at once, otherwise the experience is of little value.

Rote part singing. The teacher finds a familiar song that is easily harmonized, or locates a good song in an intermediate music textbook that was selected by its authors to introduce part singing. The class learns the melody very well. Next, the teacher divides the class into two groups. While one group sings the melody softly, the teacher sings the new part while the other group listens carefully. This is done two or three times, until some children learn the new part by rote. Then the other group sings the melody while the first group listens, and so on. Eventually the class sings both parts together while the teacher listens. Perhaps she will record the singing and play it for the singers' evaluation.

Improvising harmony. Present the class with the task of improvising parts for "Streets of Laredo," using only scale tones 3, 4, and 5. This song has been selected because it is harmonized by only two chords, I and V_7. Scale tones 3 and 5 are members of the I-chord and scale tones 4 and 5 are members of the V_7-chord. In this particular song the chords alternate regularly; this makes it easy to think in terms of choices of chord tones the singer selects to improvise his simple harmony part. The class selects the pitches it wants for each of the measures of the song (which is either on the chalkboard or on a transparency), and writes them on the chalkboard. The class next sings the two parts (the melody and the new part) together until it performs it well and is satisfied with the added part. Next, the class adds another new part by writing it the interval of a third lower. Now it has two new parts in parallel thirds. It then sings the three parts. The children evaluate the result and try to analyze what made it possible.

STREETS OF LAREDO

Cowboy Song

Leisurely

1. As I____ walked out in the streets of La - re - do,
2. "I see by your out - fit that you are a cow - boy,"

As I____ walked out in La - re - do one day,
These words he did say as I bold - ly walked by;

I spied a young cow - boy all wrapped in white lin - en,____
"Come set down be - side me and hear my sad stor - y, I'm

Wrapped in white lin - en as cold as the clay.
Shot in the breast and I know I must die."

3. "It was once in the saddle I used to go dashing,
   Once in the saddle I used to go gay;
   First down to Rosie's and then to the card-house;
   Got shot in the breast and I'm dying today.

4. "Get sixteen gamblers to handle my coffin,
   Let six jolly cowboys come sing me a song,
   Take me to the graveyard and lay the sod o'er me,
   For I'm a young cowboy, I know I've done wrong.

5. "Oh, beat the drums slowly and play the fife lowly,
   Play the dead march as they carry me along,
   Put bunches of roses all over my coffin,
   Roses to deaden the clods as they fall."

6. (Repeat Verse 1.)

Chord root parts.

Words of songs can be sung on the pitches of the chord roots—the "1" of a chord in root position (1 3 5). The letter names of the Autoharp chord designations placed above the song notation tell the reader the pitch to be sung or played. Begin with one and two-chord songs, then proceed to three-chord songs. This activity assists the comprehension of harmony because it emphasizes the chord changes.

Singing "Piano chords."

The I, IV, and V_7 "piano chords" to accompany certain two and three-chord songs can be sung. After the class has been divided into four groups, one singing the melody and the other three singing assigned chord-tone parts (high, middle, low), songs such as "Silent Night" and "Brahms Lullaby" can be performed. Write the chords[6] on the chalkboard and point to the needed chord as the song proceeds. Everyone sings the words, or those assigned the chording parts can hum or use a neutral syllable. This is a very simple kind of four-part singing that can be done in grades 4, 5 and 6, and sometimes with an exceptional third grade.

Improvising part singing.

Explore harmonizing parts "by ear," using songs such as "Goodbye, My Lover, Goodbye," "Good Night Ladies," "Kum Ba Yah," "Michael, Row the Boat Ashore," and "Sally Go Round." Others in *Singing With Children* are "Daisy Bell," "Golden Slippers," "Mary and Martha," "Hush, Little Baby," and "Sidewalks of New York."

Harmonic endings.

After a song is well-learned and the accompanying chords known, create a harmonic ending by adding a few harmonizing chord tones to be sung by part of the class. The result is a bit of two-part singing.

harmony

melody

[6]See pp. 184–188.

Singing parallel thirds "by ear"

There are some songs and parts of songs that can be sung and played in parallel thirds. *This is one of the easiest approaches to part singing.* Among these songs are "Hot Cross Buns," "Sally Go Round," "Polly Wolly Doodle," and "San Sereni." The last one is in *Singing With Children.* First review the melody thoroughly, with a strong harmonic accompaniment on Autoharp, piano, ukulele, or guitar. Oftentimes the teacher says to part of the class, "Start singing the song in this pitch," and gives them the pitch that results in a third interval from the melody. Because the harmony has been well absorbed, automatic adjustments will take place in the new part, and the class may surprise itself by singing the song at once in two parts. The two parts should then be revealed on the chalkboard or transparency in order that the children see the related parts—"see what it looks like when it sounds that way." The interval of a third should be identified by sight and by sound. On the staff it is either line-line or space-space. In subsequent lessons the teacher can help children formulate the following ideas: (1) melody with harmonic accompaniment is *homophonic* music; (2) the interval of a third in this instance is a vertical or harmonic interval as compared to the horizontal or melodic interval that appears in melodies; (3) both types of intervals might be found in a two-part song.

Composing two-part songs in thirds.

Assign children the task of composing songs or instrumental tunes having melodies that avoid the home tone; use only scale tones 2 3 4 5 6 7. Such songs or tunes can be performed in two parts, the added part being either a third lower or a sixth higher than the melody.

Thirds and sixths. Any song sung in thirds can, by inverting the parts, be sung in sixths. When this is done it often places one of the parts too high or low for comfortable singing, thus the song should be transposed into a key that better accommodates the vocal range. Examples: "Yankee Doodle" and the refrain of "Marching to Pretoria."

There are older methods of teaching part-singing which emphasize drilling on each part, then putting them together. Today the emphasis is upon helping children to hear a new part in relation to the melody and the harmony so that they hear all of the music. This principle is applicable no matter what type of part-singing is being done, whether it be round, descant, or traditional two- and three-part singing. The general outline of progress in part-singing in grades four, five, and six is as follows:

1. The learning of the melody.

2. The comprehension of the harmony (chord structure) that accompanies the melody by use of Autoharp, piano, or guitar chording, or a suitable recording.

3. The introduction of the new part in a manner that permits the children to hear the integral relation of the two parts. (Children hum the melody or sing it softly while the teacher sings or plays the new part.) Harmony must be *heard* before it is made.

4. The singing of the new part by those children who are ready for part-singing, always working for a balance in volume that permits the hearing of both parts by all of the children.

5. Introducing a third part by repeating Steps 3 and 4, adding the new part to the two parts previously learned.

6. When children have learned to feel secure in part-singing activities, then the sight-reading of part songs can be an interesting and challenging activity. When this skill is developed, Steps 1, 2, and 3 are eliminated. Since sight-singing is a complicated skill, neutral syllables instead of words are generally used at first so that the children can concentrate on the notation. The words are added when children feel secure on the parts.

In general, the voices of fifth- and sixth-grade children are unchanged and have approximately the same range, with the exception of boys in the first stage of the voice change. These voices have a range of approximately one fourth lower than the others, but remain sounding unchanged. This makes part-singing a necessity, for these boys need a lower part to sing.

Technically, it is incorrect to call immature voices soprano or alto. It is more accurate to abandon these adult terms and to call the children's voices high, low, and middle, rather than soprano, alto, and second soprano. It is the aim of the teacher that every child sing each of these parts, changing from one to another according to the directions of the moment or by being assigned them in different songs.

An interesting creative approach to singing thirds and sixths is one in which children compose songs confined within four pitches of the major scale, 3, 4, 5, and 6. After such a song has been composed and learned, a parallel third part can be added below. When this same new part is transposed one octave higher, parallel sixths result. Try this with "Sleep, Baby, Sleep."

The male teacher is at some disadvantage in teaching part-singing, since his voice sounds one octave lower than the child voice. Therefore, it is necessary for him to use some melody instrument instead of his voice when he wishes to illustrate part-singing of unchanged voices. His voice is excellent, however, in the singing of chord roots. There is seldom a changed voice among sixth-grade children, but in case there should be, the singing of special parts, such as chord roots by the male teacher along with the boy, will help the child adjust to his temporarily unique situation.

THE ELEMENTARY SCHOOL CHORUS

Among the special interest groups in the elementary school are the orchestra, band, and chorus. The instrumental groups are generally the responsibility of special music teachers but the chorus is frequently taught either by the music teacher or by a classroom teacher. Although some schools have a primary grades chorus which sings unison songs, the usual chorus is composed of fifth and sixth graders. Today's teachers are fortunate in having an improved selection of song materials to use. Not only do the series books include chants, descants, and countermelodies in addition to the standard types of two- and three-part songs, but there are valuable supplementary materials. There is no standard seating arrangement for elementary choruses. However, it is best to have the lowest and highest parts seated so that each can hear the other well. In this way the group is able to keep more accurately on pitch. In chorus work which has a goal of public performance, the children are more or less permanently assigned to one of the parts (high, middle, or low).

SEEING WHAT WE HEAR

The above discussion has considered the teaching of songs by means of guided repetitions. The teacher's plans lead from purely rote singing to understanding music concepts that help children toward reading notation. Some activities that build notational concepts include having children:

1. Compare the notation of two familiar songs of the same tempo, one which uses many eighth and sixteenth notes and another which has whole notes, half notes, and quarter notes. Guide them to discover that the "whiteness" of notation relates to long note duration and the "blackness" of notation relates to short note duration.

2. Look for familiar rhythm patterns and note patterns in the notation of selected songs.

3. Look at the notation of phrases of known songs to find out that when phrases sound the same they look the same, and when they sound different, they look different.

4. Watch the notated melody line and follow it on the page with an index finger, all the while relating high and low in pitch with high and low on the staff.

5. Relate the keyboard to notation by providing easy songs to play on the bells by number, by the note names stamped on the bars, and eventually by notation.

ANALYZING MELODIES

High-low. A class of young children compares two scale songs written differently, as follows. They are to determine which one begins high and goes low in pitch, and which one begins low and goes high.

Examples in *Singing With Children:* "Taffy" and "St. Paul's Steeple."

Melodic contour. Use parts of exemplary songs to discover that pitches can move in three general ways, up, down, or stay the same. Relate melodic contour to tension, climax, and release in melodies of songs. "I Love the Mountains" is an example, as are "Riddle Song" and "Jacob's Ladder" in *Singing With Children.* Some songs are obviously more clear in this than others, and the teacher is to select the best examples.

Multiple concepts. When older children analyze melodies, they should seek answers to questions such as: How do tones move? (scalewise, stepwise, repeated notes) What is the phrase arrangement? What is the tonal arrangement? (major, minor, pentatonic, modal, whole tone, tone row, ethnic scale, etc.) What is the range for singing? Is there evidence of tension and release? If so, how is this achieved? Is there evidence of unity and variety? If so, how is this achieved? Is there a climax? If so, how did the composer achieve it? Are there other significant aspects such as rhythm patterns, intervals, meter, tone patterns, dynamics, sequence?

USING RECORDINGS OF SONGS

Recordings can be substituted for teachers' voices in teaching songs. It is well known that children learn some songs automatically from children's recordings they play at home, and from radio and television programs. Singing commercials are frequently learned also. However, when recordings are used, many of the flexible techniques suggested above cannot be employed.

The children must sing softly in order to hear the recording. The volume of the record player can be gradually turned down as the children learn a song so that they will become increasingly independent of the recording. Another test to determine how well the children have learned a song is to have them begin singing with the recording, then lift up the needle and have them continue without its help.

The recordings that accompany the series books as well as some other song books can be of genuine value in teaching songs. They usually provide worthy examples for children to hear and imitate: they often bring to the classroom fascinating instrumental accompaniments that could be provided in no other way. They aid the teacher who studies them even though he may prefer not to use them in the classroom, because with their assistance he learns songs correctly, both rhythmically and melodically. Beginning teachers should study the recordings that accompany the series books they are to use in their classrooms. Before the fall term begins, if they hear these recordings over a period of days they will have absorbed a repertoire of songs they need to know, and will have saved time by not having to pick out each song on a keyboard instrument and learn it without a model to follow. When a child tends the record player the teacher is free to move about the room to listen to individual voices and to direct class activities. The teacher can stop singing and listen to the children—something every teacher of music needs to do. No matter how well qualified a music specialist may be, there are times when a recording will provide an effective way to teach some songs. However, recordings cannot completely take the place of the teacher's voice; younger children sometimes find it difficult to understand the diction of voices strange to them. In all of the grades, a machine is no substitute for the personality of a teacher who sings.

Many recordings that teachers use in helping children to sing are found in the catalogs of companies that make an effort to supply the music education market. For example, a favorite recording of many teachers of young children is Ella Jenkins' *You'll Sing a Song and I'll Sing a Song,* Folkways Records' FC 7664. Upon examining the Folkways catalog many more will be found. The Franson Corporation (Children's Record Guild and Young People's Records) produces albums such as *Let's Sing* (ages 6–10), *Folk Songs* (6–10) and *Songs to Sing* (6–9). The Bowmar Records Catalog lists many albums for singing including some for early childhood and for children with special needs. Other companies such as Stanley Bowmar, Classroom Materials, and the Children's Music Center are helpful in guiding the teacher to recordings that assist the singing program.

In the learning experiences listed later in this chapter, recordings can be of assistance in helping children gain many of the concepts and generalizations that comprise the study of music content. By referring to the Index, the symbol R will guide the reader to recordings and the symbol F to films, should the reader desire to employ these aids in his class presentations. *Find the concept to be studied in the Index, then look for the R and F designations.*

THE PIANO AND OTHER VOICE SUBSTITUTES

The piano or bells may be substituted for the voice or recording by teachers who lack confidence in their singing voices and do not have recordings of songs they need to teach. Words for such songs may be learned by rote or written on a transparency or the chalkboard. The teacher will then play the melody of the song. This may be repeated while the children do several of the activities of the rote singing process already described in this chapter, the instrument thus taking the place of the voice or recording. For a song of some length the phrase method may be desirable. After the playing of the entire song, the melody of the first phrase will be played; the children will mouth the words silently as it is played again. Then the children may sing this phrase with the piano; and next, sing without its support. This can be continued throughout the remaining phrase, combining some of them along the way. As the song is learned, the support of the instrument is gradually withdrawn to gain independence from it. If a child in the class is a good natural musician and has a pleasing voice, he may be an excellent teacher's assistant by singing to the class phrases or entire songs that he has learned from the teacher's playing the piano or bells. Recorder- and flute-type instruments are sometimes employed also in this approach to teaching singing.

Although it is highly desirable to have a piano in every classroom, the piano is not essential in teaching or in accompanying songs. In a normal situation where the teacher uses his singing voice, the piano has its greatest use at the end of the learning process. A song may be introduced by playing it on the piano in a simple manner. Since younger children find it difficult to hear a melody when an elaborate accompaniment is played, a simple accompaniment, permitting the melody to predominate clearly, is the most effective style of playing. During most of the learning process involved in teaching songs the piano has little use, for two reasons: (1) when the teacher is playing the piano he cannot hear the children well enough to tell if each child is singing correctly, and (2) he is in a stationary position and is unable to move through the class to hear and to help individual children with their problems. Another reason for not using the piano at this time is that if it is used constantly the children cannot sing independently and may become semihelpless without it. However, after a song has been learned, the addition of a piano accompaniment can be a thrilling and satisfying experience, adding greatly to the singer's enjoyment and to the musical effect of the performance.

Instruments

An American method that is based in large part on an instrumental approach to elementary-school music is that of Dr. Howard Doolin, *A New Introduction to Music*, General Words and Music Company, 525 Busse Highway, Park Ridge, Ill., 60068. There are four levels of instruction. Every child has a bell set to play, and the singing is combined with the playing of the instruments. The recorder and Autoharp are added later. Level One is taught from a large chart on an easel. The other three levels include sets of children's books on individual easels. There are also teacher's manuals. This method stresses letter names of the notes from the outset; syllables and numerals are not necessary for its success. However, any teacher can include them if desired. The method was written to assist the classroom teacher in providing a successful music program. However, some music specialists have also found it helpful in their teaching.

SOUND WITH INSTRUMENTS

For sound to occur, something must vibrate. Young children can experiment with a rubber band stretched across an open box. When they pluck it, they can see it quiver at a fast rate, and they can hear that this vibration makes a sound. Every time the rubber band moves back and forth, a sound wave (cycle) is formed of molecules of air. The sound waves go through the air to reach our eardrums, causing them to vibrate. Nerves carry this sensation to the brain, and our stored experiences usually tell us what kind of a sound we are hearing. The children will find that if the rubber band is pulled out far, then let go, the vibration is wide and the sound is louder; if the band is pulled a short distance, the vibration is less and the sound is soft. Through further experimentation it will be found that the lowest pitch will be sounded when the entire band vibrates, and that higher pitches will be sounded when a finger is placed on the band to shorten the vibrating portion. Thus, children may be able to generalize that the length of a vibrating object influences its pitch; the longer, the lower; the shorter, the higher. It should also be discovered that a shorter length vibrates more rapidly than a longer length.

In some woodwind instruments—the flute and piccolo—the sound is produced by a vibrating column of air, while in others— the clarinet, oboe, and bassoon—the sound is produced by a vibrating reed. By taking a bottle, and blowing across its open top, a sound can be made that comes from vibrating air. By pouring water into the bottle, the children can discover that the longer the vibrating air column, the lower the pitch is; and the shorter the vibrating air column, the higher the pitch. To imitate the vibration of the double reed of the oboe and bassoon children can flatten one end of a soda straw, cut off the corners, and practice blowing into the straw through this flattened end. When brass instruments sound, the players' lips are the vibrating agent. Some children will be able to make a circular cup "mouthpiece" with their thumb and index finger, put their lips together on it and blow into it to produce a sound with their vibrating lips. They can watch large drumheads to see that striking them causes vibrations. They can examine a piano to discover that hammers strike the strings and cause them to vibrate. When string instruments are made to vibrate, the player either plucks the strings, as the children did the rubber band, or draws a bow across them. Perhaps the children can learn from a violinist that rosin is rubbed on the horse hair in the bow to increase the friction to make the strings vibrate. Perhaps they can answer the question, "Why is it that the player is never supposed to touch the horse hair of the bow?" (Because the oil in the skin transferred to the horse hair reduces the friction needed to make the string vibrate.) As this study continues with many different instruments, consideration should be given to the material the instrument is made of, the length of the instrument, the length of the vibrating section, and the existence of *resonating chambers*, such as those of the woodblock and the violin; all of these may affect tone quality. It might be noted that science tells us it should not matter what kind of material is used for instruments having vibrating air columns. However, many musicians continue to want recorders made of wood rather than of plastic, frequently arguing about the superior tone qualities of wood and metal versus synthetic materials. Other topics of scientific or historical interest include the *vibrato* as it is used by instrumentalists and singers, the overtone series and its relation to tone quality, and the historical development of modern instruments; these topics can be investigated by older children. Some may be interested in the relation between the clavichord, harpsichord, and piano, in the evolution of the viols and the modern string family, and in the evolution of the valve instruments.

Melody Instruments

A characteristic of children is their interest in mechanical things. Making music by playing an instrument, no matter how simple the instrument, attracts them. It follows that if teachers guide this interest along the lines of learning both the skills of playing and the understanding of the elements of music, it can yield great benefits.

When melody instruments are employed to invent introductions, codas, interludes, and to play tone patterns, concepts of melody and form are being expanded. The concept of *interval* can be made clear by seeing intervals on keyboard instruments, by seeing and feeling them on blowing-type (small wind) instruments, and by comparing what is seen, felt, and heard with written intervals on the staff. The key signature is relatively unimpressive to the singer, but of undeniable significance to the player of melody instruments. Note reading becomes clearly practical and functional when the player must relate notation to the keyboard or to fingerings on a wind instrument. Instruments are also useful in studying aspects of music such as scale-line, chord-line, legato, staccato, and a host of others related to analysis and performance. Flute-type instruments lend atmosphere to American Indian music; the individually-plucked strings of the psaltery, Autoharp, guitar, and ukulele can produce imitation Oriental melodies; and the marimba contributes in an authentic manner to Latin American music. Children can use melody instruments to compose melodies. Their use combines auditory, tactile, and visual perception to build music concepts. It is theorized that some children will be more interested in trying to match tones with their voices when they produce pitches themselves on a melody instrument. Children who cannot sing well should be able to make their own music by means of instruments. Furthermore, the more experienced and gifted children can have additional musical experiences from their opportunities with instruments.

WATER GLASSES AND BOTTLES

Some teachers use water glasses and bottles as introductory experiences to keyboard instruments such as bells, xylophone, and piano. There are tuned glasses that can be used without water, obtainable from various sources on order, even from some variety stores. Other teachers employ glasses with water, knowing that this probably means some spilling and evaporation, both of which necessitate retuning because of the change in water levels. Some teachers use bottles with water, often corked or capped to keep retuning at a minimum.

By striking glasses and bottles when they are empty and when they contain water, children can make certain scientific observations. They discover that the pitch and tone quality are affected by the size and thickness of the glass or bottle. They may also discover that decreasing the amount of water raises the pitch and increasing the amount of water lowers the pitch—except in some glasses and bottles that will not tune lower no matter how much water is added. They may also discover that striking glasses or bottles with soft objects such as felt-covered mallets produces soft tones. Let the children generalize from their experimentation that: The more water one pours into a glass or bottle, the lower the pitch is. The lowest pitch is made by filling glasses and bottles full of water. The highest pitch is produced when a glass or bottle is empty. The best tone quality is produced when a soft mallet strikes the glass as if pulling the sound out, not hitting it in. Numeral names, note names, or syllable names can be painted on or written on paper stickers. Some teachers put vegetable dyes or other coloring in the water to add interest. Placing glasses on a thick cloth will result in a better tone.

Interest in playing melodies on bottles may prompt the teacher or the children to make or obtain a rack from which to suspend the bottles. When this is done, each bottle is suspended by two loops of string, one on each side of the bottle neck, to help it to hang with more stability.

The first experience in playing songs on glasses or bottles is generally with only three pitches: 3–2–1 (mi-re-do). However, it is good to compose a song with only one pitch, that of 1 (do); then a song with scale tone 1 and 2; and finally, a song with tones 1, 2, and 3, arriving at the three-pitch stage in a logical way. Known songs in the three-tone category are "Hot Cross Buns" and "Merrily We Roll Along." After this, the next step is to use four-and five-tone melodies. Teachers often devise their own three-, four-, and five-tone songs as examples, then encourage the children to compose others with scale-tones 1–2–3–4–5. After this experience has been digested, more scale tones are added until melodies are created on all eight pitches of the major scale. The pentatonic tonal organization can be used also, beginning with songs based on scale tones 5–3, then 5–6–3, then 1–2–3–5–6. It is advantageous to transfer skills acquired on glasses and bottles to bells and xylophones. Bells provide a good introduction to the piano keyboard. Some teachers prefer to go directly to them rather than introduce them by means of experimental glasses and bottles.

BELLS AND XYLOPHONES

When children have had opportunities to explore the bells for themselves, they can make a number of discoveries:

Long bars sound low pitches.
Short bars sound high pitches.
The arrangement of white keys and black keys is the same as that of the piano except that the piano has more keys.
To play a scale going up, one plays from left to right.
To play a scale going down, one plays from right to left.
A five-note (pentatonic) scale can be played on the black keys.
White keys played from C to C sound the C major scale.
If a standard bell set can be stood on end, with large bars down, and held against the chalkboard or chart paper, staff lines can be drawn from the bars to relate the keyboard to the staff.
To produce the best tone, one strikes the middle of the bar and draws the tone out rather than hitting it in.

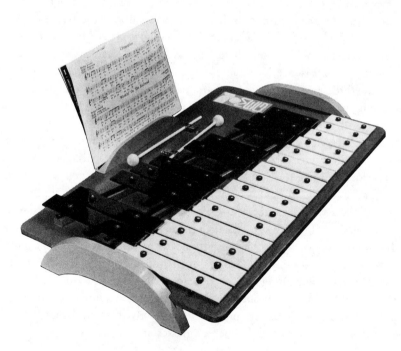

Melody Bells. Music Education Group.

The same sequence of pitches is used to initiate playing the bells as was described for glasses and bottles. *Resonator* bells are made of individual tone bars that can be taken from the carrying case if desired. For example, if children are to compose tunes with only three or four pitches, those particular bars can be removed from the set, placed in order, and played apart from the other bars to prevent possible confusion of young children when they would try to play those bars when placed in keyboard position among all the other bars. When they are removed from the set, there can be no doubt as to which ones are to be used for creating tunes.

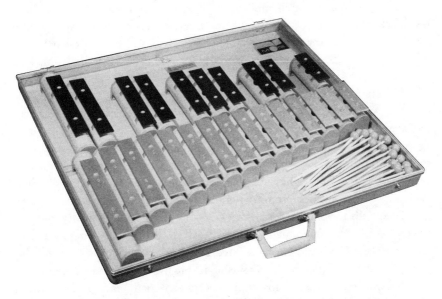

Resonator Bells. Model M.E.G. 501. Music Education Group.

Before children understand music notation, teachers guide them to play by ear and by numeral notation.[7] The scale-tone numbers can be written on the white metal keys with black crayon, or they can be placed on tagboard in back of the bells. Numeral notation could appear as follows. Notice that the "fast notes" are circled.

Hot Cross Buns	*Mary Had a Little Lamb*
3 2 1 – 3 2 1–	3212 333– 222– 333–
①①①① ②②②② 3 2 1–	3212 3333 2232 1——

---

[7]A well-known book that introduces numerical notation in kindergarten and first grade is Adeline McCall, *Timothy's Tunes* (Boston: Boston Music Company, 1943).

five-note tune

Jingle Bells

333– 333– 3512 3——
4444 433③③3223 2–5–
333– 333– 3512 3——
4444 433③③5542 1——

six-note tune

Are You Sleeping?

1 2 3 1 1 2 3 1 3 4 5–3 4 5–
⑤6⑤4⑤3 1 ⑤6⑤4⑤3 1 1 5₁ 1–1 5₁ 1–

Use C major or G major to avoid black keys. Use F major to introduce one black key (B♭). *Hot Cross Buns* and *Mary Had a Little Lamb* can be played on the group of three black keys. Some teachers prefer to introduce the piano keyboard in this way to overcome possible hesitation about the black keys later. With guidance and careful listening, young children can play songs or parts of songs in keys such as F and G major where one black key is necessary. The general procedure at first is to learn a song well by rote before attempting to play it *(listen, sing,* then *play).*

Although children may begin playing songs with the aid of numerals, they are soon looking at notation the teacher has prepared for them that includes the numerals written beneath (or above) the note they represent. Later, teachers prepare notation in which the numerals appear only with the beginning note of each measure, then only with the beginning note of each phrase, and finally they are abandoned altogether because the children have made the transition from numerals to the notes on the staff.

The bells have many uses. If a classroom teacher has difficulty with his singing voice, the instrument can be used to teach rote songs. Difficult tonal patterns in songs can be isolated and studied by means of the bells. They are often employed to establish the pitch of songs by sounding the keynote, playing tones of the tonic chord (I), then playing the starting pitch. Children can play simple parts of songs involving a single tone up to an entire scale, and they can play complete songs. Introductions, codas, and interludes—all created on the bells—can be added. Older children can write descants and other added parts to songs and play them on the bells. Bells can assist part-singing.

The xylophone is similar to the bells, but made of wood instead of metal. *Xylo* is the Greek word for wood. Because its wood strips do not vibrate as long as the metal bars of the bells, it has a more percussive quality. A more attractive xylophone is the *marimba,* which has resonators, usually metal tubes, beneath the wood strips. German music educators use the term xylophone, but prefer the terms *glockenspiel* or *metallophone* to bells. The metallophone is often lower pitched than the glockenspiel.

Other forms of bells are the step bells, which are made in the form of stair steps illustrating the ascending and descending pitches of the scale, and the glockenturm, a German instrument which is played vertically and reveals visually the relationship of keyboard and staff.

THE PIANO AS A MELODY INSTRUMENT

The piano can be used by children in connection with songs in the same informal ways the percussion instruments and bells are used. Like the bells, the keyboard provides an audio-visual tool. The piano can be used as an instrument of percussion, melody, harmony, and as any combination of these. It is therefore a superior means by which to gain concepts in music study.

Classroom teachers do not need to be pianists to teach music through keyboard experience. They need only to be introduced to it so that they can proceed in the same way the children do. In the beginning a child can play a tone that sounds "one" when the clock strikes "one" in *Hickory Dickory Dock*, as he may have done earlier on the bells. In a song that has words of importance on one or two tones, children may play these at the time they occur in the melody. The same little three-note melodies played on glasses, bottles, and bells can be played on the piano keyboard. As time goes on, four-and five-finger patterns can be used in an incidental way in both ascending and descending forms.

The resourceful teacher will gain pleasure and satisfaction in finding songs to which these simple uses of the piano are suited, knowing that by such processes children learn to listen and thus improve their singing ability at the same time. This type of keyboard experience merges with the listening process of tone-matching and makes it more of a game because of the added variety.

Another simple use of the piano is the playing of the notes according to the chord names to provide an easy added part to songs. Example: play F with the F chord, G with the G chord, and so on. Still more for children to do with the keyboard instruments include playing the rhythm of children's names with one tone or a series of tones; playing two tones that illustrate in correct pitch the concepts of high and low pitch in connection with songs; playing short tone patterns for tone-matching purposes or to add interest to songs; playing octave intervals in songs that emphasize this interval; playing other intervals in songs that feature them; playing different note values and rhythm patterns for children to respond to; playing entire characteristic phrases such as the beginning of "The Caisson Song."

Playing the bells, a small instrument, logically comes before playing the piano, a very large instrument. Whatever is done on the bells, however, applies directly to the piano because the keyboard is virtually the same.

Electric organs are used in some schools. These vary in size from small two-octave instruments to the type people purchase for home use. The larger ones can be played without disturbing others by use of earphones through which only the player can hear what is being sounded. Such instruments provide an additional type of tone quality for the classroom. The large ones have stops which produce a number of different tone qualities. Certain experiences in dynamics can be studied with the organ, and its sustained and accurate pitch is an advantage. The older (nonelectric) reed organ often has a pleasant tone that blends well with children's voices.

Matching pitch.

The use of individual resonator bars by children in relation to songs gives a helpful indication of pitch. Also, a game can be played in which each child plays his melody note each time it appears in the song. A pitch is *real* when held in the hand and struck with a mallet! There are many variations of this game. For example, "I Love the Mountains," a song used in elementary middle and upper grades can be used with six resonator bars, F, G, A, B flat, C, and D, given to as many children. When their pitch is on the first beat of any measure, they play their resonator bar on that beat. Obviously, this can be done with other songs, of course.

THE RECORDER

Very young children should have opportunity for exploration of simple types of blowing instruments such as the six-hole tin whistle or fife. Eventually one, two, or three well-sounded tones can be used with some songs and with very simple improvisations. Older children can learn to play simple wind instruments such as the Song Flute, Tonette, Flutophone, and Melody Flute. The Melody Flute sounds very much like the real flute when played well. The recorder is the easiest *adult* instrument and is somewhat more difficult than those listed above. The family of recorders can be explained with pictures, recordings, and real-life players when possible.

In general, have children learn to sing the note, notes, exercise, or song first. Then have them play the pitches on the instrument. Singing it first establishes the pitches in their minds, and makes it easier for them to play the instrument in tune. It also helps them to learn to sight-sing. For a detailed explanation of this method, refer to *Music in the Elementary School, 3rd ed.*, 1970, pp. 332–334.

The following section on the recorder is reproduced from *Basic Music, 4th ed.*, 1973, with permission of Prentice-Hall, Inc., the copyright owner.

THE RECORDER

The recorder is the ancestor of the modern flute. It was a popular instrument during the Renaissance, the Baroque, and the early Classical periods. Purcell, Telemann, and Loeillet are among the many early composers who wrote excellent music for the instrument, and contemporary composers and folk musicians are using it today. It is a popular instrument in elementary and secondary schools throughout the world.

The four different recorders used today form a family.

Soprano (descant)	tuned in C
Alto (treble)	tuned in F
Tenor	tuned in C
Bass	tuned in F

The instruments most widely used in the schools are those tuned in the key of C, the soprano and the tenor. The soprano has the advantage of low cost, and both can play music directly from the song books at the pitch indicated. However, the musically superior instrument is the alto (treble), tuned in F. It is recommended to those who will study the instrument seriously. Its advantages are its excellent tone quality combined with a more dependable tone production than the soprano.

However, most people begin their study of the recorder with the inexpensive soprano (descant) in C. The Baroque (English) fingering is preferred to the German because its use results in playing better in tune, thus only the Baroque fingering will appear here. Careful listening to pitch is essential to playing the instrument well. It helps to sing and play songs alternately so that the mental images of the pitches are reviewed and strengthened. Breath pressure is of vital importance, for the soprano can be easily overblown. Generally speaking, blow *gently*. By controlling breath pressure the player can control intonation.

The solid dots in the fingering chart on p. 173 are closed holes and the white dots are open holes. The half-closed circles require some explanation. When this symbol is used for the left thumb, it means to use the thumbnail in the hole in a manner that closes 90 percent of that hole. In this position the thumb is bent at a right angle with the hole, the flesh covers the largest part of the hole, and there is a small space left between the nail and the upper edge of the hole. This is called "pinching the octave" because the partly closed hole is used to produce pitches an octave higher.

BEGINNING TO PLAY   Hold the instrument with the left hand uppermost (nearest the mouth), with the thumb closing the thumb-hole at the back, and the first three fingers covering the highest three holes. The four fingers of the right hand cover their respective holes, with the thumb help-

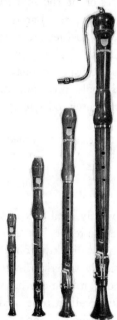

Soprano, Alto, Tenor, and Bass Recorders. Photograph courtesy of Trophy Music Company.

ing to support the recorder as it is played. Holes to be closed must be air-tight, for leakage produces unwanted sounds. Begin your practice of playing the recorder with the tones available by using the fingers of the left hand only. These tones should be mastered before proceeding to those that involve use of the right hand fingers. The five songs notated on the following pages provide an easy approach to learning to play the recorder.

Preparing to blow gently, start the tone with the tip of the tongue as if saying "doo." Stop the tone with the tip of the tongue by bringing it

HOT CROSS BUNS

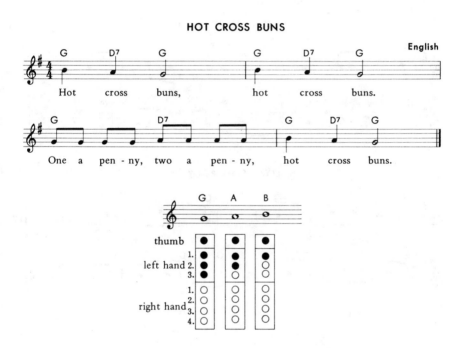

MERRILY WE ROLL ALONG

WHISTLE, DAUGHTER, WHISTLE

GO TELL AUNT RHODY

LOVE SOMEBODY

HOT CROSS BUNS

BAROQUE (ENGLISH) FINGERING FOR SOPRANO RECORDER

O = Open hole ● = Closed hole ◑ = Partially closed hole with end of left thumb and nail.

(fingering chart for notes C, D, E, F, G, A, B, C)

(second fingering chart for notes D, E, F, G, A, B, C)

behind the upper front teeth to stop the breath from entering the instrument.

Harmony Instruments

THE AUTOHARP

The Autoharp is an instrument of ancient lineage which has come to be popular in elementary and junior high schools, and is used by folk singers. The model most popular today has 15 push-button bars with felts that prevent the vibration of strings other than those that sound the chord tones desired. The 12 and 15 bar models are usually preferred to the five bar model, although it has some value in primary grades, since they can be played in more keys, making them generally more useful. The 12 bar model was once the standard instrument. Advantages of the 15 bar model are:

The addition of D major, E♭ major, and F₇ to the original 12 chords provides the primary chords for 7 keys instead of 5 keys on the 12 bar instrument.

The addition of the keys of B♭ major and D major to the original keys of C, F, and G major, and A and D minor offer forty per cent more latitude in key selection.

Five additional chords are provided in the keys of C, F, and B♭.

15-Chord Autoharp. Courtesy Oscar Schmidt International, Inc.

21-Chord Autoharp. Courtesy Oscar Schmidt International, Inc.

The 21-chord instrument is growing rapidly in popularity and may overtake the 15-chord model in usage.

Although some children in primary grades are able to play the instrument satisfactorily, it is not until the fourth grade that most children can do so. In early primary grades teachers often press the chords while children strum the strings. It is believed that guiding children to listen carefully to Autoharp chording assists the development of a feeling for harmony, which is part of the preparation for part-singing in intermediate grades. It is a substitute for the piano in situations where no piano is available, as well as being valuable for enrichment in rooms that have pianos. Hearing chord changes and playing the correct chord at the proper time are valuable for ear-training purposes, and teachers should emphasize these as listening experiences in their efforts to develop children's musicianship. The act of chording is a rhythmic response. A child who is yet unable to sing beautifully may be able to make as beautiful music on the Autoharp as anyone else; thus success on this instrument can help individual children feel a sense of accomplishment essential to good social and emotional growth. Chording on the Autoharp is an effective way to stimulate interest in the study of chords on the piano and on the staff. Another use of the Autoharp is to establish the tempo of a song by playing introductory chords in the desired rhythm.

The Autoharp is placed on a desk or table, with the corner between the two straight ends of the instrument pointing somewhat toward the player. Fingers of the left hand press firmly on the appropriate chord while the right hand strokes the full range of the strings from left to right with a pick. Sometimes the player may choose to stroke the strings on the left side of the bridge to produce a deeper-toned effect than is obtained on the right side. *Finger forms* are important, and the player needs to analyze the chord progressions he is to play, then plan the most simple and efficient way to place the correct finger on the chord. In most of the music suggested for Autoharp chording there will be no more than three chords, the tonic (I), the dominant seventh (V_7), and the subdominant (IV). The finger form for these chords in the keys of C major, G major, F major, D minor, and A minor is as follows:

	IV	V_7	I
left hand			
	ring finger	middle finger	index finger

Try the finger form in the above keys, and find the straight position and the triangular position of the fingers in this basic finger form.

For advanced strumming, the instrument is held in the arms. It then becomes an effective substitute for the guitar. Some teachers install strap fittings, wearing the strap across the left shoulder and across the back to join the Autoharp at the lower right side. See *Teaching Music with the Autoharp*, Music Education Group, Union, New Jersey 07083.

Appalachian style playing. A shoulder strap may be attached. Courtesy Oscar Schmidt International, Inc.

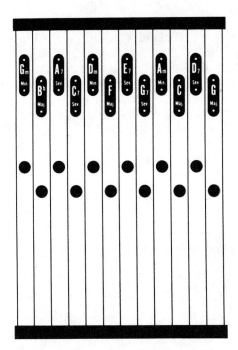

Autoharp Bridge (12-bar Model)

The strings are stroked with a pick held in the right hand, unless the player is left handed. The loud tone produced with a plastic pick is needed for most classroom singing, while the soft tone produced with a felt pick is best for solo and small ensemble singing. Picks are made in different shapes and sizes. Some are worn on a finger while others are held between thumb and index finger. Some teachers use the plastic fasteners from bread wrappers as substitutes. Others use their fingernails instead of a pick.

When teaching children to play the Autoharp, it is the usual practice to begin with songs that require only one chord to accompany, proceeding to those requiring two chords, then to songs in which three chords are necessary. It is desirable to play part of the time by rote to be sure that the children are *hearing* the chord changes, not simply playing chords mechanically. Such songs follow:

I-chord songs:	*key*
"Row Your Boat", "Little Tom Tinker"	
"Are You Sleeping?" "Farmer in the Dell," "For Health and Strength"	F major
"Canoe Song"	D minor
"Zum Gali Gali"	G minor

II-chord songs:

"Mary Had a Little Lamb," "Sandy Land," "Looby Loo,"	G major
"London Bridge," "Ten Little Indians," "Hush Little Baby,"	
"Polly Wolly Doodle"	F major
"Old Smoky," "Oats, Peas, Beans, and Barley" "Little Red	
Caboose"	C major
"Down in the Valley," "Long Long Ago," "Bow Belinda,"	
"Shoo Fly," "Susie Little Susie"	F major
"Nobody Home"	G minor
"Lovely Evening" (I-IV)	F major
"Wayfaring Stranger"	D minor

III-chord songs:

"Silent Night," Brahms' "Lullaby," "Marines' Hymn"	C major
"My Bonnie," "Jingle Bells," "Camptown Races," "Old	
Brass Wagon"	G major
"Red River Valley," "Twinkle Twinkle, Little Star," "This	
Old Man," "Hickory Dickory Dock," "Home on the	
Range"	F major
"Go Down, Moses"	A minor
"Old King Cole"	D minor

Since some two- and three-chord songs are not written in these common keys, using the Autoharp to accompany them requires *transposing* them into keys that will make it possible to play such songs on the instrument. This involves placing the fingers in the finger form of the key nearest to the original key of the song and following the I, V$_7$, and IV designations, or their equivalent in letter names. The teacher should be certain that the range of pitches in the new key is suitable for children's voices. The 15 bar model permits playing in B♭ and D major also.

A problem in the use of Autoharps is tuning them.[8] There is no universally accepted method. Ordinarily, one tunes to a piano that is in proper pitch, although a pitch pipe can be used. The strings sounding the C major chord may be tuned first (all the C's, E's, and G's), then the strings of the G$_7$ chord (all B's, D's, and F's—the G's having been tuned as part of the C chord), and next the F major chord (all A's—the F's and C's having been tuned as pitches belonging to the other chords). These three chords should then be played slowly to hear whether any of the strings need further adjusting. After this, the other strings may be tuned as in-

[8]The new Autoharps remain in tune much longer than the earlier models.

Autoharp Bridge (15-bar Model)

dividual tones of the chromatic scale (all the half-steps). Then every chord of the instrument is played slowly to determine possible need for further tuning. A child can play the pitches on the piano while the teacher adjusts the strings. As a general rule, the teacher must do the adjusting of the strings, not the children. The only cases the authors know where strings have been broken are those in which elementary school children tighten strings to the breaking point because they think they hear the pitch to which they are tuning one octave higher than it sounds. To keep the instrument in tune and to protect it, it should be kept either in the case it comes in or on a covered shelf, out of the sunlight and away from sources of heat, cold, or dampness. When the instrument is subject to changes in temperature, the expansion and contraction of the strings causes changes in their tension, hence changes in pitch.

TYPES OF AUTOHARP ACCOMPANIMENTS   Like any other musical instrument, the Autoharp should be played with good taste, and there should be logical reasons for the particular style of the accompaniment played. The mood of the song indicates whether the player uses a slow relaxed stroke (as for lullabies and quiet songs), or a strong fast stroke (as for marches and rhythmic, exciting songs). For some waltzes, an um-pah-pah style is called for. This can be made by sounding the first beat of each measure with low-pitched strings and the other two beats with high-pitched strings. A deeper, richer effect is obtained by playing on the left side of the bridge. This brings out the sound of the lower strings and omits a few of the highest pitches. The player can make an appropriate accompaniment for some Spanish-type music by chording in the rhythm of ♩. ♪♩ ♩ A bagpipe or bourdon effect is made by holding down two buttons at the same time: G major and G minor, D₇ and D minor, and A₇ and A minor. This effect is useful for pentatonic music, for some Scottish music, and for folk songs based upon the open fifth of the bagpipe or musette. Individual strings can be plucked to simulate Oriental-type music. A zither or tamburitza effect that characterizes some Eastern European folk music can be produced by two players on the same instrument. One player presses the buttons while the other strokes the strings rapidly with wooden mallets. A metal bar or object placed across the strings will produce a steel guitar effect. Minor seventh chords can be sounded when two instruments are used. For example, G-minor and B♭-major chords played simultaneously will sound the G-minor seventh chord. A minor plus C major will sound the A-minor seventh chord, and D minor plus F major sounds the D-minor seventh chord. For songs of slow tempo, a skilled player can produce both the melody and the harmony. To obtain this effect, a chord is played for each tone of the melody, and the player strums the strings only as far as the melody pitch. A harp effect is obtained by reversing the usual stroke, the player beginning the stroke with the high strings and moving the pick toward the low strings.

UKULELE AND GUITAR

If the desirability of chording experiences on the Autoharp has gained wide acceptance in elementary music education, it follows that there should be similar values in other chording instruments such as the ukulele and guitar. The ukulele has supporters from the fourth grade on, and chording on the guitar is done by some children who are ten and eleven years old.

Standard tuning on the ukulele was once G-C-E-A from low to high strings. In recent years a preference for tuning the instrument one whole step higher, to A-D-F♯-B, has developed. Thus, the ukulele beginner finds

two tunings in current use. Notice that if the teacher employs both tunings, the fingering for the common chords in G major and F major become the same, as does that for D major and C major.

Experts in ukulele playing state that while the baritone ukulele is superior in tone quality and many teachers prefer it to the soprano (standard) instrument, the soprano is best for elementary school children in terms of student hand size; it is easier for children to play. It is easily retuned in C, when this is desirable for a whole-step lower singing range, and it costs less than the baritone. Wood is preferred to plastic. Some teachers introduce

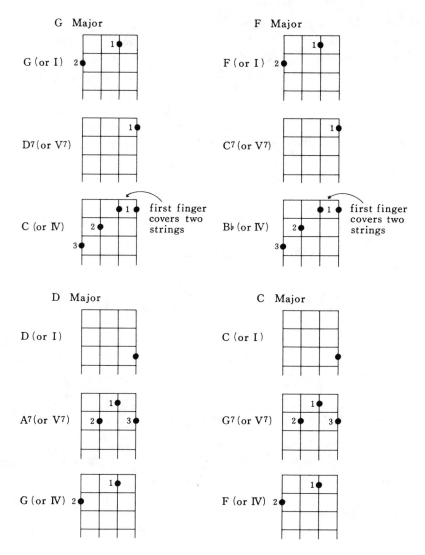

the ukulele in a way that relates to the guitar and string bass. The following describes this approach, which begins with the D tuning of the soprano ukulele: A D F-sharp B.

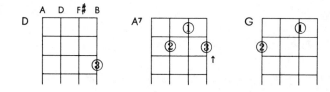

With the third finger as an anchor one can slide it up to the second fret and form:

The dominant 7th, A₇. The IV chord has one finger in common with the V₇;

One can use these fingers as pivots when he goes from one chord to another.

With these three primary chords one can play many folk songs.

The baritone, which is becoming a popular instrument for adults, is tuned a 5th below the soprano ukulele. Its first string, however, is an octave and a 5th below the soprano's first string, making its strings the same as the top four strings of the standard guitar;

Baritone Tuning:

(guitar strings)

This makes it a good instrument for beginners who may want to transfer to a standard guitar later on. The chords will be formed in the same way but will sound in different keys.

If one is using both instruments simultaneously, it is possible to stagger the teaching of these fingerings, permitting the advantage of being able to practice together. A system one teacher[9] devised to teach seven fingerings on each instrument makes possible playing all primary chords in two keys in common plus one extra key for each. Directly below these are the added fingerings for the other two strings on the guitar.

These seven fingerings are the easiest for the beginner to play. They comprise the primary triads of the keys of D, G, and C major for the ukulele, and G, C, and F major for the baritone ukulele.

Guitar chords that are easiest for the older child to play are those to follow. They are not easily learned. One clever little girl removed the lower two strings on her guitar so she could practice the baritone fingerings until her fingers grew stronger.

Also to be noted is the fact that the lower four guitar strings are the same as those on the string bass. The chord-roots are plucked with the index finger when played with other folk instruments. These can be related to chords on the guitar; this would be useful only to a student knowing the guitar chords well.

Since the string bass does not have frets, small thin strips of masking tape can be used to mark the half steps for inexperienced players.

[9]Mrs. Erma Kleehammer, University of Calgary. Calgary, Alberta, Canada.

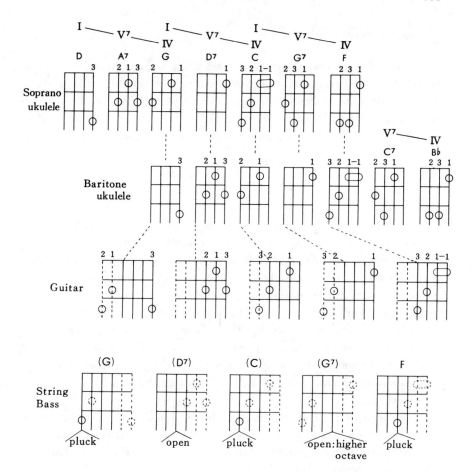

Some of the more common minor chords for the ukulele, baritone and guitar are:

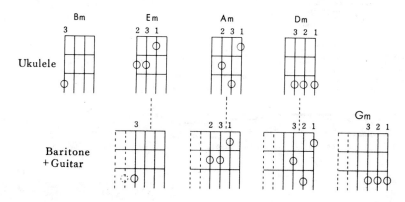

PIANO CHORDING

Since the 1 3 5 note pattern becomes a familiar one to children, being used both in their songs and in the procedure that enables the class to have a feeling for the key before singing, this is a logical note combination to use in the initial teaching of chording. This 1 3 5 chord (a major *triad* in *root position*) is also a basic concept in the study of music theory.

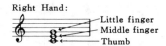

Should a child be unable to exert equal pressure through these three fingers or in any other way be unable to control them at first, he may use any combination of fingers of both hands to accomplish the playing of this chord, or he may play only the two highest notes of a three-note chord, a procedure often employed in primary grades. The teacher may help the child to play the chord in a steady walking-note rhythm, then while he continues playing in rhythm, have the class sing "Row, row, row your boat." To a child who has never played the piano, the discovery that he can accompany a well-known song in this simple manner is thrilling. There are few songs that can be accompanied by the lone 1 3 5 chord. Some were listed earlier in this chapter.

Songs that rightfully require two chords (I and V₇) but that might be usable as one-chord songs include "Old MacDonald," "Farmer in the Dell," "Three Blind Mice," "Goodbye Old Paint," "Swing Low Sweet Chariot," "Taps," and "Shortnin' Bread."

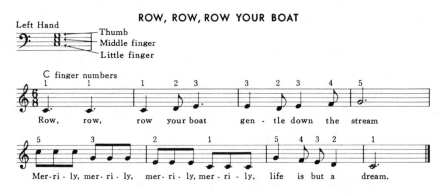

ROW, ROW, ROW YOUR BOAT

Summary of possibilities:

Play the melody with the right hand.
Play the melody with the left hand.
Play the chord with the left hand.
Play the chord with the right hand.
Play the chord with both hands.
Play the melody with the right hand and the chord with the left hand.
Play the melody with the left hand (in bass clef) and the chord with the right hand (in treble clef).
Play the chord in other forms, such as one note at a time.

How often the chord is sounded depends on how the individual feels about the song. One child may play a chord on every beat. Another may choose to sound the chord every other beat. Still another child may alter the steady pattern of chord-sounding by a pause at the end of a phrase. Children should be free to be as individually creative as possible in this simple way.

When a child has learned how to build 1 3 5 chords on different pitches such as C, F, G, and has learned to recognize the distinctive sound of the major chord, the 1 3 5 chord in minor may be easily taught. A child can soon learn that the minor chord has its own characteristic sound and that he can build both major and minor chords at will. Experience will expand the child's feeling for the difference in sound between major and minor. The mechanical difference between major and minor 1 3 5 chords is merely that the middle finger, which plays scale tone 3, is placed one halfstep lower in minor than in major. Few commonly known songs can be accompanied by the lone minor 1 3 5 chord, but children can compose such songs easily.

A song of Israeli origin that can be accompanied by the G-minor chord is "Zum Gali Gali."

If children have used the Autoharp with songs requiring two or more different chords, the addition of the V₇ chord to permit improvising a piano accompaniment to many familiar songs is relatively easy. A simple form of the chord change from I to V₇ and back to I is as follows:

Using the hand position for the 1 3 5 *chord as a starting point,* the following directions apply in *all* major keys:

right hand: The little finger remains on the same key. The fourth finger is placed one half-step higher than the third finger was. The thumb is placed one half-step lower than before.

left hand: The thumb remains on the same key. The index finger is placed one half-step higher than the middle finger was. The little finger is placed one half-step lower than before.

Many songs can be harmonized with the I and V_7 chords. Some of the most familiar were listed earlier for Autoharp chording.

Since most songs in minor keys are based on a scale in which the seventh tone is raised one half-step, practically all minor I-V_7 chord songs will have the V_7 chord played exactly the same as it is played in the major keys of the same name, i.e., the V_7 chord in G minor is the same chord as in G major. Thus, the only difference in chording would be in the I chord, which in minor would have its third (the middle note) one half-step lower than in the major chord. It is a simple matter, then, to play "Nobody Home" in G minor:[10]

NOBODY HOME

Three-Part Round

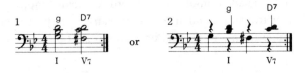

Piano chording:

[10]Some musicians abbreviate G minor by writing "g," and G major by "G."

or yet another way:

Other interesting songs in minor that use these same chords are the French carol "Pat-a-pan" and the English carol "Dame, Get Up." Percussion instruments go well with "Pat-a-pan."

The hand position for the IV chord is easier than the hand position for the V₇ chord. The "rule" for the change from I to IV is as follows:

left hand: The little finger remains on the same key. The index finger is placed one half-step higher than the middle finger was. The thumb moves up one whole step.

right hand: The thumb remains on the same key. The middle finger is placed one half-step higher than before. The little finger moves up one whole step.

The round "Christmas Bells" provides a good introduction to this chord change. Use the above chords as marked.

The familiar round "Lovely Evening" and the cowboy song "The Railroad Corral" (*This Is Music: Book 6*) are other examples of songs that require only the I and IV chords for their harmonization.

CHRISTMAS BELLS

The IV chord in minor is played by lowering the highest of the three tones of the major IV chord one half-step. An American folk song that can be harmonized with only I and IV chords is "Wayfaring Stranger":

WAYFARING STRANGER

Examples of the many songs in major keys easily chorded with I, IV, and V7 chords are "The Caisson Song," "Oh Susanna," "He's a Jolly Good Fellow," "The First Noel," "Night Herding Song," "Eyes of Texas (I've Been Working on the Railroad)," "All Through the Night," "Sing Your Way Home," "Deck the Halls," "Happy Birthday to You," "Old Oaken Bucket," "Auld Lang Syne," "Annie Laurie," "Old Folks at Home," "Reuben and Rachel," "Santa Lucia," "The Muffin Man." Others were listed earlier for Autoharp chording.

This use of the piano in the classroom can result in a teacher's learning to play comparatively well. Should any teacher desire to hasten this learning process, there are beginning piano books that employ and expand the method of chording used in this chapter; by means of these an adult can teach himself to play with more skill.

Teachers should use the loud (sustaining) pedal of the piano sparingly. A common fault of piano players is overuse of this pedal, which results in a blur of tones rather than in the clarity and distinctness children need to hear.

CHORDING WITH BELLS

The "piano chords" can be played on resonator bells effectively. Teachers use these individual tone bars in many ways. The bars can be distributed among numbers of children, each having a bar and a mallet with which to strike it. In the key of C, for example, all children who hold bells marked C, E or G, will sound them when the C-major chord is needed, and when the F-major chord is required in the harmonization of the song, all children holding bars that sound F, A, and C will strike them. Of course, they must be struck at the same instant, and this demands the close attention of the players. To produce an interesting shimmering effect, the player needs two mallets with which he strikes the bell in rapid alternation. Playing chords in this manner with appropriate songs can make truly beautiful music. Motivating a fourth, fifth, or sixth-grade class to harmonize a song in this way can initiate a study of chord structure that includes learning note names and their relation to the staff and key signature.

Hand bells can be used also, and the Melodica was mentioned earlier as an instrument on which one can play both melody and harmony.

THE SINGING CLASSROOM ORCHESTRA

When children have learned to play small wind instruments, to chord on the piano and Autoharp, and to play the bells and percussion instruments, the possibility of the singing classroom orchestra presents itself. When the teacher finds a melody line in the range of the wind instruments with the chords named, there are opportunities for combining various instruments with voices, or alternating instruments and voices. Here is a creative activity developing musical discrimination—the children and the teacher will have to orchestrate the song according to their own judgment. Children can also have experiences in conducting such orchestras. Songs that are not found in books at hand can be presented by means of projector or can be drawn on large (two by three feet) sheets of heavy paper or light cardboard and placed where all the children can see. Music can be quickly drawn on such paper. A staff liner with chalk is used to mark the staff. These chalk lines are drawn over with black crayon, freehand. When two-part songs are written, the melody part may be in black crayon while the harmony part is in another color for easier reading. Examples follow:

The *Theme from the Ninth Symphony* is an example of the very simple beginning music a classroom orchestra uses. Ordinarily, themes from the great symphonies are not applicable to this type of work. This particular theme, however, has the simplicity of folk music and is understood easily by children. It can be extended to include more of the original melody than appears here. A thrilling event after words have been set to it and the song is learned, is the teacher's playing a recording of a section of the last movement of the *Ninth Symphony*. Watching the reaction, she will find children who are fascinated listeners to "their song" and who will be interested in what Beethoven does with it. Appreciation may be at an extremely high level at this point. The key of C was chosen because it is easiest for the playing of the instruments. The key of F is preferable as soon as the fingering of B♭ is learned, because it places the singing voice in a better range.

"Come, Ye Thankful People, Come" is much more difficult and represents a later experience in the development of the classroom orchestra.

While some classroom teachers will be able to write their own class-room orchestra arrangements and make their own charts, others may not be able to do so. In these cases the music specialist becomes the helper, the arranger, and perhaps the chart-maker who assists the room teacher.

Instrumental music activities in the general music program constitute not an end in themselves but an important aid in the teaching of better listening, singing, musical discrimination, creativity, part-singing, and note-reading, and serve as an introduction to simple music theory—all in a setting that children enjoy, understand, and know to be purposeful. It is essential that instruments used in combination in the classroom be in tune with each other. It has been suggested that instruments be used en masse only one period during the week; on that day the teacher should so organize the lesson that the children are singing approximately half the time.

Teaching With Instruments

Low-high.

Relate low and high (vertical relation-ship of objects) with the keyboard left and right.

Experiment in composition.

Have individual young children select any four resonator bells. Arrange them in scale order and make up tunes on them.

Composition.

Let children invent tunes and songs on resonator bells, limited by the num-ber of bars given them. Begin with two or three adjacent pitches; ex-pand gradually to 4, 5, 6, and 8.

Composition on black keys.

Let children create pentatonic tunes and songs on keyboard black keys or on resonator bars representing a penta-tonic scale on other keys.

Scale.

Build the major scale concept (and later on, other scales) by means of children's playing them on keyboard instruments: bells, xylophone, Mel-odica, piano. Have them analyze scale patterns by examining the keyboard.

Tonal relationships.

Have a large chart of the keyboard at the front of the room so that it can be used to answer questions and solve musical problems.

Staff.

Relate bars of bell sets to line and spaces on the staff. The glockenturm does this at once. A regular bell set can be placed in a vertical position and lines drawn from it on the chalkboard or on chart paper.

Note names.

Children can learn note names by learning fingerings on small wind instruments in order to play tunes. Most bell sets have note names stamped into the metal.

Names of lines and spaces.

Musicians believe that the best way to learn names of the lines and spaces is by using note names when instruments are played; another good way is by learning the grand staff, in which one finds five lines above and below middle C.

Improvisation.

Teacher or child establishes a percussion rhythm pattern. Children take turns improvising over this pattern on selected melody instruments.

Individual practice.

Provide for individual practice and experimentation on the keyboard by using a small classroom organ with head sets so that only the player hears the sound.

Less common intervals.

For advanced children. Arrange for students to discover by means of the keyboard the two kinds of seconds, thirds, sixths, and sevenths (major or minor, or large or small). What might an *augmented* interval be? (expand a major interval by another half step.) What might a *diminished* interval be? (Contract a minor interval by another half step.) Use the keyboard, then notation to answer these questions so that the students see, hear, and feel these intervals. A question by a student, "Why are fourths, fifths, and octaves called *perfect* intervals?" is difficult to answer. The subject is not important at the elementary level, but any child's question is important to him. Technically, a perfect interval is one in which each tone of the interval appears in a major scale in which the other is *do* or *1*. This is true of fourths, fifths, and octaves, thus these are the "perfect" intervals.

Tonal memory.

A game to be played by two recorder players is one in which the first player performs a short series of pitches to be imitated by the second player.

Keyboard instruments assist note reading.

The "suggestions to the teacher" in one of the music series states that if children had access to keyboard instruments, many of the problems in teaching understanding of pitch differences, of the interval relationship of notes, and of music notation generally would be minimized. The reason is that the keyboard constitutes a highly significant *audio-visual* tool for learning. Children enjoy picking out tunes and in doing so on the bells or piano they *see, feel,* and *hear* the interval relationships of tones. This can lead to a comprehension of the meaning of notes on the staff—a comprehension frequently lacking in children whose musical experiences have been confined to a singing approach. In every classroom there should be a music learning center that includes bells and easy music to play on them. Some teachers have·a "song of the week" which children learn to play before school, after school, and during the school day. When played with a padded mallet or a pencil with a rubber eraser, this soft-toned instrument seldom disturbs other classroom activities.

Ear training with bells.

The teacher plays a few consecutive scale tones on the bells; a child is asked to come to the bells and play what he has heard. A child can make up a short tune; he then asks another child to play what he has heard. If this child does it correctly, he then has the privilege of making up a tune and calling on another classmate to remember it and play it. If a child cannot remember the tune, another is called on. The class listens and judges. (This needs to be a game, not "pressure.") The teacher asks a child to play an easy, well-known song. At first the teacher will give the starting pitch. Later, as the game grows more demanding, the child will have to find that pitch. Later, older children can "take dictation" from the teacher's playing the bells. The teacher will give the name of the first note and the key in which the dictation will be given. Then the children will write the pitches they hear on the staff in notation, either individually on paper or collectively with a flannel or magnetic board. The chalk board could be used by a number of children, each working alone.

Easy piano in the classroom.

One finger: The child plays repeated single tones such as the beginning of "Jingle Bells." He can also play a tone-matching game by striking a pitch that is within his voice range, then trying to match it vocally. *Two fingers:* The child plays repeated motives in songs when these are limited to two pitches such as scale tones 5 and 3 (*so* and *mi*). Example: "This Old Man." *Three fingers:* The scale tones 3 2 1 can be played whenever the words "three blind mice" occur in the song of that name. The tonal pattern 1 2 3 1 can be played with the words "Are you sleeping?" in the song of that name. *Four fingers:* Scale tones 4 4 3 3 2 2 1 in "Twinkle, Twinkle, Little Star" can be played when the words "How I wonder what you are," and "Twinkle, twinkle all the night" appear. Scale tones 5 5 4 4 3 3 2 can be played along with the words. "Up above the world so high," and "Like a diamond in the sky." *Five fingers*: Scale tones 5 43 21 are used at the end of "Row Your Boat" with the words, "Life is but a dream." Scale tones 5 443 2 1 are used with the words "Ten Little Indian Boys" at the end of that song. *Scales*: Some songs are based on scales and parts of scales that can be played readily on the keyboard. *Composition:* A natural outgrowth of such piano-song relationships is the composing of little tunes or songs within the limitations of three, four, and five scale tones. This activity will lead toward the use of additional scale tones. Evaluate for classroom use the songs of 5-note range listed at the beginning of this chapter by playing them with five fingers.

Adding simple parts.

A simple bell or piano part can be added to songs by asking the player to sound only the note that is the first one in each measure. While technically any song can be used for this, songs that have each measure harmonized with one chord are obviously good. The Danish song "Han Skal Leve," sometimes titled "Birthday Song," is one. Parts of some songs, such as "Weggis Song," are good to use. Songs with melody-lines that suggest scale patterns are also appropriate. The following are in *Singing With Children*: "Carrousel," "Clap Hands With Me," "Blow the Winds Southerly," "The Donkey," "Streets of Laredo."

Transposition.

Help older children develop comprehension of this concept by playing a familiar song in several keys on a melody instrument. Ask the class what they think you did. Then ask the children to find easy tunes by ear, beginning on pitches selected by the teacher.

Key signature.

This puzzle game relates to both ear training and tonal memory. The children will find that transposition demands different key signatures, which is another puzzle relating to the scale in which the song was played.

Transposing instruments.

When older children examine a band or orchestra score that they borrow from the instrumental music teacher, they will find that the music is written in a number of different keys. They may find that some instruments are built in different keys. By experimenting with notes on instruments and comparing the resulting pitch with the piano or bells, they can discover that when B flat instruments play written C, the pitch is B flat, and when E flat instruments play C, the pitch sounded in E flat. The teacher could plan a discrepant event by asking children who play instruments to all play the same song from a music textbook. This would be one way to discover which instruments are transposing instruments and which are not.

Tonal memory.

Have individual children find on the black keys of the piano or bells pentatonic melodies they know such as "Goodby, Old Paint," "Grandma Grunts," "The Riddle Song," "Nobody Knows the Trouble I've Seen," "Night Herding Song,' "Old MacDonald," "All Night, All Day," "Get on Board," "Auld Lang Syne," "Land of the Silver Birch," "The Campbells Are Coming," and "Swing Low, Sweet Chariot."

Bitonality.

Play a well-known song such as "Hot Cross Buns," using two keyboard instruments, each in a different key. "Farmer in the Dell" and "Mary Had a Little Lamb" are other candidates. Have the class judge the effect of hearing two keys at once. The effect can be altered somewhat by the tone qualities of the instruments used.

Intervals and bitonality.

Play these same tunes on the instruments at different intervals to explore further this contemporary device.

Retrograde.

Try playing a melody in retrograde (backwards). Also try this with two instruments, one playing the melody in the usual way while the other plays it in retrograde at the same time.

Adding Vocal and Instrumental Parts

Chant.

Parts of rounds can be used as repeated melodic fragments or *chants*. The "ding, dong, ding" (1, 5, 1) part of "Are You Sleeping?" is a commonly-used example of such a part that can be sung repeatedly and continuously along with the melody.

Ostinato.

If the part is played on an instrument it is called an *ostinato*. Reasons for using chants and ostinati include: 1. to provide for individual differences in singing ability and range; the lower-ranged singer can often sing a chant more easily, 2. to provide a worthwhile activity that a nonsinger can enjoy when he plays an ostinato, 3. to develop independence in a type of part-singing that prepares for harmonic part singing later on, and 4. to increase interest and enjoyment.

The following section is reproduced from Robert E. Nye and Bjornar Bergethon, *Basic Music*, 3rd ed., 1968, with permission of Prentice-Hall, Inc., the copyright owner.

CHANTS AND OSTINATI FOR I CHORD TUNES   It is easy to create a chant or ostinato to melodies which can be accompanied with only the I chord by basing it on the chord-root (1 or *do*). An example of this is the chant provided for "Little Tom Tinker," a melody that can be accompanied in its entirety with only the I chord. The chant is made up of two rhythmic motives taken from the song (♩ ♩ ♩ ♩ ♩ ♩ and ♩ ♪ ♩ ♪),

and the words attached to it are a logical comment on what is happening to little Tom:

LITTLE TOM TINKER

Practice the chant as you conduct the beat (fast ⁶⁄₈ meter). Next, divide the class into two groups, one of melody-singers and one of chanters, and sing the two parts together.

Chants such as this one are really more rhythmic than melodic, i.e., they have no melody—only one chanted pitch, and can also be played on a suitable percussion instrument.

An introduction to "Little Tom Tinker" can be created by having the chanters sing their pattern twice (four measures) before the melody singers enter. And at the end of the song the chanters can continue for another four measures to form a coda.

Scale-line chants and ostinati can also be very effective. An example of this is the following motive for "Little Tom Tinker." It has been transposed to the key of E♭ so that the chanters will not have to sing too low.

Tom - my Tink - er

Another suggestion is to sing it as a two-part round plus the chant. With the addition of the introduction and the coda you will find that this song presentation becomes something of a "winding up" and "unwinding" process which makes it seem quite impressive.

Still more can be done by adding to the chant on scale tone 1 the same chant on 3, then adding another (all with the same words) on 5. As these parts are added, you find the chant sounding in three parts (1-3-5 chord tones). With the addition of the melody, a simple form of four-part singing results. Try this.

Here is another well-known round, the melody of which can be harmonized with only the I chord.

ARE YOU SLEEPING?

Quietly

Anonymous

Among the chants and ostinati possible for this song are:

Note that scale tone 6 (D) sounds good even though it is not a chord tone. Try dividing the class into three groups. Have the first group sing the melody, the second group sing the one-note chant written below the melody, and the third group sing chant 3. Then try other combinations of chants and melody.

Other songs which can be harmonized with I chord only are "Good-bye, Ol' Paint", "Short'nin' Bread", "Row, Row, Row Your Boat", and "Old Chisholm Trail". Try creating chants and ostinati for these.

CHANTS AND OSTINATI FOR I-V₇ CHORD TUNES   Chants can be improvised for songs which are harmonized with both the I and V₇ chords by using scale tone 5 throughout the song, except at the end, perhaps, where scale tone 1 may be needed to give the chant an appropriate ending. You will recall that scale tone 5 is common to both the I and V₇ chords:

$$
I \left\{
\begin{array}{l}
5\text{\_ \_ \_ \_ \_ \_ \_}5 \\
3 \\
1
\end{array}
\right.
\qquad
\left.
\begin{array}{l}
4 \\
2 \\
7
\end{array}
\right\} V_7
$$

Therefore, a chant based on this tone will harmonize with either chord. Such chants are of the same type as those used for I chord tunes. For example, a chant for "Sandy Land" would be based on C (5) which is the common tone for the F (1) and C₇ (V₇) chords:

Sand - y   land,   Sand - y   land.

SANDY LAND

Lively   Play-Party Song

Make my liv-ing in   sand- y   land,   Make my liv-ing in   sand- y   land,

Make my   liv- ing in   sand - y   land,   La - dies, fare   you   well.

Some two-chord songs have a harmonic pattern which is repeated throughout the song. "Three Blind Mice" is one of these.

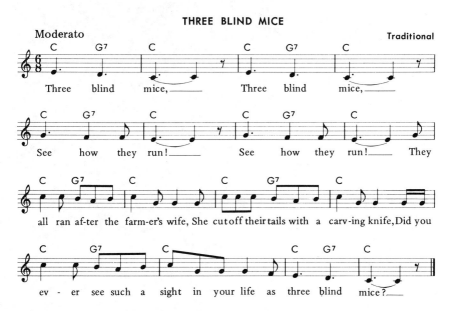

Note that the harmonic pattern C-G₇-C (I-V₇-I) is repeated every two measures, and to create an ostinato for this song you must choose chord tones that fit this pattern. As you examine this chord progression, you will discover the possibility of two ostinati (1 and 2) and also that these might be combined into a two-part ostinato (3) made up of parallel thirds.

Try all three of these ostinati.

Other songs with repeated harmonic patterns are "Grandma Grunts" and "Go In and Out the Window." You have already used scale tone 6 in chants for "Little Tom Tinker" and "Are You Sleeping?" quite effectively. This nonchord tone has the unique property of blending with both the I and V₇ chord and it is useful in creating chants for certain types of songs. Thus, the tone figure 5-6-5 makes an interesting chant for "Skip to My Lou."

SKIP TO MY LOU

American Singing Game

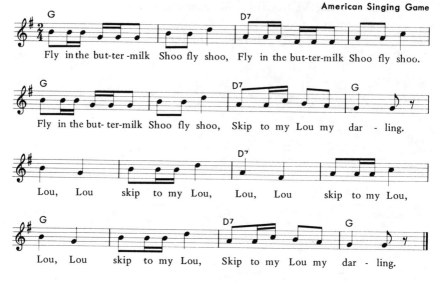

After learning the song, add this "5-6-5" chant:

To add variety to the final measures or to a coda, try:

Chants are sometimes made more enjoyable (and more effective) when the chanters stop singing for a few measures and then begin again, rather than sing the chant through the entire song. You may wish to experiment with this idea when a chant becomes monotonous.

Here is a song based on the old tune "Oh Bury Me Not on the Lone Prairie."

Sing it through several times while conducting or clapping the beats. As you sing, be sure to sustain the long notes (♩) which are *tied* over to connecting short notes (♩ ♩). After that add an accompaniment with the Autoharp and piano. Next, add a chant on 5 and 6, on the words "Leavin' Old Texas." Finally, imitate the "ridin' along" or "joggin' along" of the cowboy on his horse with percussion instruments on the rhythmic pattern. Here is how it would look:

Begin with an introduction and end with a coda.

Still another idea for "Old Texas" is to make a two-part round out of it. When you do this, leave out the chording.

I'm goin' to leave_____ old Tex-as now_____ They've got no

I'm goin' to leave _____ old _ Tex-as now

After you have mastered singing the song as a round, try adding the chant and the percussion instruments. You now have a song with three different parts being sung at one time, combined with a rhythmic accompaniment for good measure—a real accomplishment indeed.

Chants, ostinati.

Encourage children to create chants and ostinati to add variety to pentatonic songs and other songs of very simple harmonization. Begin with songs that can be accompanied harmonically with only one chord throughout.

The approach of Carl Orff.

The approach of the German composer Carl Orff to children's music includes the addition of ostinati to pentatonic melodies, thus providing a polyphonic texture. The creation of this type of music may begin with a *bourdon* (often a drone-like open fifth in the bass). From this can be developed more active bourdons produced by alternating the two pitches. Both growing from this and adding to it are the repeated tonal fragments, the ostinati. It is assumed that within these limitations children can create music that is truly children's music rather than music that is basically adult and too complex harmonically for children to comprehend fully. Bourdons that sound one octave lower are played on the alto glockenspiel or metallophone. Two mallets are used.

bourdons (alto glockenspiel sounds one octave higher)

ostinati (soprano glockenspiel, xylophone)

In the example below, begin with the bourdon for two measures, then add the ostinato for two measures, then begin the melody as the other two parts continue. You may wish to add a bit of percussion—perhaps finger cymbal and tambourine. As your improvised composition progresses, you may want the percussion to alternate with some of the other parts, or they could invent their own ostinati. On the other hand, the percussion instruments could be played only occasionally for a special accent or interesting sound effect.

improvised melody (recorder, bells)   continue

ostinati (two of them)

bourdon

This use of the pentatonic idiom is only the beginning of this aspect of the Orff approach. Like the Manhattanville Music Curriculum Project, it expands to encompass all of music. Here we are dealing with only a small part of this added resource for music teaching. The student is referred to references for further study. *Singing With Children*, 2nd ed., describes how to write a more advanced composition in the Orff style (pp. 121–123). The major references have essentially the same title. The film *Music For Children* is available from Contemporary Films, 267 West 25th Street, New York City 10001; a record album of the same title, recorded in England by Angel and marketed in the United States by Capitol Records, is available from any record shop. The books *Music For Children I Pentatonic, Music For Children II Major, and Music for Children III Minor,* can be obtained from Magnamusic-Baton, 10370 Page Industrial Blvd., St. Louis, Mo. 63132, English adaptation by Doreen Hall and Arnold Walter.

STUDIO 49 *Orff Instruments. Photograph courtesy of Magnamusic-Baton, Inc., St. Louis, Mo.*

Orff-inspired instruments can be obtained from M. Hohner, Inc., Andrews Road, Hicksville, New York; Rhythm Band, Inc., 407–409 Throckmorton Street, Fort Worth, Texas; Lyons Band Instrument Company, 530 Riverview Ave., Elkhart, Indiana 46514; Musser-Kitching (Ludwig), 1728 N. Damen Ave., Chicago, Ill. 60647; J. C. Deagan, Inc., 1770 West Berteau Ave., Chicago, Ill. 60613; Music Education Group, Garden State Road, Union, N.J. 07083; and the imported Studio 49 instruments can be obtained from Magnamusic-Baton, Inc., 10370 Page Industrial Blvd., St. Louis, Mo. 63132.

Form

Same, different.

The teacher's question, "Is the tune the same as it was, or is it different now?" is a key to helping children understand musical form. "Did the music stay the same, or did it change?" is another way to state the question. It centers attention on the phrases of songs and on sections of larger forms. It focuses attention on unity (repetition) provided by repeating the phrase or section, and on variety (contrast) provided by the phrase or section being different. These concepts should be reinforced by studying the notation of the music because one can *see* repetition and contrast in the notation.

Altering and extending melodies.

Sometimes children want to sing a melody differently than it is notated. The teacher should call attention to the difference and suggest that the class try the song both ways and decide which is best. Criteria for judgment may include ease of singing and a better communication of the message of the song. After all, children can sometimes improve songs written by adults. Melodies can be extended by introductions and codas; interludes can be improvised between repetitions of songs played by percussion and/or melody instruments.

Variations.

The children are assigned an easy, simple, familiar song tune. They are asked to rewrite it in response to the question, "In how many different ways might this tune be varied?" The answer could involve changing the melody, meter, tempo, key (from major to minor or vice versa), accompaniment, tone quality, texture, dynamics, and style. See "Variation form" in the next chapter.

Cadence.

Compare and analyze phrase endings in songs. Advanced students may be interested in the questions: How are they different when they differ? What different musical effects do the different types of cadences have? One must know his common chords well to work with this activity. The following types of cadences can be found: (1) phrase ending on V or V_7; a *half cadence*, (2) phrase ending on I preceeded by V or V_7; an *authentic cadence*, (3) phrase ending on I preceeded by IV; a *plagal cadence*; it sounds like "Amen," (4) phrase ending on an unexpected chord; a *deceptive cadence*. These concepts can be an added resource for student composers.

Learning Notation

Children are not interested in learning notation unless (1) they see an immediate useful application of it, or (2) the process of learning can be made to be fun for them. It is the teacher's responsibility to create a classroom environment in which notation is useful to the learner. One way to do this is by providing instruments for which the children need to use notation to play. Another is by providing opportunities for children to compose music they wish to save by notating it, or so that others may sing and play it. Some simple techniques of notation used earlier in this book will help the college student to realize that learning notation does not appear to be as much of a problem today as it was in earlier years. The reason is that it can become a useful part of everyday music learning. For example, the realization of the value of the keyboard as an audio-visual aid now permits the learner to see, hear, and feel the distances between pitches; notes become real to the learner rather than only spots on a staff.

Some of the generalizations and activities concerning the learning of music notation are:

1. High and low in pitch can be drawn in notes on the staff.

2. Notes can represent pitches that go higher, lower, or stay in the same place.

3. Word rhythms can be pictured in note values.

4. Note values can be dramatized by body movements and can be spoken by using selected words.

5. Rhythm patterns can be pictured in note values.

6. Tone patterns can be pictured in notes on the staff.

7. One way to learn notation is (1) learn to sing a song by rote, (2) learn to play the song by rote on a simple instrument, (3) see what you have sung and played written in notation, (4) use the notation to play and sing the song, (5) play and sing other songs from the learned notation. The goal is to progress from seeing in notation music the learner knows, to hearing in the mind what he sees in the notation of unfamiliar music.

8. Music is built in sections; sometimes these repeat exactly; sometimes they repeat in modified form; and sometimes the sections are different.

9. There are scale-lines and chord-lines in most melodies.

10. Recognition of intervals, and the ability to sing them assists the sight singer.

11. There are characteristic note groupings in the various meters. For example, the notation of ⁶⁄₈ meter looks different than that of ⁴⁄₄ meter.

12. One can find many of the chords needed to accompany songs by identifying chord tones in the melody-lines of songs.

13. The reason the singer needs to know what key a new song is written in is so that he can find out where he is, pitchwise, in the scale in which the new song is written. The last sharp to the right is 7 or *ti*, so the line

or space above it is 1 or *do*, the keynote. The last flat to the right is 4 or *fa*; one can count the lines and spaces up or down to find 1 or *do*. However, if there are two or more flats, the next-to-the-last flat to the right is 1 or *do*. As you already know, 1 and 8 are in octave apart. Some teachers do not use 8; they use 1 for both pitches.

14. Flannel boards and magnetic boards make it easy for children to notate. Some teachers use discs of felt, bottle caps, and even poker chips for the children to place on flat cardboard staffs at their desks. Even toothpicks and special sticks used in mathematics are employed by teachers in ingenious ways in having children notate the answers to problems they design.

15. Some teachers utilize a carefully graded series of charts of their own creation. Most of these are pleasant drills, accompanied by piano or guitar to make them more musical. Each chart is designed to help with a notational problem that will relate to songs that follow. Games are made of many of them. However, such drill charts form only a small part of the regular music lesson.

Manipulative note game.

Make the following figures from colored paper. The size should be generous, yet not too large to work with on the surface provided the learner. With young children the game is played without the eighth notes at first.

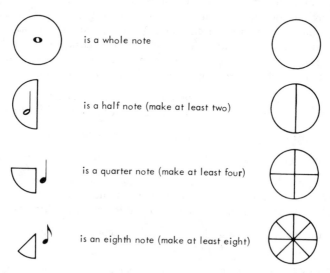

is a whole note

is a half note (make at least two)

is a quarter note (make at least four)

is an eighth note (make at least eight)

The teacher's assignment is to make a circle with any specified number of notes between 1 and 8. Each circle will eventually represent a measure of $\frac{4}{4}$ meter.

Note reading game.

The teacher makes two-measure charts of an eight-measure song, and arranges them out of order. The class sings or plays the song, and children are asked to arrange the charts in correct order. They test this by singing from the charts. Examples in *Singing With Children*: "Old Brass Wagon," "Paper of Pins," "Taffy," "Row Your Boat," "Hush Little Baby," and many others.

Note reading game.

The teacher shows untitled melodies (no words) on charts or transparencies. The child identifies the song by reading the notation silently.

Lines, spaces, and thirds.

When the interval of a third appears in a notated melody, the notes appear horizontally as either line-line or space-space. When a 1–3–5 chord pattern occurs, it is notated as line-line-line or space-space-space. Arrange for children to discover these helpful data.

Meter and notation.

Ask children to demonstrate their ability to make a familiar song eccentric by changing the meter. Challenge them to change the note values in accordance with the new meter whenever necessary. Sing the altered song from the notation; evaluate the result. Use the tape recorder so the class can evaluate more accurately. (If your school has no manuscript paper you can make your own by using the underline key on a typewriter to make a staff on Ditto carbon.)

More About Composing Music

Several suggestions follow in addition to the many made previously concerning children's compositions. The techniques of octave displacement, inversion, and retrograde are illustrated below with "London Bridge." (See *octave displacement* in the next chapter for recorded examples of that device.) The most popular approach in introducing such manipulation of melodies is by means of very simple and well-known songs such as "Baa, Baa, Black Sheep," "Three Blind Mice," "Are You Sleeping?" and "Mary Had a Little Lamb."

LONDON BRIDGE

Singing Game

Lon - don Bridge is fall - ing down, fall - ing down, fall - ing down.

Lon - don Bridge is fall - ing down, My fair la - dy. ___

Inverted

(complete it)

Retrograde

(complete it)

Octave Displacement

(complete it)

INTRODUCING SONG-WRITING TO OLDER CHILDREN

It is possible that the beginning teacher may find that the children have had no experience in composing songs. The activity can be introduced as one for the entire class, keeping in mind that the ultimate goal is to develop this creative ability into the successful composing of music by individuals. In other words, the following group process should be a stimulus for each child to write his own songs in the same way that he paints his own pictures. It can be used in grades three and above.

1. Choose words that are simple, have steady rhythmic flow, and are understood by children.

2. Write the words on the chalkboard under the staff. Discuss the meaning of the words, seeking ideas that will influence the song writing. Such ideas will include mood and anything that many reflect descending or ascending pitch.

3. Have the class read the words in unison so that a definite rhythm is established. Use clapping or stepping if necessary. The most heavily accented words or word syllables can be underlined. Measure bars can be drawn before (to the left of) these words or word syllables.

4. If this activity is comparatively new to the children, sound the tonic chord by singing 1 3 5 3 1 (do-mi-sol-mi-do), or by playing it on Autoharp or piano. If these instruments are used, it is better to play the chord sequence I V₇ I to establish a definite key feeling. If the children are experienced in song writing, this step is not necessary because they "hear with their inner ears" what they create, and the arbitrary setting of a key may interfere with the creative process.

5. Ask for suggestions to start the song. There are several approaches. In the earliest stages of learning to compose, a teacher may have all or part of the first phrase written and ask the class to finish that section of the song. This can be done by the class *thinking* what the rest of the song might be (after singing the first part several times) and finally singing it, the teacher accepting the majority opinion. Soon individuals will have melodic suggestions to offer, and the process becomes one of both group and individual contribution. The group is the controlling force, however, and exercises discrimination in choosing between versions of parts of the song that are volunteered by individuals. The composition generally proceeds phrase by phrase with the group singing frequently from the beginning of the song. The teacher notates the song as it grows in length. Those teachers who can take musical dictation will write stemless notes on the staff. Since it is necessary to proceed with rapidity to avoid lagging interest, these are usually little lines (/) instead of filled notes (•). Some teachers will prefer to use numerals or syllables and "figure" from these. Others will use the keyboard directly, and still others will employ lines on the chalkboard that indicate high and low in pitch and tonal duration.

6. Have the class decide what the meter signature is. If the bar lines have not already been placed, they can be written before the heavily accented notes. Sometimes the song will need to be transposed to a more suitable key for the voices. The key signature will be determined, as will note values. Stems, flags, beams, and dots will be added wherever necessary.

7. Autoharp or piano chords can be added as desired.

8. The children can now evaluate their song. Does it reflect the meaning of the words suitably? Does it communicate the mood desired? Can the song be improved? It is notated correctly?

9. If the song is of good quality, it should be saved by placing it in a class notebook. If it is in a key in which children can play recorder-type instruments, reproduce it on a duplicating machine so that the children may use notation at home in playing the song for their parents.

OPERA

Children can write their own miniature operas by choosing a story and adding to it both songs they know and songs they will write for their plot. They can plan solos, duets, trios, and choruses, write an accompanying instrumental score, and add their version of a ballet if this suits them. Such an activity can help children to identify with opera rather than regard it as an alien form, as some may do.

HAIKU

The Japanese haiku poem can be created, then set to music using a Japanese scale. Accompanying instruments can be added rather delicately, with gong, bells, woodblocks, finger cymbals, and a light rattle being appropriate in many cases. The poem includes a central idea, a suggested or inferred location, reference to seasons of the year, and seventeen syllables in three lines, although the latter is not always held to. An example might be:

> *The late poppy bloom*
> *Withers in the cold.*
> *Orange petals are falling.*

Japanese scales (pentatonic scales with half-steps):

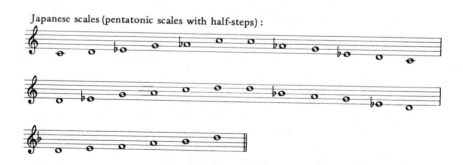

Summary

This chapter was concerned with teaching strategies in which songs and pitched instruments were primary means by which children learned music concepts and music skills. The teacher should now be able to design plans of marked variety which could include the independent types of strategies studied in Chapter Three and the song-and-instrument types in this chapter. Chapter Five will provide additional resources: recordings and films.

REFERENCES

American Orff Schulwerk Association, Arnold Burkart, Executive Secretary, School of Music, Ball State University, Muncie, Ind. 47306.

BACON, DENISE, "Controversy on Kodály," Readers' Comment, *Music Educators Journal*, September, 1969, pp. 3–16.

"Bibliography of Negro Music," *Music Educators Journal*, January, 1970, pp. 113–120.

BURAKOFF, GERALD, AND LAWRENCE WHEELER, *Music Making in the Elementary School*. New York, 157 W. 57th St. 10019: Hargail Music Inc. 1968. Student's and Teacher's Editions. Recorder, voice, bells, and percussion instruments.

Concordia Publishing House, St. Louis, Mo. 63118: Carols with instruments. "Shepherds in Judea," "The Sleep of the Child Jesus," "Cradle Hymn," "The Bells of Paradise."

DOOLIN, HOWARD, *New Introduction to Music*. Park Ridge, Ill.: General Words and Music. 525 Busse Highway 60068, 1968. Level One: Pitch and Duration of Tone; Level Two: Pitch and Duration of Tone Using Notation; Level Three: Modes and Form; Level Four: Harmony Chart, student books on easels, teachers' manuals.

GOULD, OREN A., "Developing Specialized Programs for Singing in the Elementary School," *Bulletin No. 17*, Council for Research in Music Education, University of Illinois, n.d.

Handy-Folio Music Company, 5100 W. 82nd St., Minneapolis, Minn. 55437: *Sing At Sight Series*, and *Choral Method Series*, n.d.

HAYNES, MARGARET S., AND RICHARD A. COOLIDGE, *Owls, Pussy Cats, Cabbages, and Kings*. Dubuque, Ia.: Kendall-Hunt Publishing Co., 1973. Composed modal and tone row songs for elementary-school use. Some serial pieces for piano also.

Highland Music Co., 1311 N. Highland Ave., Hollywood, Calif., 90028: *American Indian Songs; Folk Songs of Africa; Latin-American Songs; Favorite Songs of Japanese Children; Children's Songs of Mexico*, n.d.

Kodály Musical Training Institute, 525 Worcester St., Wellesley, Mass. 62181.

KODALY, ZOLTAN, *Bicinia Hungaria I, II; Let Us Sing Correctly; 101 Exercises in Intonation*, and other books. Oceanside, N.Y.: Boosey & Hawkes, n.d.

LANDECK, BEATRICE, *Songs to Grow on; More Songs to Grow On*. New York: Marks and Sloane, 1950, 1954. Recorded by Folkways Records.

LEWIS, ADEN G., *Listen Look and Sing*, Vol. I, Teacher's Edition. Morristown, N.J.: Silver Burdett Co., 1971. A Kodály sequence.

MARSH, MARY VAL, *Explore and Discover Music*. New York: Macmillan Inc., 1970.

NASH, GRACE, *Today With Music*. Port Washington, N.Y.: Alfred Publishing Co., Inc., 1973. A classroom method for K–3 for voice, rhythm, and melody instruments.

NYE, ROBERT, AND BJORNAR BERGETHON, *Basic Music: Functional Musicianship for the Non-Music Major*, 4th ed. Englewood Cliffs, N.J.: Prentice-Hall Inc., 1973.

NYE, ROBERT, AND VERNICE NYE, *Music in the Elementary School*. 3rd ed. Englewood Cliffs, N.J.: Prentice-Hall, Inc., 1970. Chap. 9 and 10.

NYE, ROBERT, VERNICE NYE, NEVA AUBIN, AND GEORGE KYME, *Singing With Children*. 2nd ed. Belmont, Calif.: Wadsworth Publishing Co., 1970.

RICHARDS, MARY HELEN, *Pentatonic Songs for Young Children*. Belmont, Calif.: Fearon Publishers, Inc., 1967.

———, *Threshold to Music*. Belmont, Calif.: Fearon Publishers, Inc., 1964.

SCOTT, RICHARD, *Clap, Tap and Sing* (for grades 2–5); *Sevenfold Choral Method* (for grades 5–7). Minneapolis, Minn.: Handy-Folio Music Company, n.d.

SZABO, HELGA, *The Kodály Concept of Music Education*. Oceanside, N.Y.: Boosey & Hawkes, 1969.

WHEELER, LAWRENCE, AND LOIS RAEBECK, *Orff and Kodály Adapted for the Elementary School*. Dubuque, Ia: Wm. C. Brown Music Publishers, 1972. Pt. 2.

WIEDINMEYER, CLEMENT, *Play-Sing-Chord Along*. Delaware Water Gap, Pa.: Shawnee Press, Inc., n.d.

WILSON, HARRY R., *Old and New Rounds and Canons*. Delaware Water Gap, Pa.: Shawnee Press, Inc., 1943.

Autoharp Instruction

NYE, ROBERT, AND MARGARET PETERSON, *Teaching Music With the Autoharp*, 1973. Union, N.J. 07083: Music Education Group.

Classroom Instrument Suppliers

Music Education Group (MEG), Garden State Road, Union, New Jersey 07083.

Peripole, Inc., P.O. Box 146, Lewiston Road, Browns Mills, N.J. 08015.
Rhythm Band, Inc., P.O. Box 126, Fort Worth, Texas 76101.

Guitar Instruction

EISENKRAMER, HENRY E., *Strum and Sing: Guitar in the Classroom*. Evanston, Ill.: Summy-Birchard Co., 1969.

SILVERMAN, JERRY, *Graded Guitar Method*. New York: The Big Three Music Corp., 1970.

TIMMERMAN, MAURINE, AND CELESTE GRIFFITH, *Guitar in the Classroom*. Dubuque, Ia.: William C. Brown Company Publishers, 1971.

Recorder Instruction

BUCHTEL, FORREST, *Buchtel Recorder Method*, Book 1. Park Ridge, Ill.: Neil A. Kjos Music Company, 525 Busse Highway, 60068, n.d.

EARLE, FREDERICK, *Trophy Elementary Recorder Method, Baroque System*. Cleveland, Ohio: Trophy Music Co., 1278 W. 9th St. 44113, n.d.

LANAHAN, WALTER D., *Melody Method for the Recorder*. Laurel, Md.: Melody Flute Co., n.d.

NEWMAN, HAROLD, AND GRACE NEWMAN, *Music Shall Live—Singing and Playing with the Recorder*. New York City: Hargail Music Press, 157 W. 57th st. 10019, n.d.

RELATED AUDIO-VISUAL MEDIA

Hello, I'm Music: EMC Corporation, 180 E. 6th St., St. Paul, Minn. 55101. Six color filmstrips, six records or three cassettes, 240 worksheets and a teacher's guide. Melody, rhythm, harmony, form, and tone color are presented to children.

Man and His Music: Keyboard Publications, 1346 Chapel Street, New Haven, Conn., 06511, 1973–74. Includes student magazines, listening records, sound filmstrips, and teacher guides for music, social studies, art, and humanities classes in grades 4–12.

The Sight and Sound of Music: Shawnee Press, Delaware Water Gap, Pa. 183327. A vocal sight reading course for third and fourth grades. Books, recordings, projections, teaching aids, and lesson plans are provided.

What is Music?; Wind Sounds; String Sounds; Percussion Sounds; New Sounds in Music: Churchill Films, 662 N. Robertson Blvd., Los Angeles, Ca. 90069. A popular series of music education films.

5

learning music with recordings and films

Recordings and films have enabled the teacher to bring into the classroom sounds and sights that would otherwise be impossible for the children to experience. Careful selection of these important resources has added immeasurably to the learning of music. This century has seen recording advance from the days of the "talking machine" on which comedians told jokes to the magnificent sound systems of today that reproduce faithfully the sounds of myriad kinds of music. It has seen the movies develop from the silent "flickers" to the impressive color and sound films of today, and the invention of television, which has placed the New York Philharmonic Young People's Concerts and the Public Television programs in the classroom. These developments have had a tremendous impact upon education in general.

Films and Filmstrips

To use motion pictures effectively, teachers preview them carefully, selecting them in accordance with the needs and problems of the class. A good film is authentic, up-to-date, and on the child's level of comprehension. The best source for music educators is the most recent edition of the *Film Guide for Music Educators*, published by the Music Educators National Conference, 1201 Sixteenth Street, Washington, D.C.

Films are selected to contribute to the concepts, generalizations and objectives toward which the children are working. Teachers should be aware of any places in a film where there are difficult ideas which will require additional explanation, and provide for these. Prior to the showing of a film, a teacher might ask, "What do you think a film of this title might tell us?" and list the ideas the children present. This assists them to search actively for ideas they hope to find expressed or explained in the film. After the showing, the teacher will ask if the film showed them what they hoped for, and if it did not, what it did reveal to them. In all of this, teachers' questions are to guide the children's thinking toward the ideas, concepts, and generalizations of most significance. Some specific suggestions of ways to use films follow:

A. Purpose: to acquire information to be generalized.
    1. "What did you learn from this film?"
    Technique: An open question followed by listing of information.
    2. "What do we have listed about melody and form?" "How do these items relate to each other?" "How is this information related to what we know about rhythm?"
    Technique: Relate points of information to each other and to what the learners know about other elements of music.
    3. "Can we state this in a way that makes clear what the relationship is?"
    Technique: Try to draw a generalization from the class.
    4. "Can we combine all that we know about melody, rhythm, and form into a statement that relates to all the other elements of music?"
    Technique: Try to combine sub-generalizations into one broad generalization.

B. Purpose: to verify generalizations developed earlier.
    1. What did we find in the film that would indicate to us that our sentence relating melody and form is true or not true?
    2. Continue this process of verification and clarification with other earlier developed generalizations.

C. Purpose: to test generalizations developed earlier.
    1. Show a film of a new, but related musical experience.
    2. "If we were to visit this country and listen to its music, what would we expect to hear?"

D. Purpose: To acquire specific data.
    1. "As we watch this film, let's find as many new ideas as we can about melody and form."
    2. List data and incorporate it into charts for later study.

An important use of films for individual instruction is the three-to-ten minute 8 mm cartridge which the learner injects into a specially-designed projector. Children of all school ages can operate these machines. In the viewing and listening center a student or a small group of students may view 8 mm single concept films or 35 mm filmstrips. Filmstrips accompanied with recorded sound may be viewed while listening to the recorded commentary or music related to the film.

Filmstrips are made by many companies; the Jam Handy Organization, Bowmar Records, and the Society for Visual Education produce sound filmstrips concerned with music stories, music fundamentals, composers, and instruments of the orchestra. Filmstrips can also be made by teachers with a 35 mm camera and the assistance of either a school audio-visual expert or advice from a photography supply house. They are rather inexpensive, are easy to store, and convenient to use. Some purposes will require only a few frames, while others will use the entire filmstrip.

Schools having closed circuit television with taping facilities can video-tape important musical events and replay them in the classroom for further analysis and discussion.

Transparencies

Opaque projections of pages in a book, pictures, drawings, single copies of songs, scores, can be used in a darkened room. The opaque projector is the one device that will make it possible for a class to examine their notated compositions without the teacher having to make transparencies of them.

With the aid of an overhead projector and a sheet of transparent plastic, music teachers or students can face the class while drawing music notation to illustrate a problem at hand. To project a creative production or to present parts of the entire song, they can point to notation or pictures on transparencies as they are shown on the screen. By making overlays, they can add notation to a musical score or sections of the orchestra one by one until the full orchestra is shown. Because rooms need not be darkened, and the student or teacher can face the class while referring to the transparency, overhead projectors are easy to use and they serve to "focus" the attention of the class. Care should be taken to place the screen high so that no "machinery" blocks the view of any child, and to slant the screen so that the bottom is farther from the projector than the top.

Among the uses of overhead transparencies are showing illustrations of conducting patterns, themes of symphonic works, drawings or pictures of instruments, building triads and their inversions, comparing different scales, notes, beats and rests. A teacher can plan a review of music fundamentals with the use of overlays; he first shows the staff, then adds leger lines, then names of lines and spaces, clef signs, and the grand staff. It is much easier to show this with overlay transparencies than by means of a chalkboard. The musical themes for Bowmar Orchestral Library Series 3 are now presented compactly on one cell to be flashed on a screen. Teaching is becoming more screen-centered.

Selecting Recordings

This book began its music learning experiences with strategies that do not require the use of song books and recordings. It then progressed to learning music through the use of songs and pitched instruments. This section will deal with learning music by means of recordings.

Recordings are usually selected in terms of their clarity of presentation of the specific aspects of music the children are studying. The teacher needs to choose recordings which emphasize the musical elements he wants the children to find while listening. The conceptual approach to teaching music provides its own clear outline by which teachers can analyze recordings for class use. One teacher[1] made a large chart that can be used with any recording or with an entire collection of educational recordings. Her headings, which were written horizontally across the top of the chart, were as follows: composer, title, sources, general feeling, rhythm, dynamics-tempo, melody, harmony, texture, tone quality, national origin, style period, additional comments. These headings served as criteria as she listened to each recording. She wrote only in the spaces beneath the headings that named outstanding characteristics of the music. For example, in the instance of Anderson's *The Girl I Left Behind Me*, she found the general feeling *lively*, the rhythm featured by *march rhythm and syncopation*, the melody contained *augmentation and diminution*, the form was *theme and variations*, the national origin was *Irish folk*, and the style *20th century*. The other spaces were left blank because she found nothing outstanding relating to those headings. Later, when she searched for music featuring a specific musical element, she could look down a column on her chart and select from the compositions accordingly. For example, she could choose recordings for quiet listening (under general feeling), for studying polyphony (under texture), for studying woodwind tone qualities (under tone qualities), and for studying accents (under dynamics and tempo). She con-

[1]Mrs. Madeline Tews, Springfield Schools, Oregon.

tinued working with her chart until it consisted of a number of long sheets of paper and it contained every record in one collection of recordings.

Such information might be condensed in a card file. There are a number of ways in which entries can be made on cards, one of which appears below. By making duplicate cards, the teacher can have a file at his desk and a central file available to all.

Composer	Number of Record or Album
Title	Sources of information
	about the music
Music Elements Emphasized	Comments:

Catalogs offer assistance to teachers who are seeking recordings for specific uses. They are published by concerns such as the Children's Music Center, Folkways Records, Bowmar Records, and RCA-Victor. The catalog of the Children's Music Center classifies recordings in relation to all commonly taught units of school work. Further assistance is provided by teacher's guides which accompany the school record collections. The *Bowmar Orchestral Library* consists of three series comprising 36 ungraded albums, accompanied by wall charts of themes printed on heavy cardboard. Series Three adds themes on transparencies, lesson plans, and record groove spreads for ease in finding places on the discs. *Adventures in Music*, a graded series of albums by RCA-Victor, is widely used.

Readiness to listen to music is influenced by a child's maturity level and by the music listening he has had in his out-of-school environment. The teacher plans with these in mind. A child's interest in listening is more likely to be keen when he can understand a large part of what he hears. Therefore, he is more ready to respond when the content of the music relates to his past experiences, and when the music contains familiar elements, particularly rhythmic and melodic. Recognizing familiar melodies in new settings assists motivation. A list of recorded music of this type based on familiar songs follows (pp. 223–225). Further motivation comes from teachers' plans that include asking the children to answer specific questions and to solve specific problems by listening carefully to what they are to hear.

All children are likely to enjoy listening to recordings that possess some of the following characteristics: (1) potential for active physical response; (2) a distinct mood; (3) songlike melodies; (4) beautiful tone qualities; (5) a story or message in the music; (6) content that relates to their experience and interest; (7) length in relation to their genuine interest. Older children with musical experience background have the ability to be more analytical in their responses to music than younger children.

Composer	Title	Song or Themes
BARLOW	The Winter's Passed	"Wayfaring Stranger," "Black Is the Color of My True Love's Hair"
BEETHOVEN	String Quartet Op. 59, No. 2	Russian hymn "Praise to God" (*This Is Music* Book 4)
	Symphony 8, Second Movement, Third Theme	"The Metronome" (Adventures in Music 6 v. 1)
	Symphony 9, Fourth Movement	"United Nations Hymn" ("World Anthem") *This Is Music* Book 6
	Wellington's Victory	"For He's a Jolly Good Fellow"
BLOCH	America	"Yankee Doodle," "Old Folks at Home," "Hail Columbia."
BRAHMS	Academic Festival Overture	"Guadeamus Igitur" (student song often found in series books for grades 7–8) (Bowmar #76)
CAILLIET	Variations on Pop Goes the Weasel	"Pop Goes the Weasel" (Bowmar #65) (Adventures in Music 4 v. 1)
CHOPIN	Fantasy Impromptu	"I'm Always Chasing Rainbows"
COPLAND	Appalachian Spring	"Simple Gifts" (Bowmar #75)
	Billy the Kid, Fourth Theme	"Goodbye, Old Paint"
	Lincoln Portrait	"Camptown Races," "Springfield Mountain" "Pesky Sarpent")
	Rodeo	"Hoe-Down" (Adventures in Music 5 v. 2) (Bowmar #55)
DOHNANYI	Variations on a Nursery Tune (for older children)	"Twinkle, Twinkle, Little Star" (piano and orchestra)
DVORAK	Symphony 5	"Swing Low, Sweet Chariot" (First Movement, Third Theme) "Going Home" (Second Movement, First Theme)
GOULD	American Salute	"When Johnny Comes Marching Home" (Adventures in Music 5 v. 1) (Bowmar #65)
GOULD	Cowboy Rhapsody	"Goodbye, Old Paint," "Home on the Range"
	Variations on When Johnny Comes Marching Home	"When Johnny Comes Marching Home"

Composer	Title	Song or Themes
GRAINGER	Londonderry Air	"Londonderry Air" (Adventures in Music 4 v. 2)
GROFE	Death Valley Suite	"O Susanna" (Adventures in Music 4 v. 1)
GUION	Turkey in the Straw	"Old Zip Coon" (same tune)
HARRIS	Folk Song Symphony	"Irish Washerwoman," "Bury Me Not on the Lone Prairie," "Streets of Laredo," "Turkey in the Straw," "When Johnny Comes Marching Home."
HAYDN	"Emperor" Quartet in C Major	"Glorious Things of Thee Are Spoken" ("Austrian National Hymn") Appears in several of the music series.
HINDEMITH	Trauermusic (Funeral Music)	"Old Hundred." Both melody and harmony are manipulated.
HUMPERDINCK	Hansel and Gretel, Prelude to Act 1	"Prayer," "Song of the Gingerbread Children," "Partner, Come and Dance With Me."
IVES	Second Symphony	"Columbia, Gem of the Ocean," "Camptown Races," "Reveille," "Joy to the World," "Long Long Ago," "Old Folks at Home"
KAY	Western Symphony	"Red River Valley," "The Girl I Left Behind Me," "Golden Slippers," "Jim Along Josie" (Vox Recording)
McBRIDE	Mexican Rhapsody Pumpkineaters Little Fugue	"Hat Dance," "Rancho Grande," "La Cucaracha" "Peter, Peter, Pumpkin Eater" (Bowmar #65)
McDONALD	Children's Symphony	"Farmer in the Dell," "Jingle Bells" (Adventures in Music 3 v. 2)
MAHLER	First Symphony, Third Movement	"Are You Sleeping?"
MUSSORGSKY	Boris Godunov, Coronation Scene	"Praise to God" (This Is Music Book 4)

Composer	Title	Song or Themes
NELSON	Kentucky Mountain Portraits	"Cindy," "Skip to My Lou," "Paw Paw Patch"
QUILTER	A Children's Overture	"Girls and Boys Come Out to Play," "St. Paul's Steeple," "Dame Get Up and Bake Your Pies," "Over the Hills and Far Away," "The Frog and the Crow," "The Frog He Would A-Wooing Go," "Oranges and Lemons," "Baa Baa Black Sheep"
ROSSINI	William Tell Overture	"Lone Ranger Theme" (Bowmar #76) (Adventures in Music 3 v. 1)
SIBELIUS	Finlandia	"Song of Peace" and other titles
SOWERBY	Irish Washerwoman	"Lane County Bachelor" and other titles
STRAVINSKY	Greeting Prelude	"Happy Birthday to You" (Columbia Record *Instrumental Miniatures*)
TSCHAIKOVSKY	1812 Overture	"Russian National Hymn" and other titles
	Symphony 4, Fourth Movement	"The Birch Tree" (Adventures in Music 6 v. 2)
VARDELL	Joe Clark Steps Out	"Old Joe Clark" (Mercury Recording)
VAUGHAN-WILLIAMS	Fantasia on Greensleeves	"What Child Is This?" (Greensleeves") (Adventures in Music 6 v. 2)

While some recordings are made to appeal to specific age levels, music in general is not; it is a communication by a composer for anyone who can grasp its meaning. A movement from a symphony is generally too lengthy, and when used will be reduced to an excerpt. However, length must be measured in terms of interest; children can listen for long periods of time if they are truly interested. For young children this may mean physical responses; for children of all ages, music can be used as a background to other activities if the mood is one that is not distracting or disturbing. In the long run, whether or not a particular recording should be used on a particular level depends upon its appropriateness on that level in terms of the teacher's objectives. Besides exemplifying music concepts, other purposes may include presenting beauty for its own sake without comment, use for quality background listening before and after school, during rest periods, and during some other activity when such music adds aesthetic quality to the environment. The same recorded music may serve one purpose, such as rhythmic response, at lower levels and another purpose, such as the study of tone quality, form, or harmony, at a higher level.

Listening to Program Music

Children often listen to stories from recordings which are told with music in the background to add interest and color. They are examples of music being used to enhance another subject. The educational objectives are not concerned with music.

When program music is used in music classes, attention is eventually centered on *how* the music suggests the story, description, or mood. In preparation for a more extended experience in listening to this type of music the teacher studies the selection and analyzes it in terms of the musical elements discussed in this book. He will then relate these elements to the story or description. He may also be familiar with information about the composer, his life and times. He will plan questions, may place a list of guiding statements or words on the chalkboard, or plan some other way to guide the listening of the class to help them discover the musical meaning of the work. He will have questions planned for use after the class has heard the recording.

There are many different types of program music, and they demand different approaches. In some instances it is necessary to tell the children the story before they hear the music; in others they can be free to make up their own stories (which may be as good or better than the composer's), but in all cases they are to explain how the elements of music are used to describe the mood, description, or story. Obviously, the older children will be able to give the more precise analysis, while young children will express these ideas in more simple terms. The teacher encourages the children to explain the music to the extent they are able, later supplying whatever information is necessary. As in other aspects of music, the lesson is planned in a way that results in general success, not bewilderment or frustration.

Sometimes it adds variety and encourages divergent thinking to tell the name of a recording before the children hear it, and ask them, "If you composed a piece of music with this title, what would you do to convey the idea to the listener?" "How would you use the music elements to help the listener understand your meaning?"

If a teacher asks children to imagine a story suggested to them by an unnamed composition, there are no wrong answers; the thinking is again divergent. Their imagined stories may be entirely different from the composer's story. However, the child has the responsibility to explain what happens in the music to justify his story. It is this that makes the experience a musical one rather than one in story-telling. Some children may not hear a story. It will then be their responsibility to tell what they did hear, and their answers should be in terms of the elements of music.

Listening to Absolute Music

Absolute or "pure" music is that which has no extra-musical meaning. It exists for its own sake as a work of art. With this type of music the teacher and children work directly with the elements of music—the melodies, tone and rhythm patterns, tone qualities, form, and so on. Repetition and contrast, tension and release, cool and warm, will be listened for. The function of form and tone qualities will be examined and discussed free of any program. A large amount of music has no story aspect, and children need to be clear in their classification of music into the two types—program and absolute. Thus, "story music" must not be over-emphasized.

Remember that children need the opportunity to compare and analyze music in order to develop ability to discriminate and to make value judgments. They do not fully accept value judgments made by adults; they need to be helped to make their own.

Listening to Contemporary Music

Contemporary music sometimes provides marked contrasts with other music. For example, the children have learned that music always communicates something, which may be a mood, description, story, beauty for its own sake, the working out of a particular form or some challenge the composer assigned himself, or the conscious or unconscious reflection of a period or nation in historical context, or the personality of the composer. Against this concept of communicating something, the children may be challenged by a contemporary work that is claimed by its composer to communicate nothing; it is to be recognized only for what it is. The children's minds are then pitted against the composer's with the question, "Can a composer write music which does not in some way reflect the age in which he lives?" "Is there something about this music that may communicate something about the decade in which he composed it?" "Is there something about this music that can be recognized as ageless or timeless, thus acceptable in any age?" "Is there something about this music that exists only for itself and nothing else?" Again, older children can be challenged with this type of divergent thinking which has its convergent possibilities also.

Today's children are conditioned to the sounds of electronic music they hear while watching certain television programs, and the concept of the tape recorder as a source of musical sounds should be well understood and practiced in classroom composition. Children now work with small computers and may be able to understand better than many older people that they can be used in composition, that the major problem is how the computer is programed, and that the number of possibilities is incredible. The point of view of the music educator is that children need to be exposed to every type of music. This does not mean that they are expected to *like* every type of music. To understand something about every type of music gives the child knowledge by means of which he can decide whether or not he likes it; this is his personal business. He needs to explore the different kinds of music somewhat like the scientist examines classifications of plant and animal life under a microscope. Contemporary music takes its rightful place with all the other types of music as part of the world of organized sound. An interesting aspect of composing with a tape recorder is that notation can be by-passed; this makes it easy for children to do. No one knows with certainty the future of electronic music; its possible position in music history has been compared with that of the beginnings of opera in 1600. In some teacher education programs, a laboratory course in electronic music is required. Experimental music seems to be a reflection of our time. Picasso said, "Strangeness was what we wanted the people to think about, because we were aware that the world was becoming very strange and not exactly reassuring." Contemporary music has tended to reject emotion as a necessary component of art; this is in part a reaction against the emotion-filled romantic music of the nineteenth century. The concept that art is beauty is rejected by many contemporary composers, painters, and sculptors; these people try to portray concepts of reality as they see it, whether this is inspiring or degrading. In music, this results in some radically changed concepts of tonality, harmony, melody, consonance, and dissonance from those held for centuries before. People who do not or cannot accept such changes criticise this music as being overintellectual, mechanical in nature, and lacking in emotional meaning. Whether the listener likes this music or not seems not to be the question. It is here, it exists, and each listener is called upon to examine it in a situation in which final judgment is not yet possible. Children can be helped by letting them discuss what they like and do not like about it without trying to lead them into a final judgment. Experience with contemporary music has been a part of the study of every musical element in this book. If this approach is followed, contemporary music will take its place among all the other types, and children should be relatively open-minded about it.

Some bridges can be built between the music of today and that of the past. For example, the following aspects of form in music can be found in both contemporary and baroque music: ostinato figures, bourdon bass, pedal point (one long-held pitch usually in the bass above which changing harmonies take place), and improvisation. There are forms of music common to all periods, such as two-part, three-part, variation and rondo. If we go back far enough in music history we find the use of tonalities other than major and minor. The non-western musics of Asia and Africa lead in some ways toward contemporary music because they are different from most of the music we know best. Baroque-style music of groups like the Beatles and the Swingle Singers is helpful when comparing it with authentic baroque music; it helps children to associate the present with the past. Orff, Bartók, Hindemith, Britten, and Kodály are contemporary composers who have written music for children which teachers should study and evaluate for classroom use. Included in listening in the primary grades to instrumental music, and in singing activities, there should be recordings and songs with expanded tonality (so that the children are not restricted in their classroom experience to only major-minor tonality), free rhythm, and asymmetrical forms. These are gradually appearing in later series books.

Recordings Today

The number of recordings available today and the number of companies producing them stagger the imagination. To compile a complete listing of this ever-changing body of material is probably an impossibility.

Thus, the listing of recordings and other aids to music learning in this chapter is only a small sample of what is available. However, such listing should be a profitable introduction for the reader; it introduces him to a search for better teaching materials that will continue throughout his professional life as a teacher. Since recordings are continually being discontinued or newly introduced, the reader is advised to consult his record dealer before ordering many of the items listed.

SOUNDS AND TONE QUALITIES

Recorded examples are used by teachers to focus attention on sounds and tone qualities and to stimulate children's imaginative uses and adaptions of what they hear in their own compositions.

Recording

Unconventional sound sources.

Cage: Second Movement, *Amores.* Wood sounds. Time 58,000.
Cage and Harrison: *Double Music.* Eight rice bowls. Time 58,000.
Harrison: *Canticle No. 1,* on *Concert Percussion.* Time 8,000.
Oliveres: *Sound Patterns.* Mouth sounds. Oddyssey 3216–0156.
Partch: *The World of Harry Partch.* Hand-made instruments; an invented tonal organization of 43 tones within the octave. Columbia MS 7207.
Sounds of New Music (Cage, Leuning, Ussachevsky, Varese). Reverberation, tape loops, music concrete. Folkways FX 6160.

Prepared Piano
Cage: *Amores No. 1.* Children can be inspired by this to try for new sounds on the Autoharp.
Cowell: *Banshee.* A banshee is a female ghost that warns of approaching death. Children can think in terms of Halloween and use the Autoharp to imitate the sounds made on the prepared piano. On *Sounds of New Music*, Folkways FX 6160.

Electronic Music
Badings: "Ragtime" from *Evolutions.*
Epic BC 1118.
LeCaine: *Dripsody.* A drop of water
makes music on a tape recorder. On
Electronic Music, Folkways FM
3436.
Leuning: *Gargoyles,* for violin and
synthesizer. On *Columbia-Princeton
Electronic Music Center,* Columbia
MS 6566.
Luening and Ussachevsky: *Poem in
Cycles and Bells for Tape Recorder
and Orchestra.* Composers Record-
ings Inv. CRI 112.
Varèse: Déserts, Angel S–36786

When discussing tone qualities, the terms *tone color* and *timbre*
(tám-bur) are often used. Tone color is a term borrowed from art; it implies
that tone qualities are accomplished in music in the same general way the
artist selects and combines colors in painting. Timbre is the French word
for tone quality. Thus, tone quality, tone color, and timbre mean the same
thing: the difference in sound between tones of the same pitch when produced by different instruments or voices. For example, the same pitch played
on a violin, a trumpet, or a flute varies greatly in tone quality.

In music education of the past there was emphasis on identification
of the sources of tone—the specific instrument or voice that produced it.
Research has shown that very young children can learn to do such identification. However, merely trying to identify sources of tone has apparently
been an unsuccessful approach to learning, since the majority of adults are
surprisingly lacking in knowledge of musical instruments, and few can
identify many with accuracy. The child's curiosity should be encouraged—
what is there in the construction of a given instrument that produces its
particular tone quality; how the player of the instrument can affect tone
quality by his manner of playing; why particular tone qualities are selected
by composers as the most suitable to enhance melodies and harmonies; the
effect of range on tone quality; how tone quality interrelates with melody,
harmony, texture, and form to make music more attractive. If the study of
tone quality can be based on the reasons for the employment of particular
instruments in a composition, the mechanical construction of those instruments, and the method of playing them, then the identification of the
instrument or combinations of instruments should become part of a logical
scheme of things rather than the memorizing of isolated facts.

A contemporary phenomenon that makes sound identification more difficult is the major part the technician plays in the recording studio. Using many controlled microphones, he can exaggerate or diminish the sound of an instrument electronically. In some popular recordings the technician becomes almost as important as the players or singers. Some sounds are distorted purposely, making identification of the source more difficult. In addition to this there are electronic sounds from computers as well as from electric organs; this is another class of sounds to identify. They are commonly heard as part of television background music and on recordings of some popular music.

STRINGS   The string family of the orchestra is made up of the violin, viola, cello, and double bass (string bass, bass viol). They are approximately the same shape except that the violin is the smallest, the viola somewhat larger, the cello so large that the player must sit in a chair and rest the instrument on the floor, and the double bass so very large that the player ordinarily stands up to play it. These instruments are called "the first family of the orchestra." Study of the seating plan of an orchestra will explain one reason why. Listening carefully to symphonic music will reveal that the strings are truly the backbone of the orchestra, with the brass, woodwinds, and percussion sections assisting by adding many contrasting tone qualities.

The string instruments produce a variety of tone qualities within their family. The violin, viola, and cello use *vibrato*, a slight varying of pitch produced by rapid movement of the left hand while pressing down on a string. The term *con sordino* means with a mute; when the mute is attached to the bridge, the device that supports the strings, the tone becomes smaller and more nasal. These instruments produce *harmonics*, higher pitches of reduced resonance with flute-like tones that occur when the player touches, but does not press down on a string, and bows very lightly on that string. When these instruments are played by plucking strings, this is called *pizzicato*; it produces still another tone quality. A short, fast stroke played in the middle of the bow with a slight bounce from the string is *spiccato* bowing. Double stops, the playing and bowing of two strings at once, gives another effect. The *tremulo* produces a rather tense impression; it is done by moving the bow back and forth a short distance at an extremely fast rate. A flute-like effect is made by *sur la touche*, a slight bowing over the finger board, and a glassy effect, *sul ponticello*, is made by bowing very close to the bridge. An unusual orchestral effect is the *col legno*, which means using the wood of the bow rather than the hair. The *glissando* is produced by playing scale passages with many tiny movements of the left hand to change the pitch in almost a sliding effect. The normal tone qualities of these instruments can be described in various ways. A beginning can be made with these:

> *violin:* The string instrument that most resembles the qualities of the human voice; great versatility in range of expression; extremely sensitive tone qualities.
>
> *viola:* a veiled and nasal quality; darker in color than the violin.
>
> *cello:* the bass violin; a deep masculine voice of soulful quality.
>
> *double bass:* very low, heavy tone quality; it often sounds one octave lower than the cello.

Children, older students, and adults should be asked to demonstrate these instruments. While films and recordings are helpful, nothing takes the place of a good, well-qualified, live performer.

The harp is another string instrument; the player is seated with the string section of the orchestra. It can be compared to the piano in some ways; it has a range of six octaves and a fifth. There are seven foot pedals, each of which can be pressed down two notches, each notch representing one halfstep. The harp makes splashing, cascading effects. The *glissando* is used frequently to produce these. Harmonics are sounded by placing the palm of the hand in the middle of the strings; this places the pitch one octave higher than normal, making possible a quality of mystery. A different effect is made by plucking strings close to the sounding board.

The keyboard instruments include the piano, harpsichord, and celesta. The tone qualities of the piano should be thoroughly explored; special experimental effects can be made. In the piano, felt hammers strike the strings; the harpsichord strings are made to vibrate by means of a plucking mechanism. The celesta is basically a percussion instrument. Its keyboard causes hammers to strike the steel bars of what approximates a type of glockenspiel (bell set). The tone is of unusual light quality; a famed celesta piece is "Dance of the Sugar Plum Fairy" from the *Nutcracker Suite* of Tschaikovsky. The harpsichord—older than the piano—was the favorite keyboard instrument at the time of Haydn and Mozart. Its tone quality is considerably lighter than the piano, and it has less expressive capability. The Young People's Record 411, *Said the Piano to the Harpsichord*, is informative, and it communicates to children.

Stringed instruments not part of the symphony orchestra include the guitar, banjo, ukulele, mandolin, lyre, zither, Autoharp, and others. These should be explored to identify the tone qualities they produce. There is excellent guitar literature, much of it from Spanish sources; children should know of Segovia and others who play the classical guitar. Bowmar 84 includes a guitar selection.

Examples of recordings portraying tone qualities of the symphony strings include:

Scheherazade Suite, Rimsky-Korsakov	violin cadenzas
Flight of the Bumblebee, Rimsky-Korsakov, Bowmar 53	violin
Eine kleine Nachtmusik, Mozart, Adventures in Music 4 v. 1	strings
Danse Macabre, Saint-Saëns, Bowmar 59	viola plays second theme
"The Swan," *Carnival of the Animals*, Saint-Saëns, Bowmar 59, Adventures in Music 3 v. 2	cello
"Elephants," *Carnival of the Animals*, Saint-Saëns, Bowmar 51; AM 2 v 2	double bass
"Jimbo's Lullaby," Debussy, Bowmar 51	double bass

Suggested films include:

Listening to Good Music: The String Quartet	Encyclopaedia Britannica Films
The String Choir	Encyclopaedia Britannica Films
The String Trio	Coronet Instructional Films
The Trio	World Artists, Inc.
String Sounds	Churchill Films

WOODWINDS The woodwind instruments not only blend well with the strings of the orchestra, but they add other interesting tone qualities which can be used in the performance of melodies or subsidiary parts that contribute to the effect the composer plans to achieve. It is of interest that the woodwinds in the concert band seem to take the place of the strings in the orchestra; for example, when one looks at a concert band, he finds many clarinets instead of many violins.

The modern flute is a descendant of the recorder. It is a *transverse* flute, which means that one holds it at right angles to the mouth and blows across a hole in the side of it. The recorder is an end-blown flute. While it is said that the best recorders are made of wood, the modern flute is generally made of silver. Its tone quality varies with the range. Low pitches are relatively big and somewhat breathy, while higher tones become increasingly bright and penetrating with ascending pitches. An impressive flute solo at the beginning of a composition that emphasizes tone qualities is in Debussy's *Afternoon of a Faun,* followed by colorful effects on a harp. (Remember that a *faun* is a creature from rural Roman mythology, a man principally human, but with a goat's tail, pointed ears, short horns, and sometimes cloven feet.) Another favorite composition featuring flutes is Tschaikovsky's "Dance of the Toy Flutes," from the *Nutcracker Suite,* Bowmar 58. The piccolo is a small flute, half as long, and pitched one octave higher. It plays the highest pitches of any instrument in the woodwind family, and its tone quality is exceedingly brilliant and penetrating. A favorite piccolo solo is in Sousa's *Stars and Stripes Forever,* Bowmar 54, Others are found in the "Chinese Dance" from Tschaikovsky's *Nutcracker Suite,* Bowmar 59, and "Entrance of the Little Fauns" by Pierné, Bowmar 54.

The most commonly found clarinet is the B♭ instrument; some of the children who are studying this single reed instrument can demonstrate it. There is a family of clarinets, with the E♭ being smaller and higher in pitch, and the alto and bass being lower, as would be expected. There are other less common clarinets, including the clarinet in A and the double bass in B♭, the latter being an octave lower than the bass clarinet. The B♭ clarinet has three registers, each with a different tone quality. The lowest is rich and full-bodied, the middle is sometimes breathy and is the most difficult to make sound well; the highest is brilliant and versatile. This variety of tone qualities gives the clarinet a good deal of breadth of expression. Examples include Prokofiev's *Peter and the Wolf,* Saint-Saëns' "Cuckoo in the Deep Woods," from *Carnival of the Animals,* Bowmar 51, and the second movement of Rimsky-Korsakov's *Scheherazade Suite.* Clarinets are made of wood, ebonite, and occasionally of metal.

The saxophone is seldom used in orchestras, but widely used in bands and dance bands. There is a family of saxophones, including soprano, alto, tenor, baritone, and bass. The most commonly seen are in the following order, alto, tenor, and baritone. These are in most school bands and in many dance bands. Although they have cane reeds like clarinets, they are made of metal. The tone quality of the instrument is such that it blends with other woodwinds or brass instruments. This tone quality can be changed markedly by the player, thus can be sweet, raucous, or brusque as desired in certain types of jazz and dance music.

The oboe family includes all the double reed instruments. The oboe is about the same size as the B♭ clarinet. The English horn is an alto oboe and the bassoon is the bass instrument of the family. The contrabassoon is an octave lower than the ordinary bassoon. The oboe tone quality is often described as nasal, pastoral, oriental, and plaintive. *Peter and the Wolf* demonstrates the oboe tone quality, as does the second movement of Tschaikovsky's *Symphony No. 4* and his "Puss in Boots and the White Cat," from the *Sleeping Beauty*, Adventures in Music 3 v. 1. The English horn has a pear-shaped bell which is one source of its melancholy tone quality. Examples of its sound appear in the "Largo" of Dvořák's *New World Symphony*, Sibelius' *Swan of Tuonela*, and "Puss in Boots and the White Cat," mentioned above. Children should discover how the bassoon is built, since the design permits it to have a great length of tube. (The contrabassoon has over sixteen feet.) Besides serving as a bass instrument, its tone blends well with the French horn and enables it to play solo passages of distinction. While its tone quality is rather even except at extreme high and low ranges, it has a certain versatility which enables it to project plaintive, gruff, and humorous impressions. It can play over a wide range with legato and staccato articulation. Examples are found in "In the Hall of the Mountain King," from *Peer Gynt Suite*, by Grieg, Adventures in Music 3 v. 2, and Bowmar 59; "Berceuse" from Stravinsky's *Firebird Suite*; the second movement of Tschaikovsky's *Symphony No. 4*; and in *Rondo for Bassoon and Orchestra*, Children's Record Guild 1009. The grandfather theme in *Peter and the Wolf* is played by a contrabassoon.

Additional variety in the performance of woodwind instruments is attained by legato and staccato tonguing, as well as double, triple, and flutter tonguing. Double tonguing can be explained by letting out the breath with a series of repeated "t-t" tonguings; triple tonguing is a repeated "t-k-t." There are of particular importance in flute playing.

The film *Introducing the Woodwinds*, Indiana University, introduces the instruments of the woodwind quintet to children. These are flute (and piccolo), clarinet, oboe, bassoon, and French horn—the brass instrument that possesses a tone quality which blends with both the woodwinds and the brasses. *Wind Sounds*, Churchill Films, treats of woodwinds and brasses.

BRASSES Children can quickly find a major difference between a bugle and a trumpet, or cornet, in that the bugle lacks valves. They can then discern why the bugle can play only bugle calls whereas the other instruments can play both bugle calls and melodies. They should study the valve and its length of tubing to find what valves do to the length of the air column, and how much each valve lowers a pitch. They will see that the cornet is shorter than the trumpet, and they will hear that its tone quality is less brilliant. The player has a great deal to do with the sound of these instruments; he can produce tones of both coarse and pleasing qualities at will. The baritone is a larger instrument found in bands; the melophone is an instrument about the size of a French horn but which lacks the golden quality of the French horn tone; it is used for marching bands and for students who may later progress to the more difficult French horn. The tubing of the French horn should be examined to try to determine how long the instrument would be if it were a straight horn like the alphorn, a folk instrument from the Alps. Both tone quality and pitch are influenced by a practice called *stopping*, which is the insertion of the hand into the bell. Mutes made of metal, wood, or cardboard change the tone qualities of the cornet, trumpet, French horn, and trombone. Both school band and dance band players of trumpet and trombone can demonstrate their several types of mutes in the classroom. While the cornet and trumpet have the most commanding tones, the French horn has the tone that blends with other instruments the best, although it can be bold and brassy when this is desired. The tones of these instruments can be varied by legato and staccato tonguing, double and triple tonguing, flutter tonguing, and the use of mutes. Four sizes of trombones are used in the symphony orchestra, the most common being the tenor. This instrument and an occasional bass trombone will be seen in school bands. The trombone and baritone have larger mouthpieces than those of the cornet, trumpet, and French horn; this results in a tone quality of less brilliance, but of more dignity and solemnity. Children will be interested in how the trombone's slide shortens or lengthens the air column in place of the valve mechanism. Because of the slide, trombones can produce a *portamento*, which is a gliding from one tone to another through all degrees of pitches. The lowest pitched instruments of the brass family are the tubas and sousaphones. The sousaphone is the instrument carried on the shoulder of its players in marching bands; its huge shiny bell makes an impressive appearance. New plastic materials are being used today in place of metal in order to reduce the weight the player must carry. The tuba player is seated in the orchestra and appears occasionally in the band. As expected, these bass instruments have the largest mouthpieces. As told in the children's recording, *Tubby the Tuba*, Decca Records, the tuba seldom plays melodies. Instead, it normally supports the band as the primary low bass instrument, and it assists the double basses of the orchestra. Its tone is deep and its execution somewhat ponderous.

Examples of brass instrument tone qualities include:

"Finale," *William Tell Overture*, Rossini, Adventures in Music 3 v. 1; Bowmar 76   Trumpet
"Changing of the Guard," *Carmen Suite*, Bizet, Adventures in Music 3 v. 2

Peter and the Wolf, Prokofiev	French horn
"Nocturne," *Midsummer Night's Dream*, Mendelssohn	
"Third Movement," *Symphony No. 3*, Brahms	
"Prelude to Act 3," *Lohengrin*, Wagner	Trombone
Stars and Stripes Forever, Sousa, Adventures in Music 4 v. 2; Bowmar 54	
"Bydlo," *Pictures at an Exhibition*, Moussorgsky, Adventures in Music 2; Bowmar 82	Tuba
"Departure," *Winter Holiday*, Prokofiev, Adventures in Music 2 v. 1	

PERCUSSION

Examples of percussion instrument tone qualities include:

Danse Macabre, Saint-Saëns	
"Dagger Dance," *Natoma*, Herbert, Adventures in Music 3 v. 1	Cymbals, Drums
Semper Fidelis, Sousa, Adventures in Music 3 v. 2	Cymbals, Drums
"In the Hall of the Mountain King," *Peer Gynt Suite*, Grieg Adventures in Music 3 v. 2; Bowmar 59	Drums, Timpani
"Tarantella," *Fantastic Toy Shop*, Rossini, Adventures in Music 3 v. 2; Bowmar 56	Tambourine
The Alligator and the Coon, Thomson, Adventures in Music 3 v. 2	Xylophone
Said the Piano to the Harpsichord, Young People's Record 411	Piano, Harpsichord
"Pianists," *Carnival of the Animals*, Saint-Saëns, Bowmar 51	Piano
Chopin, Liszt, Debussy piano pieces; Grieg and Rachmaninoff concertos	Piano

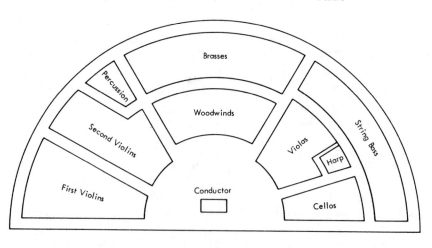

Recordings to stimulate children to compose percussion music.

Toccata for Percussion, Carlos Chavez, Columbia CMS 6447; HBR 21003, 2 discs

Concerto for Percussion and Small Orchestra, Darius Milhaud, Capitol HBR 21003, 2 discs

Ionization, Edgard Varèse, Columbia MS 6146, also on Folkways' *Sounds of New Music*, FX 6160

Identifying classes of instruments.

Third Movement of Symphony No. 4, Tschaikowsky, BOL #71 (Bowmar Orchestral Library)

Specific instruments.

King's Trumpet, The, Franson Corporation, 225 Park Avenue South, New York, N.Y. 10003, Children's Record Guild (CRG) 5040 (ages 5–8)

Licorice Stick: Story of the Clarinet, Franson, Young People's Record (YPR) 420 (ages 6–10)

Guitar Music from the Courts of Spain (Romera) Mercury

Pan the Piper, on Columbia CL 671

Peter and the Wolf (Prokofieff), on Columbia CL 671

Popular Classics for the Guitar (Bream), RCA Victor

Rusty in Orchestraville, Capitol Records

Said the Piano to the Harpsichord, Franson YPR 411

Tubby the Tuba, Decca (ages 6–7)

Wonderful Violin, The, Franson YPR 311 (ages 6–10)

Instruments of the orchestra.

Several manufacturers have albums under the title *Instruments of the Orchestra*: Capitol, Columbia, Decca, Vanguard, Victor

Child's Introduction to the Orchestra, Golden Records

Orchestra and Its Instruments, The, Folkways

Symphony Orchestra, The, Decca

Films and filmstrips.

Churchill Films, 622 N. Robertson Blvd., Los Angeles, Calif. 90069: *What is Music?*, *Wind Sounds*, *String Sounds*, *Percussion Sounds*, *New Sounds in Music*

Instruments of the Symphony Orchestra, (recordings with six filmstrips), Jam Handys, 2821 E. Grand Blvd., Detroit, Mich., 48211

Meet the Instruments, (recordings with two filmstrips), Bowmar Records, 622 Rodier Drive, Glendale, Calif., 91201

Music for Young People Series, NET Films Service, Indiana University, Bloomington, Ind. 47401; *Introducing the Woodwinds, Percussion, Pulse of Music*, and more

Musical Books for Young People, a series of six filmstrips, Society for Visual Education, 1345 Diversey Pkwy., Chicago, Ill., 60614. Strings, brass, woodwinds, percussion, keyboard, and folk instruments. (ages 9–13)

Symphony Orchestra, The, Encyclopedia Britannica Films, 425 N. Michigan Ave., Chicago, Ill., 60611. Traces growth of the symphony orchestra from string quartet to the modern orchestra. (ages 9–11)

Toot, Whistle, Plunk and Boom, Walt Disney. A humorous cartoon film available free of charge from C. G. Conn, Ltd., Educational Films Services, Elkhart, Ind., 46514. For all elementary grades.

We Make Music, Film Associates, 11559 Santa Monica Blvd., Los Angeles, Calif., 90025. *The Violin, The Bassoon*, and more

Music and Movement

For the very young, music and movement are natural partners. Children have the innate urge to listen to music with their entire bodies, not only with their ears. Jacques-Dalcroze understood this when he organized his method of learning music based upon body movements. Free rhythmic interpretation can be one logical activity for which to use recorded music. It allows children to experiment—to try different rhythmic movements in response to the music they hear. They first listen to the music. After listening and thinking how they might respond, they move, each in his own way, as they listen to the music again. There are some simple guidelines to follow as they move, such as not to touch other children or get in anyone's way, and to all move in the same direction. In a small classroom perhaps only four or five children will do the moving, after which the teacher can select others to take their places. In a large room such as a gymnasium the entire class can move at one time.

Free rhythmic response.

My Playful Scarf, Franson Corporation CRG 1019 (ages 2–4)

Ravel: "Laideronette, Empress of the Pagodas" from *Mother Goose Suite*, BOL 57 (Bowmar Orchestral Library Album 57)

Moussorgsky: "Bydlo" from *Pictures at an Exhibition*, AM 2 v 1 (Adventures in Music, Grade 2)

Donaldson: *Under the Big Top*, BOL 51

Lecoq: "Gavotte" from Mlle. *Angot Suite*, BOL 53

Moussorgsky: Ballet of the Unhatched Chicks" from *Pictures at an Exhibition*, AM 1 v 1

Animals and Circus, BOL 51

Bach: "Badinerie" from *Suite No. 2 in B Minor*, AM 3 v 1

Pierné: *Entrance of the Little Fauns*, BOL 54; AM 2 v 2

Tschaikowsky: "March" from *The Nutcracker Suite*, BOL 58

Pierné: *March of the Little Lead Soldiers*, BOL 54

Prokofiev: "March" from *The Love for Three Oranges*, BOL 54

Pictures and Patterns, BOL 53

FUNDAMENTAL MOVEMENTS

Fundamental movements is a term used in physical education. It describes simple, basic movements such as walking, running, skipping, and galloping. Series books for kindergarten and first grade contain helpful song and piano material as well as suggestions for teaching such movements. Also, teachers can quickly learn to use percussion instruments or a few notes on the piano keyboard to improvise rhythms for the simple movements to which children learn to respond. In these early levels the teacher should not expect every child to respond in the same way; some children need time to experiment before being able to do what the others do. It is ncessary that children learn fundamental movements because command of them is essential to being able to engage in free rhythmic play, some action songs, and singing games and dances. Each child needs time in which to explore *his own* tempo. Thus, at first the teacher observes and use the child's natural tempo before asking him to conform to one predetermined by the teacher.

Further understanding of fundamental movements can be gained by using songs that suggest impersonation (imitative play). Children who are five and six years old tend strongly to *be* what they may impersonate, such as the horses that gallop and the rabbits that hop. The teacher may tap a drum, play a piano, or use a recording, and ask the children what it makes them feel like doing. From their prior experience should come such movements as clapping, walking, running, skipping, galloping, sliding, hopping, and jumping. Through the freedom of children to respond to the rhythms of music they can discover other body movements which may include swinging, pushing, bouncing, pulling, bending, stretching, and striking. During all of this the teacher controls the learning situation by helping children relate familiar physical responses to the music they hear. The teacher should do this in such a manner that each child feels he has made his personal contribution.

Walking.

Children may develop different types of walking by pretending they are different characters or animals. Marching is an outgrowth of walking. Walking is normally relaxed and swinging.

Thomson: "Walking Song" from *Acadian Songs and Dances*, AM 1 v 1

Kabalevsky: "Pantomime" from *The Comedians* (big steps) AM 1 v 1

Moussorgsky: "Bydlo" from *Pictures at an Exhibition*, (lumbering steps), AM 1

Prokofiev: "Departure" from *Winter Holiday* (fast steps), AM 2

Rossini: "Finale" from *William Tell Overture*, AM 3 v 1

Herbert: "Dagger Dance" from *Natoma*, AM 3 v 1

Handel: "Bourrée and Menuetto" from *Royal Fireworks Music*, AM 3 v 2

Grieg: "In the Hall of the Mountain King" from *Peer Gynt Suite*, AM 3 v 2

Marching.

While the interest of young children in marches focuses on body responses, the older children may be interested in comparing and analyzing different march styles. Military band marches can be compared with the favorite marches of the young children—those having to do with toys, dwarfs, and such. Older children could add to these the march movements of Beethoven's *Third Symphony* and Tschaikowsky's *Sixth Symphony* as well as the march from Prokofiev's opera, *The Love For Three Oranges* and the "March and Cortege" from Gounod's opera, *The Queen of Sheba.*

Rossini-Britten: "March" from *Soirees Musicales*, AM 1 v 1

Herbert: "March of the Toys" from *Babes in Toyland*, AM 2 v 1

Vaughan-Williams: "March Past of the Kitchen Utensils" from *The Wasps,* AM 3 v 1

Lully: "March" from *Ballet Suite*, AM 3 v 2

Sousa: *Semper Fidelis*, AM 3 v 2

Grieg: "Norwegian Rustic March" from *Lyric Suite*, AM 4 v 1

Sousa: *Stars and Stripes Forever*, AM 4 v 2

Gould: *American Salute*, AM 5 v 1

Coates: "Knightsbridge March" from *London Suite*, AM 5 v 2

Running.

Running on tiptoe is commonly stressed; the movement should be kept light.

Gluck: "Air Gai" from *Iphigenie in Aulis*, AM 1 v 1

Bizet: "The Ball" from *Children's Games*, AM 1 v 1

Hopping.

Hopping is done on one foot.

Moussorgsky: "Ballet of the Unhatched Chicks" from *Pictures at an Exhibition*, AM 1 v 1

Bach: "Gigue" from *Suite No. 3*, AM 1 v 1

Gretry: "Gigue" from *Cephale et Procris*, AM 1 v 1

Gretry: "Tambourin" from *Cephale et Procris*, AM 2 v 1

Jumping.

Jumping is done with both feet together. Overly heavy movements are to be avoided.

Massenet: "Aragonaise" from *Le Cid*, AM 1 v 1

Bizet: "Leap Frog" from *Children's Games*, AM 1 v 1

Meyerbeer: "Waltz" from *Les Pateneuers*, AM 2 v 1

Skipping or Galloping.

Skipping is a step, hop, first on one foot and then on the other. Children enjoy a large fast skip that gives them the feeling of moving high in the air. When galloping, one foot is kept ahead of the other throughout, and the back foot is brought up to meet it. Heels never touch the floor.

Bach: "Gigue" from *Suite No. 3*, AM 1

Gretry: "Gigue" from *Cephale et Procris*, AM 1

Whirling.

Massenet: "Argonaise" from *Le Cid*, AM 1

Rossini-Respighi: "Tarantella" from *The Fantastic Toy Shop*, AM 3 v 2

Swaying, rocking.

These movements can relax children after the stimulation of the more active movements. Swaying trees, branches or flowers are often imitated, as are swings, the pendulum of a clock, rocking a baby to sleep, and rowing a boat.

Bizet: "Cradle Song" from *Children's Games*, AM 1 v 1

Delibes: "Waltz of the Doll" from *Copelia*, AM 1 v 1

Fauré: "Berceuse" from *Dolly*, AM 2 v 1

Shostakovitch: "Petite Ballerina" from *Ballet Suite No. 1*, AM 2 v 1

Offenbach: "Barcarolle" from *Tales of Hoffman*, AM 3 v 1

Saint-Saëns: "The Swan" from *Carnival of the Animals*, AM 3 v 2

Chabrier: *España* (for a spirited swinging), AM 4, v 1

Sliding, gliding. Waltzing.

Prokofiev: "Waltz on Ice" from *Children's Suite*, AM 3 v 2

Tschaikowsky: "Waltz" from *The Sleeping Beauty*, AM 4 v 2

Khachaturian: "Waltz" from *Masquerade Suite*, AM 4 v 2

For specific suggestions, study the Teachers Guides for the *Adventures in Music* albums. Older children can study the waltz with the purpose of expanding that concept. The *Adventures in Music* albums provide many different types to study. Contrast the Viennese and American concepts of waltz.

Review of fundamental movements.

When working with recordings that illustrate several different movements, small groups of children can be asked to respond appropriately whenever their assigned movement is heard.

A Visit to My Little Friend, Franson CRG 1017 (ages 2–4)

Animals and Circus, BOL 51

Marches, BOL 54

Nature and Make Believe, BOL 52

RHYTHMIC DRAMATIZATION

Rhythmic dramatization implies that the child is able to respond physically to rhythm, melody, mood, tempo, dynamics, and instrumentation. First he listens to the music to ascertain how an action or a story is suggested. He then associates the action or story with related aspects of the musical elements. In the instance of a story, some call these "cues." Finally, he creates his dramatization. The Teacher's Guide for *Adventures in Music* recordings are helpful.

Bartók: "Bear Dance" from *Hungarian Sketches*, AM 3 v. 2
Ibert: *The Little White Donkey*, AM 2 v 1
Kabalevsky: "March and Comedian's Gallop" from *The Comedians*, AM 3 v 1
Lully: "March" from *Ballet Suite*, AM 3 v. 2
Grieg: *Norwegian Dance*, BOL 63
Debussy: "Golliwog's Cakewalk" from *Children's Corner Suite*, BOL 63
Grieg: "Ase's Death" from *Peer Gynt Suite No. 1*, BOL 59

Tempo and dynamics.

Debussy: Fêtes (Festival), BOL 70
Honegger: *Pacific 231*

Percussion reviewed.

Strike Up the Band, Franson CRG 5027 (ages 5–8)
Children can play a game to identify percussion instruments. The order on the recording is drum, cymbal, wood block, jingle bells, sticks, triangle, tambourine

Beat (pulse).

Offenbach: "Barcarolle" from *Tales of Hoffman*, AM 3 v 1
Gounod: "Waltz" from *Faust Ballet Suite*, AM 3 v 1
Herbert: "Dagger Dance" from *Natoma*, AM 3 v 1
Dvořák: *Slavonic Dance No. 7*, AM 4 v 2
various marches

Fermata, ritard, accelerando.

These interrupt the regular beat.
Brahms: *Hungarian Dance No. 5*, BOL 55
Shostakovitch: "Petite Ballerina" from *Ballet Suite No. 1*, AM 2 v 1

ANIMALS, MACHINES, AND NATURE DESCRIBED IN MUSIC

Imitating animals seems to be a natural interest of young children, thus recordings such as those that follow have good possibilities for listening-moving-dramatizing activities. Older children should be asked, *"How does the music describe the animal?"* Their answers should be in terms of the elements of music—rhythm, melody, tempo, dynamics, harmony, and instrumentation.

Rimsky-Korsakoff: *Flight of the Bumble-Bee*, BOL 52

Respighi: *The Birds*, Mercury 90153; "Prelude" from, BOL 85

Liadov: *Dance of the Mosquito*, BOL 52

Griffes: *The White Peacock*, AM 5 v 1

Saint-Saëns: "The Swan" from *Carnival of the Animals*, AM 3 v 2

Machines.

Villa-Lobos: "Little Train of the Caipira" from *Bachianas Brasileiras No. 2*, AM 6 v 2

Honneger: *Pacific 231* (a railroad locomotive of World War I)

Mossolov: *Iron Foundry*, on *Sounds of New Music*, Folkways FX 6160

Nature.

Debussy: "Reflections in the Water" (piano music and an example of impressionist style)

Debussy: "Nuage" (Clouds), BOL 70

Thomson: *The River*, Vanguard 2095

Smetana: *The Moldau* (a river in Czechoslavakia)

Debussy: *La Mer* (The Sea), section from, BOL 70; AM 6 v 2

Ives: *Three Outdoor Scenes*, Composers Recordings CRI 163

Grofe: *Death Valley Suite*, Capital T-272

Grofe: *Grand Canyon Suite*, BOL 61

Beethoven: *Symphony No. 6*, "Pastoral"

Debussy: *Clair de Lune* (Moonlight)

Vivaldi: *The Four Seasons*

OTHER RHYTHM-RELATED CONCEPTS

Tempo, fast.

Corelli: "Badinerie" from *Suite for Strings*, BOL 63
Kabalevsky: "Intermezzo" from *The Comedians*, BOL 53
Rossini-Respighi: "Tarantella" from *The Fantastic Toy Shop*, AM 3 v 2

Tempo, slow.

Ravel: "Pavanne of the Sleeping Beauty" from *Mother Goose Suite*, BOL 57
Corelli: "Sarabande" from *Suite for Strings*, BOL 63

Fast and slow.

Slow Joe, Franson YPR 9003 (ages 6–10)

Accelerando.

Grieg: "In the Hall of the Mountain King" from *Peer Gynt Suite*, AM 3 v 2; BOL 59

Accent.

Prokofiev: "Departure" from *Winter Holiday*, AM 2
Shostakovitch: "Petite Ballerina" from *Ballet Suite No. 1*, AM 2 v 1
Rossini-Respighi: "Can Can" from *The Fantastic Toyshop*, AM 2 v 1
Herbert: "Dagger Dance" from *Natoma*, AM 3
Rossini-Respighi: "Tarantella" from *The Fantastic Toyshop*, AM 3
Debussy: *Iberia* (beginning of)

Legato (articulation).

Also music for resting
Stravinsky: "Berceuse" from *Firebird Suite*, AM 1 v 1
Fauré: "Berceuse" from *Dolly*, AM 2 v 1
Bizet: "Cradle Song" from *Children's Games*, AM 1 v 1
Offenbach: "Barcarolle" from *Tales of Hoffman*, AM 3 v 1
Waldteufel: *Skater's Waltz*, BOL 55
Brahms: Waltz in E-flat
Rubenstein: *Melody in F*

Staccato (articulation).

Moussorgsky: "Ballet of the Unhatched Chicks" from *Pictures at an Exhibi-*

tion, AM 1 v 1

Anderson: *The Syncopated Clock,* Keyboard Junior Recordings

Prokofiev: "March" from *Summer Day Suite,* AM 1 v 1

Herbert: "March of the Toys" from *Babes in Toyland,* AM 2 v 1

Stravinsky: "Dance Infernale" from *Firebird Suite,* BOL 69; Keyboard Junior Recordings

Vaughan-Williams: "March Past of the Kitchen Utensils" from *The Wasps* AM 3 v 1

von Suppé: *Light Cavalry Overture*

Meter.

Game: Select recordings that are clear examples of specific meters. Play these, asking the children to identify the meter they hear. One way to help them solve the problem is to tell them to make the hand and arm go *down* on the strong accent of the first beat of the measure, then raise the arm slightly for each of the intervening beats until the next strong downbeat comes. They should count the downbeat as "one," and continue to count the intervening beats. The last number before the next downbeat tells the listener the number of beats in the measure. From this he may be able to determine the meter (time signature).

Schubert: *March Militaire,* BOL 54 (two beats, $\frac{2}{4}$ meter)

Sousa: *Stars and Stripes Forever,* AM 4 v 2 ($\frac{2}{4}$ meter)

Bach: "Gigue" from *Suite No. 3,* AM 1 v 1 (two beats, $\frac{6}{8}$ meter)

Berlioz: "Ballet of the Sylphs" from *Damnation of Faust,* AM 1 (three beats, $\frac{3}{4}$ meter)

Delibes: "Waltz of the Doll" from *Copelia,* AM 1 v 1 ($\frac{3}{4}$ meter)

Ippolitov-Ivanov: "Cortege of the Sardar" from *Caucasian Sketches,* BOL 54 (four beats, $\frac{4}{4}$ meter)

Herbert: "Dagger Dance" from *Natoma,* AM 3 v 1 ($\frac{4}{4}$ meter)

Offenbach: "Barcarolle" from *Tales of Hoffman*, AM 3 v 2 (⁶⁄₈ meter)

Changes in meter.

Cailliet: *Pop Goes the Weasel* (variations) AM 4 v 2 (⁶⁄₈, ¾, ⁴⁄₈, ¾, ²⁄₄)

Copland: "Street in a Frontier Town" from *Billy the Kid*, AM 6 v 1

Piston: "Tango of the Merchant's Daughter" from *The Incredible Flutist* (⁵⁄₈), Mercury 90423

Less common meters.

Tschaikowsky: "Second Movement," from *Symphony No. 6* (⁵⁄₄)

Ginastera: "Wheat Dance" from *Estancia*, AM 4 v 2

Copland: "Hoe-Down" from *Rodeo*, AM 5 v 2

Guarnieri: *Brazilian Dance*, AM 6 v 2

Brubeck: *Time Out*, Columbia CL 1397

Brubeck: *Time Farther Out*, Columbia CL 1690 (⁷⁄₈)

Ravel: "Fourth Movement" from *Trio* (⁵⁄₄, ⁷⁄₈)

Polyrhythms.

Copland: "Street in a Frontier Town" from *Billy the Kid*, AM 6 v 1

see *The Study of Music in the Elementary School: A Conceptual Approach*, Charles L. Gary, ed. (Music Educators National Conference, Washington, D.C., 1967), pp. 47–50

see *Source Book of African and Afro-American Materials for Music Educators* (Music Educators National Conference, Washington, D.C., 1972) for two beats against three, p. 34.

Rhythm patterns.

Bartók: "Bear Dance" from *Hungarian Sketches*, AM 3 v 2

Cui: *Orientale*

Tschaikowsky: "Fourth Movement" from *Symphony No. 4*

Beethoven: "Second Movement" from *Symphony No. 8*

Ibert: "The Little White Donkey" from *Histories No. 2*, AM 2

Bizet: "Habanera" from *Carmen*, BOL 56

Debussy: "Golliwog's Cakewalk" from *Children's Corner Suite*, BOL 63

Milhaud: "Copacabana" from *Saudades do Brazil*, AM 4 v 2 (Ask children to find and identify the four major patterns used by the composer.)

Bolero pattern.   Ravel: *Bolero*

Beguine pattern.   Porter: *Begin the Beguine*

Habanera pattern.   Bizet: "Habanera" from *Carmen*

Gottschalk: "Grand Walkaround" from *Cakewalk*, AM 5 v 1

Benjamin: *Jamaican Rhumba*, BOL 56

Syncopation.   Gottschalk: "Grand Walkaround" from *Cakewalk*, AM 5 v 1

Debussy: "Golliwog's Cakewalk" from *Children's Corner Suite*, BOL 63

Copland: "Hoedown" from *Rodeo*, AM 5 v 2; BOL 55

Charbrier: *España*, AM 5 v 1 (also for study of the beat)

MISCELLANEOUS RHYTHM REFERENCES

Bowmar Records, Inc.
622 Rodier Drive
Glendale, California 91201   age level

Holiday Rhythms	4–7
Rhythm Time No. 1 (fundamental movements)	4–7
Rope Jumping and Ball Handling	5–7
The Rainy Day Record	6–8
Another Rainy Day Record	6–8
Singing Games, Albums 1 and 2	4–8
Singing Games and Folk Dances, Album 3	4–8
Folk Dances, Album 4	7–10
Folk Dances, Album 5	7–11

Folk Dances, Album 6	10–13
Square Dances and Round Dances, 3 albums	9–14
Rounds and Mixers, 2 albums	5–9
Play Party Games, 2 albums	8–11
Ethnic Dances: *Mexico, Hawaii, Canada*	

Capitol Records Distributing Corporation
1750 North Vine Street
Hollywood, California 90028

Listen, Move, Dance, Vols. 1 and 2
    Vol. 1, side one: "Moving Percussion"; side two: "Electronic Sound Pictures"
    Vol. 2, side one: "Music for Quick and Light, Quick and Strong, and Slow and Light Movements"; side two: "Electronic Sound Patterns"

Children's Record Guild and Young People's Records
Franson Corporation
225 Park Avenue South
New York, New York 10003   age level

Do This, Do That CRG 1040	2–4
Drummer Boy, CRG 1015	2–4
Eensie Beensie Spider, CRG 1002	2–4
Folk Songs for Singing and Dancing, YPR 8005/6	6–10
I Am a Circus, CRG 1028	2–4
Let's Dance, CRG 5021	5–8
Little Indian Drum, YPR 619 (drum talk)	2–5
Little Red Wagon, CRG 1004	5–8
Merry Toy Shop, CRG 1022	2–4
My Playful Scarf, CRG 1019 (creative)	2–4
My Playmate, the Wind, YPR 4501 (creative)	4–5
Nothing To Do, CRG 1012 (fundamental movements)	2–4
Out of Doors, YPR 724	2–5
Ride 'Em Cowboy, CRG 5001	5–8
Skittery Skattery, CRG 1005	2–4
Slow Joe, YPR (fast and slow)	6–10
Strike Up the Band, CRG 5027	5–8
Swing Your Partner, YPR 9002	6–10

Sunday in the Park, CRG 1010	2–4
Trains and Planes, YPR 706	2–5
When I Was Very Young, CRG 1031	2–4
When the Sun Shines, YPR 617	2–5
Whoa! Little Horses, Lie Down, YPR 714	2–5

Columbia Records, Inc.
799 Seventh Avenue
New York, N.Y. 10019 — age level

Jum-A-Jingles (rope skipping, ball bouncing)	6–8
Lead a Little Orchestra (conducting)	6–8

Folkways Records
121 West 47th St.
New York, New York 10011

Adventures in Rhythm (Ella Jenkins)	9–11
Dance Along (rhythm improvisations)	5–8
Rhythms for Children	5–8
Rhythms of the World	
Skip Rope Games	5–8
American Play-Parties	8–11

Methodist Church Publishing House
407 Church Street
Nashville, Tennessee

World of Fun Folk Dances
New World of Fun Series

RCA Victor *Dance-A-Story* Records (storybook record combinations)
Ginn and Company, Boston, Mass. 02117
Ginn and Company, 35 Mobile Drive, Toronto 375, Ontario, Canada

Little Duck	5–7
Noah's Ark	5–9
Magic Mountain	5–11
Balloons	4–11
The Brave Hunter	5–8

Flappy and Floppy	3–7
The Toy Tree	4–7
At the Beach	5–11

RCA Victor Educational Sales
155 E. 24th Street
New York, N.Y. 10010
The World of Folk Dances series

Rhythms Productions Educational Records
8869 Venice Blvd.
Los Angeles, California 90034

There are many other sources. See your physical education-dance department for more suggestions.

Among the helpful catalogues are:

Children's Music Center Catalog
5373 West Pico Blvd.
Los Angeles, Calif. 90019

Phonograph Records and Filmstrips for Classroom and Library
157 Chambers Street
New York, N.Y. 10007

EXEMPLARY FILMS

Building Children's Personalities with Creative Dancing, University of California Extension Division Film 5844. For teachers. May be obtained from UCLA Educational Film Sales Department, Los Angeles, California, and from Dance Films, Inc., 130 West 57th Street, New York, N.Y., 10019.

Dance Your Own Way, UCLA Educational Film Sales Department; also from Dance Films, Inc.

Discovering Rhythm, United World Films, Universal Education and Visual Arts, 221 Park Ave. South, New York, N.Y., 10003. Concepts in rhythm for children from preschool to seven years.

Let's Begin With the Beat, EMC Corporation, St. Paul, Minn. 55106. A sound-filmstrip.

Pantomimes, Brandon Films, New York, N.Y. 10019. How the body communicates ideas.

Reading Music: No. 2, Finding the Rhythm, Coronet Films, 65 E. S. Water Street, Chicago, Ill. 60601.

What is Rhythm? and *Discovering Dynamics in Music*, BFA Educational Media, 2211 Michigan Avenue, Santa Monica, Calif. 90404.

Be sure to utilize the *Film Guide for Music Educators*, published by the Music Educators National Conference.

Music-Art Relationships

While it should be emphasized that music and art are totally different media—one is aural and the other visual—colors in art and tone colors in music are thought to have some relationship. Rhythm, melody, and dynamics also may be reflected in art. Children can explore these concepts by listening to music of contrasting nature, such as the Debussy and Shostakovitch below. The titles should not be given. The music should be repeated a number of times while the children work with chalk, crayon, or brush to interpret through art the rhythms and tone colors they hear. Remember that there are "cool" and "warm" sounds and colors.

> Debussy: "Nuages" from *Nocturnes*, BOL 70
> Offenbach: "Barcarolle" from *Tales of Hoffman*, AM 3 v 1
> Shostakovitch: "Polka" from *Age of Gold*
> Stravinsky: "Dance Russe" from *Petrouchka*, BOL 80

Polyphony, Harmony, and Texture

Ostinato

> Pierne: *March of the Little Lead Soldiers*, BOL 54
> McPhee: "Ostinatos" from *Tabuh Tabuhan*, Mercury MG 50103
> Cowell: "Ostinato Pianissimo" on *Concert Percussion*, Time 8000

Descant

> *Growing Up With Music*, Bowmar Records. Five albums based on the descant books by Beatrice and Max Krone, Neil A. Kjos Music Co., Park Ridge, Ill.

Rounds and canons

> *Let's Sing a Round*, Bowmar Records
> *Round and Round*, Franson YPR 431, (ages 6–10). From round to canon to fugue.
> Franck: *Violin Sonata*, last movement (a beautiful example)

Polyphony
Sousa: *Semper Fidelis*, AM 3 v 1. Have children explore this march to discover the different melodies and how Sousa combines them.

FUGUE

The fugue is a rather complex polyphonic form. A theme (subject) is introduced by two or more voices in turn, developed in what can be considered another section, then restated in the final part of the form. If children should describe a fugue after listening to it carefully, they might say that when one voice or instrument states a theme and then continues playing another melody while a second voice states the theme a fourth lower or a fifth higher, the beginning of a fugue has been created. The melody the first voice plays or sings when the second voice sounds the theme is called the "countersubject." This process may continue with the entrance of other voices, each beginning with the subject. This first section is called an *exposition*. It is followed by a free section consisting of statements of the subject, often in altered forms, and "episodes," something akin to interludes, based on tone patterns or rhythm patterns found in the subject and countersubject. Sometimes there is a *stretto* near the end, when the voices sound the subject in a way in which there is overlapping of the entrances. The subject is restated at the end to establish unity.

The fugue may appear somewhat complicated by its description, and the teacher must use good judgment in knowing how far to expect a class of eleven-year-olds to proceed with it. Depending on the group, going into fine detail will be something only advanced children will find interesting. However, the entire class can detect the unique beginning and the texture of the fugue; even young children can do this.

Fugue.
McBride: *Pumpkineater's Little Fugue*, BOL 65
Thomson: *Fugue and Chorale on Yankee Doodle*, BOL 65
Scarlatti: *Cat's Fugue*, Keyboard Junior Recordings
Bach: *Little Fugue in G Minor*, BOL 86, AM 6 v 1
Bizet: "Farandole" from *L'Arlesienne Suite No. 2*, AM 6 v 1

Major and minor.

Lecuona: "Andalucia" from *Suite Andalucia,* AM 4 v 1 (includes a canon)

Mozart: "Romanze" from *Eine kleine Nachtmusik,* AM 4 v 1

Charpentier: "Oh Muleback" from *Impressions of Italy,* AM 5 v 1

de Falla: "Spanish Dance" from *La Vida Breve,* AM 6 v 1

Harmonic intervals: thirds and sixths.

Tschaikowsky: *Italian Caprice* (a prominent theme is in thirds)

Mendelssohn: *Symphony No. 4,* first movement (theme two has a two-part melody in thirds)

Charpentier: "On Muleback" from *Impressions of Italy,* AM 5 v 1 (theme three has a two-part melody in thirds and sixths)

Common chords.

Mozart: "Romanze" from *Eine kleine Nachtmusik,* AM 4 v 1 (I, V_7, and IV chords can be heard and identified)

Ginastera: "Wheat Dance" from *Estancia,* AM 4 v 1

Milhaud: "Copacabana" from *Saudades do Brazil,* AM 4 v 2

Autoharp chording.

Tuning the Autoharp, Rhythm Band, Inc., Fort Worth, Texas

Tuning Your Autoharp, Oscar Schmidt —International, Union, N.J.

Contemporary harmony.

Bartók: *Concerto for Orchestra.* Quartal harmony (chords built in fourths)

Milhaud: "Laranjeires: from *Saudades do Brazil,* AM 4 v 2 (dissonance, bitonality)

Milhaud: "Copacabana" from *Saudades do Brazil,* AM 4 v 2 (bitonality, dissonance)

Hindemith: *Mathis der Maler,* Columbia (harmony constructed of fourths and fifths)

Harris: *Folk-Song Symphony,* Vanguard (contemporary harmonizations of U.S. folk songs)

Honneger: "March from *King David*, Vanguard (polytonality: three keys at one time)

Ives: "Putnam's Camp" from *Three Places in New England*, BOL 75; Columbia; Mercury (bitonality; describes two bands playing in different keys). Also "Fourth of July," Columbia MS-6889 and *Variations on America*, Columbia MS-7269 and Victor LSC-2893

Copland: "Circus Music" from *The Red Pony*, AM 3 v 1 (tone clusters, polytonality)

Webern: *The Complete Music*, Columbia (tone row music)

Sounds of New Music, Folkways FX 6160 (electronic music) tone clusters: see music of Charles Ives and Henry Cowell

TEXTURE

Ask questions to help children develop a vocabulary of terms descriptive of texture such as light, heavy, thick, thin, and degrees of these. Use recordings in which children can easily compare a thick texture with a thin texture. Compare the combining of melodic lines in polyphony with threads in weaving tapestry.

Saint-Saëns: "The Swan" from *Carnival of the Animals*, AM 3 v 2 (homophonic texture)

Ligeti: "Atmospheres" from *Space Odyssy*, Columbia MS 6733

Bach: *Little Fugue in G Minor*, AM 6 v 1; BOL 86

Exemplary Films

Elements of Composition (New York Wind Ensemble), NET Film Service, Bloomington, Ind. 47401 (melody, harmony, rhythm, and counterpoint)

Discovering Melody and Harmony, BFA Educational Media, 2211 Michigan Ave., Santa Monica, Calif. 90404 (Harmony is added to melody through use of descant and thirds and by playing instruments)

Harmony in Music, Coronet Instructional Films, Chicago, Ill. 60601 (introduces harmony and chords, ages 10–13)

Let's Get Together, EMC Corporation, St. Paul, Minn. 55101 (harmony, age 10 and up)

Music, The Expressive Language, Sutherland Productions, 201 N. Occidental Blvd., Los Angeles, Calif. 90026 (rhythm, melody, harmony, reading music, for ages 9–11)

Two-Part Singing, Johnson Hunt Productions, Hollywood, Calif. 94105 (ages 9–11)

Refer to *Film Guide for Music Educators*, Music Educators National Conference.

Form

FORM IN MUSIC

It is the practice today to consider two kinds of form. One is form *in* music; the other concerns forms *of* music. The first consists of aspects of music relating to generalizations such as: melodies can be divided into logical parts; melodies can be extended and altered. The second is concerned with the larger forms of music such as song forms, suites, and symphonies.

Children can discover natural divisions of melodies comparable to a sentence in speech in answer to the questions, "Is the tune the same now or is it different?" and "Is it different or is it almost the same?" This division is called the phrase. Phrases are often thought of as being four measures in length, and while most of the songs in the series books seem to demonstrate this, phrases can be found in these books that vary from two to eight measures. The important idea is not their length as much as it is that melodies can be divided into logical parts called phrases. This, of course, is the generalization teachers want children to make. Sometimes two phrases relate to each other in a special way; these two phrases are called a *period*. They can be improvised in the classroom by the teacher singing the first phrase and children taking turns improvising the second phrase; the teacher sings a "question," and the child sings an "answering" phrase.

Sometimes an entire phrase or a part of the melody within a phrase is found to be repeated on a different degree of the scale, either higher or lower than the first appearance of the phrase or note pattern. This was identified as the *sequence* in the analysis of melody in Chapter 4.

Identifying *same* or *different* is the key to understanding form. Young children's experience with this is at first more physical than it is intellectual. The teacher suggests that they move their bodies in relation to what they hear in the music. Among the suggestions is to draw from children how they might "act out" the music to show when it was the same and when it was different. In learning to recognize different phrases or larger contrasting sections of music, children may change movements or steps, reverse directions, and play different kinds of percussion instruments. Phrase repetition and difference are found in the songs children sing and in recorded music to which they listen. As in all aspects of teaching music, teachers select very clear examples of the phrase or larger sections of music when their objective is to help children distinguish "same" and "different." Very young children can compare Bartók's *Bear Dance*, which consists of repeated A sections separated by interludes, with Prokofiev's *Waltz on Ice*, (both in Adventures in Music 3 v. 2), which has three different sections in simple rondo form— ABACA. Their discoveries may include that music is made of different tunes or parts; sometimes these are the same, sometimes they are different, and some music has more parts than other music. Teachers can use visual aids, such as hats, costumes, streamers, masks, dancers, and colors, to dramatize same and different parts of music. To emphasize this in phrases, one group of children can be asked to sing phrases that are alike and another group those that contrast—boys and girls, those with black hair and those with brown hair, those with rubber-soled shoes and those with leather-soled shoes, and so on. Children can play finger cymbals to mark the ends of phrases; this gives them a purpose for listening carefully. Older children can classify phrases as being alike, different, and almost alike; they can study the notation of recorded music or familiar songs to form the generalization that when phrases look alike, they sound alike.

Teachers have learned that some older children are usually not greatly interested in phrases and some other structural aspects of music. While from an artistic point of view form is highly important because all works of art have form, and while scholars have written that form is the most fundamental aspect of music learning, children of elementary-school age do not always agree with the scholars. These children are practical people, and they are not impressed unless they can understand the *function* of phenomena like form. The function of form seems to be to provide in different ways for two opposing concepts, *unity* and *contrast* or variety. Children who have acquired concepts of unity and contrast may find meaning in form. For example, when children are confronted with a phrase order such as *a a b a*, or *a b a c a*, and the teacher asks, "What is there in this tune that gives us a feeling of variety or contrast?" and "What is there that gives us a feeling of unity?" the function of form is made clear. Phrases *b* and *c* provide variety, and phrase *a* provides unity with its repetitions. Understanding this brings added meaning to the form of their own compositions. There are a number of interesting discoveries when they apply the principles of unity and contrast. Perhaps they will decide that the sequence serves both; it offers unity because it is a repetition, but it offers variety because the pitch is different.

Another generalization which concerns form is that melodies can be extended and altered by composers in various ways. By listening to music, making music, and creating music, children discover and use introductions, codas, and interludes. Introductions and codas are usually derived from melodies, but an interlude is often a contrasting section. Repetition is an obvious way to extend melodies. *Thematic development* is a term that describes what composers do with themes (tunes) they use in their larger compositions. When themes are developed they are extended or altered in many ways, including augmentation, diminution, canon, inversion, retrograde, and octave displacement. These are only a sampling of what composers do with the two themes in the middle (development) section of sonata-allegro form.

Before we leave forms *in* music, we should again refer to unity and variety. Aspects of form should be tested and analyzed by children in these terms. The various forms of melodic alteration sometimes contain both elements. For example, an inverted melody has a natural relation with the original melody; because of this there should be some degree of unity found in it. The children can discover that the rhythm remains the same, providing rhythmic unity. The inverted melody sounds different, however, so variety is also achieved by the inversion. Eventually children will discover that they must analyze unity and variety in terms of the elements of music. Unity may be attained by *repetition* of rhythm, melody, harmony, texture, tempo, dynamics, and tone quality. Variety may be attained by *changes* in rhythm, melody, harmony, texture, tempo, dynamics, and tone quality. When the form *of* music is understood, form can be added to the above list of musical elements. This infers that teachers' questions can be quite to the point. "How is unity achieved in this composition?" "Was there repetition of any of the above elements of music?" "How was contrast achieved?" "Was there any change in any of the above musical elements?" "How did it change?" In this way analytical thinking is guided, and the function of these aspects of form is made clear to the learner. Form becomes a logical scheme of things.

FORMS OF MUSIC

Songs in the music textbooks can usually be easily analyzed according to their phrases. Some phrases will be found to be repeated note-for-note, some repeated with changes, and some contrasting and different. Songs such as "Au Claire de la Lune," "The Blue Bell of Scotland," "The Marines' Hymn," "O Susanna," and "Long, Long Ago," have clearly defined phrases, both repeated and contrasting. Most of the songs in the textbooks are printed with one phrase on each stave. When songs are not printed that way, commas, semicolons, and periods in the texts, or rests in the melody offer semireliable clues as to the length of phrases. Songs can be one-part (unary) such as "Whistle, Daughter, Whistle," with a phrase arrangement of *a a*; two-part (binary) such as "Go Tell Aunt Rhody," with a phrase arrangement of *a b*; and three-part (ternary) such as "Twinkle, Twinkle, Little Star," with a phrase arrangement of *a a b a.*

From the child's point of view, identifying phrases and larger sections in terms of letters of the alphabet is not very appealing or even as logical as some other ways. To dramatize phrase differences, some teachers find that freeing the children to draw the form in their own creative ways can attract interest and induce far more learning. For example, phrases *a b a* might be:

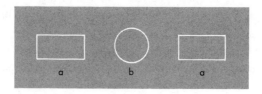

The sections of a rondo could be:

Another form might be drawn as:

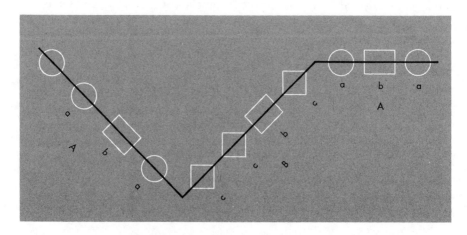

Using colors adds more interest because color highlights the contrasts. Some children will draw objects rather than the geometric designs illustrated here. The evaluative criterion is, "Does this drawing tell us clearly what the form is?" or "Does it show us all the parts in their true order?"

The A B A sectional form is common to many larger compositions. It is the same principle as the *a b a* phrase arrangement except that the concept is expanded into large sections instead of only several phrases.

SEQUENCE:

Carpenter: "The Hurdy-Gurdy" from *Adventures in a Perambulator*, AM 5 v 2

THEMATIC DEVELOPMENT.   Thematic development as a means of extending melodic-rhythmic ideas can be studied by having older children explore the beginning of Beethoven's Fifth Symphony. "What different things did the composer do with his short idea?" "List them." (The first thing Beethoven did was to write a sequence.)

TWO-PART (BINARY) FORM

Ginastera: "Wheat Dance" from *Estancia*, AM 4 v 1
Handel: "Bourrée" and "Menuetto" from *Royal Fireworks Music*, AM 3 v 2; BOL 62
Milhaud: "Copacabana" from *Saudades do Brazil*, AM 4 v 2
Respighi: "Danza" from *Brazilian Impressions*, AM 5 v 2
Bach: "Badinerie" from *Suite No. 2 in B Minor*, AM 3 v 1

THREE-PART (TERNARY) FORM

Brahms: *Hungarian Dance No. 1 in C Minor*, AM 5 v 2
Debussy: *En Bateau*, BOL 53
Offenbach: "Barcarolle" from *Tales of Hoffmann*, AM 3 v 1
Schumann: "Traumerei" from *Scenes of Childhood*, AM 4 v 2: BOL 63
Stravinsky: "Berceuse" from *Firebird Suite*, AM 1

Tschaikowsky: "Trepak" from *Nutcracker Suite*, BOL 58
Vaughan-Williams; *Fantasia on Greensleeves*, AM 6 v 2
Walton: "Waltz" from *Facade Suite*, AM 6 v 2

COMPOUND TERNARY FORM   The compound ternary form is one in which each of the A B A sections may be a binary or ternary form within itself. It is found in classical minuets of Haydn and Mozart.

Bizet: "Minuetto" from *L'Arlesiene Suite No. 1*, AM 4 v 2
Haydn: "Menuetto" from *Symphony No. 6 in G Major*, BOL 63
Mozart: "Menuetto" from *Divertimento No. 17 in D Major*, AM 5 v 2
Mozart: "Minuet" from *Symphony No. 40 in G Minor*, BOL 62
Sousa: *Stars and Stripes Forever*, AM 4 v 2 BOL 60

RONDO   The principle of the rondo is a basic theme or section, A, which is alternated with two or more contrasting themes. Children sometimes compare its scheme with a sandwich. The shortest rondo is A B A C A. If one compares A to a slice of bread and B and C to different sandwich fillings, the result is a special kind of double-decker sandwich. Longer rondos may be A B C A B A or A B A C A D A. The rondeau is similar; it is an extension of the latter example using a different contrasting section each time; only A repeats. A beginning concept of the rondo is acquired by young children in simple ways. This might begin with establishing a beat, then asking the class to say the name of the school ("Oak Ridge School") followed by the name of a child, then the name of the school followed by the name of another child, and so on. The teacher's questions will help the class to realize the scheme of what they are doing—what is the same and what is different. Next, the same rondo principle is done with percussion instruments and even with rows of objects in the room. From here the children apply the scheme to short melodies and soon they are composing rondos. To help them compose, the teacher may write the recurring section of a rondo on the chalkboard and assign groups of children (or individual children) to extend the composition according to the plan, which might be A B A C A B A.

Rondo for Bassoon and Orchestra, Franson YPR 1009 (ages 6–10)
Beethoven: "Scherzo" from *Symphony No. 7*, BOL 62
Dvořák: *Slavonic Dance in C Minor*, AM 4 v 2
Hayden: "Gypsy Rondo" from *Trio in G Major*, BOL 64 (A B A C A Coda)
Khachaturian: "Waltz" from *Masquerade Suite*, AM 4 v 2 (A B A Interlude C A B A)

Mozart: "Romanze" from *Eine kleine Nachtmusik,* AM 4 v 1 (A B A C A
 Coda)
Prokofiev: "Waltz on Ice" from *Winter Holiday,* AM 3 v 2
Smetana: "Dance of the Comedians" from *Bartered Bride,* AM 6 v 2; BOL
 56
Tschaikovsky: "Waltz" from *Sleeping Beauty,* AM 4 v 1
Kodály: "Viennese Music Clock" from *Háry János Suite,* AM 2 v 1; BOL
 81

VARIATION FORM   This form is an extension of the concept of altering melodies. However, as the learner's concept of variation grows, he finds
that the music can be varied in terms of its melody, rhythm, harmony, texture, tempo, dynamics, form, tone quality and its general style. This can
make listening to variations somewhat like a mystery which gradually re-
solves itself as the listener detects which musical elements the composer
changes in order to create the variation. Generally there is a theme (melody),
followed by the different treatments of it. Unity is provided by the theme,
which is always present in some form; variety is provided by the changing
of any of the musical elements. There is a form of variations in which a
melody or chord progression is repeated over and over, with variety coming
from changes in the other elements.

> *Hot Cross Buns,* Franson CRG 5005 (ages 5–8)
> Guarnieri: *Brazilian Dance,* AM 6 v 2; BOL 55
> Anderson: *The Girl I Left Behind Me,* AM 5 v 2
> Copland: "Simple Gifts" from *Appalachian Spring,* BOL 65
> Cailliet: *Variations on Pop! Goes the Weasel,* AM 4 v 1; BOL 65
> Ives: *Variations on "America,"* Louisville Records
> Kraft: *Variations for Percussion Instruments,* BOL 83
> Gould: *American Salute,* AM 5 v 1; BOL 65

VARIATION FORM: TEACHING   The Cailliet *Variations on Pop! Goes
the Weasel,* listed above, can be useful as an example of how to help children learn the principles of the form. Its sections are as follows:

Introduction and theme:	Can the children sense the meter? Can they tell if a full orchestra is playing? Can they hear whether or not one section of the orchestra predominates?
1. Fugue	In a fugue, the same melody is played at different times by different instruments at different pitch levels, but it

gives the impression of a round because of the entries of these parts. Does it sound that way here? What is the order of the entering instruments? (Six instruments are emphasized before the entire orchestra plays the tune.)

2. *Minuet*

What is the meter in this formal dance, the minuet? Hear two melodies played at once. Which instrument plays the melody and which plays another tune? Can *augmentation* (playing the melody in longer note values) be identified?

3. *Adagio*

What elements of the music produce the mood here, and what do you think this mood is? A new tune is introduced, a Jewish wedding song.

4. *Music box*

What is a music box? What instruments are used to sound like a music box? What did the composer do to make the "oomp pa pa" effect?

5. *Jazz*

What meter does the composer choose here? Listen to the trumpet with the "Wa Wa" mute. What do you think the player does with his mute to make this sound? How does the composer make the music sound like jazz? What happens to the melody this time? Now ask the children to define "variation form" in their own words. Ask them in how many ways a melody can be varied in a variation form.

SONATA-ALLEGRO FORM   The sonata-allegro form is an expanded A B A form. Its plan is a statement of two different themes followed by a development of those themes as a contrasting section, then a restatement of the themes to provide unity. Sometimes one of the themes will be in a familiar song-form. The first theme is apt to be masculine and vigorous while the second theme may be feminine and lyrical, thus providing contrast. Often there are transitional passages between this first part of the form, the *exposition*, and the second part, the *development*. In the development section the themes and parts of themes are treated in many different ways, and the listener may identify inversion, rhythmic alteration, sequence, change of key, and many other techniques composers use in creating variety. The final section is the *recapitulation*, in which there is a restatement of the themes, often followed by coda. This form is used as the first movement of a symphony, sonata, concerto, quartet and quintet, as well as appearing in some overtures and other forms.

> Schubert: "First Movement" from Symphony No. 5, AM 5 v 1
> Mozart: "First Movement," from Symphony No. 40, BOL 71
> Prokofiev: Classical Symphony, BOL 73

THE SUITE   The suite has an interesting history which some advanced children may want to research. The suites we hear today are often dance suites in which a series of related dances constitute the composition, the ballet suite, the opera suite, and suites based on dramatic (stage) works. The dance suites are usually made up of dances of the sixteenth and seventeenth centuries, the allemand, courante, saraband, gigue, and a number of others. The suites based on stage works such as opera, ballet, and drama, are selections taken from music written for these works and arranged for concert performance. Still other suites are written on ideas such as philosophy, psychology, and geography.

Dance suites	Bach: *English Suites*
	Handel: *Harpsichord Suites*
Ballet suites	Tschaikovsky: *Nutcracker Suite*, BOL 58
	Stravinsky: *Petrouchka Suite*
	Ravel: *Daphnis and Chloe Suite No. 2*, BOL 86
	Rimsky-Korsakoff: *Scheherazade Suite*, BOL 77
Based on stage works	Grieg: *Peer Gynt Suite*, BOL 59
	Walton: *Facade Suite*
Opera suites	Bizet: *Carmen Suite*
	Menotti: Suite from *Amahl and the Night Visitors*, BOL 58
Geographical suites	Grofé: *Grand Canyon Suite*, BOL 61
	Grofé: *Mississippi River Suite*, BOL 61

TONE POEM   The symphonic poem or tone poem is a work for symphony orchestra in which the form is dictated by a story, a description, or a character.

> Strauss: *Til Eulenspiegel and His Merry Pranks* (a lengthy work for older children)

Moussorgsky: *Night on Bald Mountain*, BOL 81. This short tone poem is a favorite at Halloween time.
Saint-Saëns: *Danse Macabre*, BOL 81. (Another Halloween favorite)

OPERA, ORATORIO, CANTATA These are large vocal works. The opera is a stage play in which the words are sung and in which the singers are accompanied by an orchestra. There may be duets, trios, quartets, sextets, and other ensembles, a chorus, and even a ballet. The *recitative* is a rather declamatory vocal style that attempts to imitate speech; an *aria* is a solo; an *arioso* is midway between the recitative and aria.

Menotti: *Amahl and the Night Visitors* (can be used in its entirety at Christmas)
Humperdinck: *Hansel and Gretel* (use selections from, and relate to the story)
Bizet: *Carmen* (use selections from, and the story)
Rossini: *William Tell Overture* (an opera overture to hear, and the story), BOL 76; AM 3 v 1
Verdi: *Aida* (use selections from, and the story)
Britten: *The Little Sweep* (can be used in entirety)
Mozart: *The Magic Flute* (selections from, with simplified story)
Child's Introduction to Opera, Childcraft Records, Album 38. (includes *Barber of Seville*, *Amahl and the Night Visitors*, and *Hansel and Gretel*)

MULTIPLE CONCEPTS

Jurey: *Design in Music*, Bowmar Records (an album)
Contains the following:
Waltz: A B A form; Rondo: A B A C A; Theme and Five
Variations; Symphony in Miniature:
    First Movement: Sonata-Allegro Form with the songs "Erie Canal" and "Red River Valley"
    Second Movement: Song Form with "All Through the Night" and "All the Pretty Little Horses"
    Third Movement: Scherzo Form with "Merrily We Roll Along" and "Good Night Ladies"
    Fourth Movement: Rondo Form with more children's game songs (transparencies for overhead projector containing themes of all compositions are available)

EXEMPLARY FILMS AND FILMSTRIPS

Discovering Form in Music, BFA Educational Media, 2211 Michigan Avenue, Santa Monica, Calif. 90404 (phrases and sections)
Forms of Music: Instrumental, Coronet Instructional Films, 65 E. South Water St.,

Chicago, Ill., 60601 (sonata, concerto, symphony, and tone poem; for advanced children)

Let's Discover the Design, EMC Corporation, St. Paul, Minn. 55101. (ages 10 and up)

Music Stories, filmstrips in color with recordings, Jam Handy Organization, 2821 East Grand Ave., Detroit, Mich., 48211 (*Hansel and Gretel, The Nutcracker Suite, Peer Gynt Suite, Firebird Suite, The Sorcerer's Apprentice*)

Opera and Ballet Stories, filmstrips in color with recordings, Jam Handy Organization, 2821 East Grand Ave., Detroit, Mich., 48211 (*Lohengrin, The Magic Flute, Barber of Seville, Die Meistersinger, Coppelia*)

Symphony Orchestra, Encyclopedia Britannica Films, 425 N. Michigan Ave., Chicago, Ill., 60611. (Traces growth of symphony orchestra from string quintet to the modern orchestra) Enjoyable for ages 9–11

Young People's Concert Series (Leonard Bernstein): *What Makes Music Symphonic? What Is a Concerto?; What is Sonata Form?* McGraw Hill Films, 330 W. 42nd St., New York, N.Y., 10036. Each one an hour. Ages 10 and up. Also inquire at local Bell Telephone Office for possible free availability.

Music of Other Cultures

One of the recent trends in music education is an interest in music of the world. While there have been songs from Western Europe and Latin America in music textbooks, Africa and Asia, where the majority of the people on the earth reside, have been poorly represented. Efforts are now being made to learn more about the indigenous music of all the world's peoples. We become involved with generalizations such as:

1. The early history of the development of music in any country has a direct influence on the present and future types of music in that country.

2. The music of any country is undergoing more or less constant change.

3. The music of any country reflects the people's concerns in every aspect and area of life—social, esthetic, religious, political, and economic.

4. The music of most cultures has been altered and influenced by music from another or other cultures.

5. Folk songs in all societies undergo constant change which reflects the changes taking place in those societies; both words and melodies may change over the years (Example: Songs about "choo-choo" trains are not written today because the modern diesel engine does not make that sound.)

6. The music of a particular culture has a distinctive style that differentiates it from all other cultures.

7. Every society, no matter how primitive, has found a need for music, and has created its own types of music to serve its purposes.

8. The music, art, language, literature, architecture, recreation, food, clothing, and political and social customs of a people serve to bind them together into a national or cultural unit.

Music is sometimes considered solely as an art to be studied, and sometimes considered solely as an art that reflects humanity. This implied division is in many respects artificial, since music as an art is rooted in the lives of people. Both social studies and ethnomusicology demand that music be studied *in the context* of the society and times of which it is an expression. An example is the minuet, which became an official French court dance in 1650, and eventually became an expression of a courtly and aristocratic society. Its restraint and sophisticated artificiality reflected the patterned dignity and courtesies of the eighteenth-century ruling class. As this aristocratic society began to weaken, the minuet began to decline in importance as a dance, but became a movement in symphonies of Haydn and Mozart at a faster tempo, not danceable. This finally evolved to become the *scherzo* (literally joke) movement of Beethoven symphonies. Music is always communicating something, whether it is feelings of restraint or of freedom, a folk singer's reaction to his environment, aspects of a specific culture, or a sophisticated reflection by a professional composer of that culture.

Songs, dances, and instruments yield data about people's beliefs, values, and how they live or lived. Through the music of various people and times, children can discover *who they are*, and can find their places in the cultural stream that began in the past and will flow into the future. New songs explain the concerns of the present day, while old songs are a means of understanding the past and its influence on the present. The historian and the anthropologist find music an essential ingredient of a culture, society, or tribal organization; thus it is one of the essentials of a civilized state of being. Music is not necessary for mere physical survival, but it is an ingredient which helps make survival worthwhile; it is a quality factor for living which indicates degrees of cultural sophistication.

The school music of Japanese children is similar to that of American children, while the original, authentic Japanese music occupies a minority position. The native Japanese music stems historically from Chinese culture, causing the Japanese child to find himself amid two cultural streams of music. The excellent film, *Folk Songs of Japan*, useful for age eight and up, can be obtained from the nearest Japanese consulate (color, 29 min.). It portrays the beauty of the Japanese countryside while taking the listener through examples of all types of folk music including a contemporary popular song performed at a ski resort by young people. The combination of Japanese and American influences in this song encourages children's analyses of the music.

As children explore Asiatic music by means of television, recordings, films, and books, they will discover that concepts of music which differ from our common scales and harmonizations have a utility, charm, and worth of their own. Rhythm and melody, often accompanied by a simple drone, characterize the music of India. The scale and melodic structure is found in the *raga*, of which there are hundreds. Each of these has from five to seven pitches and one or two secondary pitches. The performer elaborates and improvises on the raga of his choice. Each raga has non-musical implications which could be some feeling or emotion, a season, or a time of day. This music is horizontally conceived; there is no harmony as we know it—only the drone. Both melody and rhythm are more sophisticated than their counterparts in western music, although our composers are being increasingly influenced by Indian concepts of melody and rhythm. The *tala* is the rhythmic structure, organized into a number of beats with recurring accents. Approximately thirty talas are in common use. Some are regular in meter, such as $4 + 4 + 4 + 4$ beats, while others are irregular, such as the eleven-beat $7 + 2 + 2$. The musician improvises rhythmically on the basis of the tala. Three popular instruments are the *sitar*, a many-stringed fretted instrument, the *tabla*, a double drum, and the *tamboura*, a long-necked unfretted instrument with drone strings.

The mixing of eastern and western music has taken place in the popular music field with the raga-rock concept. Arabic music is a worthy study, as is the *gamelan* music of Indonesia which influenced Debussy and other composers. Something to avoid is thinking of nonwestern music as stereotypes. It is infinitely varied. For example, there are many differences in the music of one section of a country like Nigeria from other sections; the same is true of China and almost every country. The music of Africa has been influenced by music of Asia, Arabian music, and music of the West, with Central Africa providing music more indigenous than other sections of that continent. American Indian and Hawaiian music are of special interest to people of the United States. American Indian music, generally speaking, utilizes steps smaller than our half-steps, uses a percussion accompaniment of drums, rasps, and rattles, employs the flute as a solo instrument, has no structured harmony, and has chant-like melodies which do not conform to the European scales. Original Hawaiian music has been practically destroyed by European musical influence, but researchers have managed to reconstruct some of it.

Native Hawaiian music was largely chant, centered about one pitch. Harmony was absent; the form was mainly of short repeated chants with instrumental interludes to provide contrast. The modern Hawaiian style resulted when missionary hymns and the Portuguese guitar were introduced. The guitar evolved to become the modern ukulele. Recordings are available for classroom use which take the listener to the culture, nation, region, or even tribe, and permit him to study the authentic music of the selected people.

Recordings are a necessity when studying the music of the world, but listening to fascinating authentic music can have its problems when children are called upon to analyze it and to describe it. One problem is that of identifying the meter. Often the solution is an easy mathematical one; identify the two-beat and three-beat segments. This was discussed in Chapter Four under *Complex Compound Meters*, with the Greek song *Gerakina* as an example of such grouping of beats.

Another problem is identifying instruments. Because there are probably thousands of standard folk instruments, this becomes virtually impossible. Yet, the ear can classify the instruments heard so that class discussion about them can take place. The following classification has proved to be helpful.

string
    plucked
    struck
    bowed
    stroked
wind
    open hole (flute-type)
    single reed
    double reed
    brass
membrane (drum-type)
    pitched
    unpitched
percussion
    metal
    wood
    stone
    body sounds

Other headings to assist analysis are:

vocal sounds
rhythm
   regular beat
   flexible
pitch
   straight (true and unwavering)
   bent (swooping up or dropping down; unsteady)
melody, type of
harmony, if any
form (unity-contrast)

One can expect varying tonal (scale) organizations. Tempo and dynamics should be easily described. Acceptable tone qualities are different in various cultures.

The October, 1972 issue of the *Music Educators Journal* concerned music in world cultures. It contained nineteen articles on world musics, a glossary, a bibliography, discography, and filmography. It affords the reader greatly more than is possible to include in this textbook, so the authors refer him to that publication for books, recordings, and films for use in this interesting new area of emphasis. Among the many available films are those of BFA Educational Media, 2211 Michigan Ave., Santa Monica, Calif. 90404, "Discovering the Music of Africa," and others of a *Discovering Music* series that includes music of the middle ages, Latin America, the Middle East, India, Japan, Jazz, American Folk Music, and American Indian Music.

The final Contemporary Music Project *Newsletter*, dated Spring, 1973, contains a recommended list of recordings of Asian and African music thought to be useful for teaching purposes. It was submitted by Robert Trotter, Dean, School of Music, University of Oregon. Those preceded by one asterisk are especially recommended; a second asterisk indicates that extensive notes are provided to help orient the listener.

JAPAN:

   Bell Ringing in Empty Sky, Solo Flute (Shakuhachi) music. Nonesuch 72025
   Music from the Kabuki. Nonesuch 72012
   Japanese Koto Classics. Nonesuch 72008
   Gagaku, Ancient Japanese Court Music. Everest 3322

SOUTHEAST ASIA:

**Traditional Music of Thailand.* Institute of Ethnomusicology, UCLA, Los Angeles, 90046. Includes an excellent booklet by David Morten.
Music from Cambodia. UNESCO Anthology, Bährenreiter 30L 2002
Music from Vietnam I. UNESCO 30L 2022

INDONESIA:

Golden Rain (Bali).Nonesuch 72028
Gamelan Music of Bali. Lyrichord LLST 7179
The Jasmine Isle (Java). Nonesuch 72031
Gamelan Semar Pegulingan (Gamelan of the Love God) (Bali). Nonesuch Bali. H-72046
Music for the Balinese Shadow Puppet Plays, Gender Wayang. Nonesuch H-72037

CHINA:

Shantung Folk Music and Traditional Instrumental Pieces. Nonesuch H-72051

AFRICA:

**Mbira Music of Rhodesia.* University of Washington Press, Seattle
The African Mbira. Nonesuch 72043
**Music of the Dan Territory.* Ocora, OCR 17
**Music of Central Africa (Musique centrafricaine).* Ocora, OCR 43
**Black Africa, Panorama of Instrumental Music (Afrique noire, Panorame de la musique instrumentale).* BAM LD 409A
**Nigeria—Hausa Music I.* UNESCO 30L 2306

INDIA:

Sarangi, Voice of a Hundred Colors. Nonesuch 72030
**The Anthology of Indian Music, Vol. I.* World-Pacific WDS 26200 (three records and extensive notes)
Drums of North and South India. World Pacific WPS 21437
Indian Drums. Connoisseur Society CS 1466
West Meets East, Ravi Shankar and Yehudi Menuhin. Angel 36418
The Sound of Subbudlakshmi. World Pacific WPS 21440
The Music of India (South). Nonesuch 72003
**Ustad Ali Akbar Khan, Raga Chandranandan.* Connoisseur Society
Bhavalu/Impressions, South Indian instrumental music. Nonesuch 72019

PERSIA (IRAN), THE MIDDLE EAST:

The Persian Santur. Nonesuch 72039
The Living Tradition: Music from Iran. Argo ZFB 51
**Music from Turkey. Living Tradition,* Argo ZRG 561
Music from the Middle East (Syria, Iraq, Palestine). Living Tradition, Argo ZRG 532

TIBET:

***Anthology of Asian Music: Tibet.* AST 4005 (Anthology Record Corp.), 135 West 41st, N.Y. 10036

AFGHANISTAN:

Music of Afghanistan. UNESCO 30L 2003

Summary

This chapter was concerned with recordings and films as resources for the teacher in organizing lesson plans. These and other materials are also used to equip individual and small group learning centers or stations. Recordings were discussed in relation to planning for listening to various types and sounds of music and for using them to help children expand their knowledge of the elements of music. Both recordings and films were recognized as essential aids in learning about the musics of the world. Thus, the teacher's plans should now include a large variety of materials and learning experiences.

REFERENCES

BAIRD, PEGGY, *Music Books for the Elementary School Library.* Washington, D.C.: Music Educators National Conference, 1972.

Electronic Music Issue, *Music Educators Journal.* Washington, D.C.: Music Educators National Conference, November, 1968.

Film Guide for Music Educators. Washington, D.C.: Music Educators National Conference, 1968.

GARY, CHARLES L., ed., *The Study of Music in the Elementary School—A Conceptual Approach.* Washington, D.C.: Music Educators National Conference, 1967. See references to recordings throughout the book.

HUMPHREYS, LOUISE, AND JERROLD ROSS, *Interpreting Music Through Movement.* Englewood Cliffs, N.J.: Prentice-Hall, Inc., 1964.

Learning to Listen to Music. Morristown, N.J.: Silver Burdett Company, 1973. Five LP records with narrated lessons, Teacher's Manual, forms for student response, detailed lesson plans. For grades 4–9.

Music Resources Library. New Haven, Conn.: Keyboard Junior Publications. Fifty-seven boxed units for grades 4–7. Each unit contains material for the child to read, a teacher's guide, a long-play record, an enlarged thematic chart, and pictures for classroom display. The units are concerned with elements of music, nature and music, composers, musical stories, and ethnic music (social studies relationships).

SMITH, ROBERT B., *Music in the Child's Education.* New York: The Ronald Press Company, 1970. The lists of recordings at the ends of chapters are helpful.

appendix a

Books That Harmonize With Elementary School Children[1]

Biographies

BURCH, GLADYS, AND JOHN WOLCOTT, *Famous Composers For Young People.* New York: Dodd, Mead, 1939. $3.50. Gr. 4–9. Includes brief sketches of twenty of the world's greatest composers: Palestrina, Bach, Handel, Gluck, Haydn, Mozart, Beethoven, Schubert, Mendelssohn, Chopin, Schumann, Liszt, Wagner, Verdi, Foster, Brahms, Tchaikovsky, Grieg, MacDowell, Debussy.

BURCH, GLADYS, AND JOHN WOLCOTT, *Modern Composers For Young People.* New York: Dodd, Mead, 1941. $3.50. Gr. 4–9. Brief biographies of twenty middle-nineteenth century composers. Mussorgsky, Dvorak, Rimsky-Korsakov, Humperdinck, Elgar, Delius, Strauss, Sibelius, Scriabin, Vaughan-Williams, Schoenberg, Ravel, Carpenter, de Falla, Respighi, Bartok, Stravinsky, Griffes, Prokofiev, Gershwin.

DEUCHER, SYBIL, *Edvard Grieg, Boy of the Northland.* New York: Dutton, 1946. $4.50. Gr. 3–7. This delightful story about Edvard Grieg will cause children to enjoy his music even more than they already do.

———, *The Young Brahms.* New York: Dutton, 1949. $3.95. Gr. 3–7. An entertaining description of Brahms' life from age 6 to 16. Includes many of his compositions.

GOUGH, CATHERINE, *Boyhoods of Great Composers: Books I and II.* New York: Walck, 1960. $4 each. Gr. 4–6. Both books describe events in the lives of

[1]Courtesy of the Oregon State Department of Education, Delmer Aebischer, Music Consultant.

277

composers of interest to young people. Book I includes Handel, Mozart, Schubert, Mendelssohn, Grieg, Elgar. Book II includes Bach, Beethoven, Verdi, Chopin, Tchaikovsky, Vaughan-Williams. Incidents included are primarily anecdotal, having little to do with the importance of these men as composers.

MIRSKY, REBA PAEFF, *Beethoven*. Chicago: Follett, 1957. $3.50. Gr. 5–7. Beethoven's many struggles, disappointments and successes are emphasized in this book.

———, *Brahms*. Chicago: Follett, 1966. $4.98. Gr. 5–7. "A well-rounded picture of the composer's personality, his times, and his music." (McClurg. *Book News*).

———, *Haydn*. Chicago: Follett, 1963. $4.98. Gr. 5–up. The author describes Haydn's childhood and life as a court musician which climaxed with the composing of "The Creation."

———, *Mozart*. Chicago: *Follett*, 1960. $4.17. Gr. 4–6. "An entertaining account of Mozart's life and work, including excerpts from his letters." (American Library Assn.)

POSELL, ELSA Z., *American Composers*. Boston: Houghton Mifflin, 1963. $3.50. Gr. 4–up. An explanation of American music and twenty-eight brief stories of the musical background of composers, their personalities, manner of composing and style. Composers included are: Barber, Bernstein, Copland, Cowell, Creston, Dello Joio, Foss, Foster, Gershwin, Gould, Griffes, Grofe', Hanson, Harris, Hovhaness, Ives, Kay Lockwood, MacDowell, Mennin, Menotti, Moore, Piston, Porter, Riegger, Schuman, Sessions, Sousa, Still. (ALA)

———, *Russian Composers*. Boston: Houghton Mifflin, 1967. $3.50. Gr. 4–6. Biographical sketches of 17 composers including Glinka, Khachaturian, Mashovskii, Mussorgsky, Prokefiev, Rachmaninoff, Rimsky-Korsakoff, Shostakovich, Stravinsky, Tshaikovsky and others.

SURGE, FRANK, *Singers of the Blues*. Minneapolis: Lerner, 1969. $3.95. Gr. 5–up. An introduction to "blues" for young readers, plus biographies of singers and photographs of each. Singers included are: Ma Rainey, Bessie Smith, Blind Lemon Jefferson, Leroy Carr, Rabbit Brown, Leadbelly, Blind Willy Johnson, Big Bill Broonsy, Billie Holiday, Lonnie Johnson, Big Joe Williams, Tommy McClennan, Furry Lewis, Lightnin' Hopkins, Muddy Waters, Sonny Terry, Brownie McGhee.

WHEELER, OPAL. Various titles listed below. New York: Dutton. Anecdotal incidents from composers' personal lives, written in story form with dialogue. The more recognizable works are included, also simple piano arrangements.
Adventures of Richard Wagner. 1960. $3.95. Gr. 3–7.
Frederick Chopin, Son of Poland. (2 books) *Early Years. Later Years*. 1948. $3.95. Gr. 3–7.
Handel at the Court of Kings. 1943. $3.95. Gr. 3–7.
Ludwig Beethoven and the Chiming Tower Bells. 1942. $4.70. Gr. 3–7.
Paganini, Master of Strings. 1950. $4.50. Gr. 3–7.
Peter Tschaikowsky. 1953. $3.95. Gr. 3–7.
Peter Tschaikowsky and the Nutcracker Ballet. 1959. $4.50. Gr. 3–7. (ALA)
Robert Schumann and Mascott Ziff. 1947. $3.95. Gr. 3–7.
Stephen Foster and His Little Dog Tray. 1941. $4.50. Gr. 3–7.

————, AND SYBIL DEUCHER, Various titles listed below. New York: Dutton. Same as preceding entry, with co-author.

Edward MacDowell and His Cabin in the Pines. ND. $4.50. Gr. 4–8.

Franz Schubert and His Merry Friends. ND. $3.50. Gr. 4–7. (ALA)

Joseph Haydn: The Merry Little Peasant. ND. $3.91. Gr. 4–7.

Mozart, the Wonder Boy. 1941. $3.95. Gr. 4–7.

Sebastian Bach: The Boy from Thuringia. 1937. $3.75. Gr. 4–7.

WICKER, IREENE, *Young Music Makers: Boyhoods of Famous Composers.* Indianapolis: Bobbs-Merrill, 1961. $3.95. Gr. 4–6. Stories with emphasis on musical talent and home life of Bach, Chopin, Gershwin, and others.

Folk Music

BERGER, DONALD P., *Folk Songs of Japanese Children.* Rutland, Vt.: Tuttle, 1968. $6.00. This book will be of value to teachers since it discusses the melody, rhythm, form, scale and meters used in Japanese folk music. A variety of song materials such as seasonal songs, lullabies, and play songs are included. Teacher oriented.

BERTAIL, INEZ, *Nursery Song Book.* New York: Lothrop, Lee & Shepard, 1947. $4.50. Gr. K–3. More than 150 nursery songs, with simple piano accompaniments. Directions for singing games are included.

BONI, MARGARET B., *Fireside Book of Folk Songs.* New York: Simon & Schuster, 1947. $6.95. Gr. 5–up. A collection of 147 favorite songs, including sea chanteys, cowboy songs, hymns, railroad songs, spirituals and Christmas carols. Easy piano accompaniments by Norman Lloyd. Information about each song and category of songs included.

CARMER, CARL, *America Sings: Stories and Songs of Our Country's Growing.* New York: Knopf, 1950. $6.19. Gr. 5–11. Stories of America's work songs and such legendary characters as Big Foot Wallace, Spadebeard and Philetus Bumpus. Music is included. Useful for social studies and folk lore as well as music classes.

DIETZ, BETTY W., AND MICHAEL BABATUNDE OLATUNJI, *Musical Instruments of Africa: Their Nature, Use and Place in the Life of a Deeply Musical People.* New York: John Day, 1965. $6.50. Gr. 4–6. Emphasizes the importance of music in the lives of native Africans. It pictures and describes the making of native instruments and their use in ritual and dance. Included are a list of records, an LP record of African music recorded in Africa, a glossary, and reading list. Useful for teachers.

DIETZ, BETTY W., AND THOMAS CHOONBAI PARK, *Folk Songs of China, Japan, Korea.* New York: John Day, 1964. $4.97. Song materials plus explanatory notes, accompaniments and English translations. Pronunciation guide and many helps for teachers. Pencil drawings. Recording included.

FELTON, HAROLD W., *Cowboy Jamboree; Western Songs & Lore.* New York: Knopf, 1951. $3.94. A collection of 20 songs cowboys sing plus the legends and history concerning them.

FRASER, SIMON H., *Pooh Song Book*. New York: Dutton, 1961. $4.95. Gr. 1–4. Fifteen of Pooh's hums set to music; also fourteen poem songs from "When We Were Very Young"; plus a setting of the "King's Breakfast."

HOFMANN, CHARLES, *American Indians Sing*. New York: John Day, 1967. $6.29. Gr. 3–6. How songs and lives of these people knit together, why and how they made music, why songs were so important to daily living. Last chapter deals with Indian music of today. Recording included. Useful to teachers and students.

HUGHES, LANGSTON, *Famous Negro Music Makers*. New York: Dodd, Mead, 1955. $3.00. Gr. 4–7. Biographies of seventeen outstanding Negro music makers from folk singers to symphony conductors, and jazz musicians to church musicians. Artists included are: Fisk Jubilee Singers, James Bland, Bert Williams, Bill Robinson, Leadbelly, Jelly Roll Morton, Roland Hayes, William Grant Still, Bessie Smith, Duke Ellington, Ethel Waters, Louis Armstrong, Marian Anderson, Bennie Benjamin, Mahalia Jackson, Dean Dickson, Lena Horne. Photographs are excellent. Useful to teachers and students.

————, *First Book of Jazz*. New York: Franklin Watts, 1955. $3.75. Gr. 6–up. A history of jazz, as related to the life of Louis Armstrong. Begins with African drums and continues through work songs, jubilees, swing and bebop. Excellent record list included. Teachers and students.

JOHNS, ALTONA T., *Play Songs of the Deep South*. New York: Associated Publishers, 1944. $2.65. Gr. K–2. A collection of play songs which have been sung by black children in the south for many generations. Directions for rhythmic games are also included.

JOHNSON, JAMES WELDON, AND ROSAMUND JOHNSON, *Lift Every Voice and Sing*. New York: Hawthorn, 1970. $4.95. Gr. 3–6. Book contains lyrics and simplified musical score for a song written by James Weldon Johnson. This song is sung with reverence by the Negro race. Striking illustrations.

KELLY, JOHN M., *Folk Songs Hawaii Sings*. Rutland, Vt.: Tuttle, 1963. $4.95. Gr. 3–up. Supplies background on music of Asia and Polynesia plus song materials in native languages. Also contains pronunciation guide and English translations. Teacher oriented.

LANDECK, BEATRICE, *More Songs to Grow On*. New York: Morrow, 1954. $8.95. Gr. K–4. Folk songs with suggestions for dramatization and rhythm instrument accompaniment. Teacher oriented.

————, *Songs to Grow On*. New York: Morrow, 1950. $8.95. Gr. K–4. A collection of 60 American folk songs for children, including suggestions for activities. Musical arrangements are simple. Useful for teachers.

SACKETT, S. J., *Cowboys and the Songs They Sang*. Settings by Lionel Nowak. W. R. Scott, 1967. $5.95. Gr. 4–7. A "history of cowboy life and lore is woven around a selection of cowboy songs of the ranch and the range." (McClurg, Book News) Excellent western photographs.

SEEGER, RUTH CRAWFORD, *American Folk Songs for Children*. New York: Doubleday, 1948. $4.50. Gr. K–5. Ninety folk songs from various parts of the country to be sung and dramatized. Accompaniments are simple. Introductory chapters discuss value of folk music and the use of folk music with children. Useful for teachers.

———, *American Folk Songs for Christmas*. New York: Doubleday, 1953. $5.70. Gr. K–5. A collection of 50 American folk songs about Christmas. Sources of songs and holiday celebration are included. Useful material for teachers.

———, *Animal Folksongs for Children*. New York: Doubleday, 1950. $3.50. Gr. 1–6. Forty American folksongs describing such animals as the cross-eyed gopher and the snake who baked a hoecake. Useful for teachers.

WHITING, HELEN ADELE, *Negro Art, Music, and Rhyme, Book II*. New York: Associated Publishers, 1967. $1.40. Gr. 2–3. A "reader" type book for primary children dealing with Afro-American art, crafts, song, dance and rhyme. Attractive illustrations.

YURCHENCO, HENRIETTA. *Fiesta of Folk Songs from Spain and Latin America*. New York: Putnam's 1967. $3.96. Gr. 2–6. "Here are 34 folk songs—singing games and dances, songs for Christmas, and songs about people, animals and nature." (Booklist) Teacher oriented.

See also *Stories*, p. 286.

History and Origin of Music

BRITTEN, BENJAMIN, AND IMOGEN HOLST, *Wonderful World of Music*. New York: Doubleday, 1968. $3.95. Gr. 5–up. Magnificently illustrated book concerning the historical development of music and the related arts; ancient to modern cultures are included.

CRAIG, JEAN, *Story of Musical Notes*. Minneapolis: Lerner Publications, 1962. $2.75. Gr. 4–7. This book presents the history of musical notation. It contains excellent examples of each method of music writing.

DAVIS, MARILYN K., AND ARNOLD BROIDO, *Music Dictionary*. New York: Doubleday, 1956. $4.25. Gr. 5–7. An illustrated music dictionary containing over 800 definitions of words, terms, and instruments. Pages are large, definitions concise and illustrations are black and white sketches interesting for children.

GREENE, CARLA, *I Want to Be a Musician*. Chicago: Children's Press, 1962. $2.75. Gr. K–3. An excellent history showing the development of musical instruments and rhythm. Includes cavemen beating on logs, shepherd horns, reeds, a short explanation of counting and a description of present day instruments.

HUGHES, LANGSTON, *First Book of Rhythms*. New York: Franklin Watts, 1954. $2.95. Gr. 3–5. A delightful way to introduce children to the rhythms all around them. Includes rhythms of nature, rhythm in sounds, in design, and in movement, and serves as excellent motivation for a study of rhythm.

LERNER, SHARON, *Places of Musical Fame*. Minneapolis: Lerner Publications, 1962. $2.75. Gr. 4–7. A description of famous music halls such as Carnegie Hall, Lincoln Center, La Scala, Covent Garden, and many others.

NORMAN, GERTRUDE, *The First Book of Music*. New York: Franklin Watts, 1955. $2.95. Gr. 4–6. An introduction to the elements of music (rhythm, melody, and harmony), together with the development of music from past to present. Brief biographies of composers and explanation of the instruments are also included.

SELIGMANN, JEAN, AND JULIET DANZIGER, *Meaning of Music: A Young Listener's Guide.* Waco, Texas: World, 1966. $4.95. Gr. 5–9. An introduction to the elements of music (rhythm, melody, harmony, tempo), the families of instruments and famous composers. Photographs and line drawings.

SPENCER, CORNELIA, *How Art and Music Speak to Us.* New York: John Day, 1963. $3.95. Gr. 5–up. Awakens children to the fact that man has expressed his deepest feelings and thoughts through the arts. A beautifully written book deserving of a place on the library shelf.

SURPLUS, ROBERT W., *Alphabet of Music.* Minneapolis: Lerner Publications, 1962. $2.75. Gr. 4–7. The elements of music are presented in an interesting manner for young children. An excellent guide to building awareness of what music is all about.

————, *Story of Musical Organizations.* Minneapolis: Lerner Publications, 1962. $2.75. Gr. 4–7. A history of musical performance organizations including bands, orchestras, choirs, chamber music groups, dance bands and combos. The music they play is also discussed.

Instruments

BALET, JAN B., *What Makes an Orchestra.* New York: Walck, 1951. $4.75. Gr. 4–6. An introduction to each instrument of the orchestra, what is looks like, how it is played, what "color" it adds to the ensemble.

BUNCHE, JANE, *An Introduction to the Instruments of the Orchestra.* Racine, Wisc.: Golden Press, 1962. $2.79. Gr. 3–up. An illustrated story of musical instruments from early drums to the modern orchestra.

COLLIER, JAMES, *Which Musical Instrument Shall I Play?* New York: Norton, 1969. $3.93. Gr. 4–6. Intended as an aid to children in selecting the instruments they wish to play. The reader is guided through the families of instruments and informed of their characteristics and method of playing. Electrically amplified instruments are also discussed. Photographs are excellent. Interesting shots of hand positions are included.

COMMINS, DOROTHY BERLINER, *All About the Symphony Orchestra and What it Plays.* New York: Random House, 1961. $2.95. Gr. 5–9. A story of the symphony orchestra discussing the individual instruments, the conductor, and the music played. Contains sketches of 46 composers. Drawings by Warren Chappell, also photographs.

CRAIG, JEAN, *Heart of the Orchestra.* Minneapolis: Lerner Publications, 1962. $2.75. Gr. 4–7. The story of the violin, viola, cello, bass violin, and early string instruments; their role in the orchestra; similarities and differences; and how they are played.

————, *Woodwinds.* Minneapolis: Lerner Publications, 1962. $2.75. Gr. 4–7. A delightful introduction to members of the woodwind family. Attractive illusstrations and little known facts concerning the instruments are also presented.

DAVIS, LIONEL, AND EDITH DAVIS, *Keyboard Instruments*. Minneapolis: Lerner Publications, 1962. $2.75. Gr. 4–7. The development and history of the piano, harpsichord and other keyboard instruments. The "why" and "how" of the keyboard.

GILMORE, LEE, *Folk Instruments*. Minneapolis: Lerner Publications, 1962. $2.75. Gr. 4–7. Ten folk instruments of today are presented to children in an interesting fashion including history and how they are made and played. Instruments include the square dance fiddle, accordion, harmonica, Jew's harp and bagpipes.

HUNTINGTON, HARRIET E., *Tune Up: The Instruments of the Orchestra and Their Players*. New York: Doubleday, 1942. $3.25. Gr. 5–8. Photographs illustrate how shapes of instruments and handling by players combine to produce intricate sounds.

KETTLEKAMP, LARRY, *Drums, Rattles and Bells*. Morrow, 1960. $3.56. Gr. 4–6. The development of percussion instruments presented in an interesting fashion; includes illustrations and directions for making instruments such as waterglass carillon, drums and rattles.

————, *Flutes, Whistles and Reeds*. Morrow, 1962. $3.56. Gr. 4–7. The importance of wind instruments in the orchestra, their history, and directions for easy to make pipes and whistles.

————, *Horns*. New York: Morrow, 1964. $3.56. Gr. 4–7. How animal horns, shells, and tusks contributed to the development of today's horn family.

————, *Singing Strings*. New York: Morrow, 1958. $3.56. Gr. 4–7. Instruction for constructing simple stringed instruments, as well as a discussion and illustrations of the various instruments: guitar, violin family, harp and piano.

LACY, MARION, *Picture Book of Musical Instruments*. New York: Lothrop, Lee and Shepard, 1942. $3.95. Gr. 3–7. Concise pen and ink drawings show how instruments have been used, past and present.

LEVINE, JACK, AND TAKERU LIJIMA, *Understanding Musical Instruments—How To Select Your Musical Instrument*. New York: Frederick Warne, Inc., 1971. $3.95. Gr. 6–9. Two music teachers describe the different orchestral instruments, as well as some not found in the orchestra, and tell how each one is played. A useful list of recordings that feature the individual instruments is included. Illustrations show each instrument and the way it is held. A good reference book for both students and teachers.

POSELL, ELSA, *This Is An Orchestra*. Boston: Houghton Mifflin, 1950. $2.90. Gr. 4–6. Excellent photographs and descriptions of the instruments of the orchestra, plus helps for choosing and purchasing an instrument. Famous instrument makers, habits of practice, and suggestions for building a home record collection.

RICHARDSON, ALLEN L., *Tooters, Tweeters, Strings & Beaters*. New York: Grosset & Dunlap, 1964. $2.50. Gr. 1–4. An instrument book for young readers consisting of poetic jingles concerning each instrument of the orchestra; also includes guessing games.

SLOANE, ERIC, *The Sound of Bells*. New York: Doubleday, 1966. $2.75. Gr. 4–7. Descriptions of many kinds of bells and how they were used throughout the history of our country, including the Liberty Bell. Describes the ringing of the bells on Independence Day and encourages the return of this custom.

SMITH, PETER, *The First Book of the Orchestra*. New York: Franklin Watts, 1962. $2.95. Gr. 4–6. The four families of instruments are illustrated and described; includes a list of recorded listening suggestions.

SURPLUS, ROBERT W., *Beat of the Drum*. Minneapolis: Lerner Publications, 1962. $2.75. Gr. 4–7. The drum—from tree stump to modern drums of the symphony orchestra. Other percussion instruments are also presented.

———, *Follow the Leader*. Minneapolis: Lerner Publications, 1962. $2.75. Gr. 4–7. The story of conducting and its development through the years. Special emphasis is given the conductor, program planning, and musical scores.

TETZLAFF, DANIEL B., *Shining Brass*. Minneapolis: Lerner Publications, 1962. $2.75. Gr. 4–7. The story of brass instruments with attention given to size, shape and appearance.

WEIL, LISL, *Things That Go Bang*. New York: McGraw-Hill, 1969. $4.50. Gr. 3–6. Many things go bang! A glimpse into the percussion world—from the gong to the xylophone. Includes suggestions for making instruments and music for a "kitchen combo."

Opera

BULLA, CLYDE R., *The Ring and the Fire, Stories from Wagner's Nibelung Operas*. New York: Crowell, 1962. $4.95. Gr. 5–up. A brief biography of Richard Wagner's life accompanies his stories of "The Rhinegold," "Valkyrie," "Siegfried," and "The Dusk of the Gods." Musical themes are included. Illustrated with woodcuts.

———, *Stories of Favorite Operas*. New York: Thomas Y. Crowell, 1964. $4.95. Gr. 4–6. Twenty-three opera stories with notes on composers and performances. Included are: "Marriage of Figaro," "Don Giovanni," "The Magic Flute," "Barber of Seville," "Lucia di Lammermoor," "Tannhauser," "Lohengrin," "Tristan and Isolde," "Mastersingers of Nuremberg," "Parsifal," "Rigoletto," "Il Trovatore," "Aida," "Faust," "Carmen," "Manon," "Cavalleria Rusticana," "I Pagliacci," "La Boheme," "Tosca," "Madame Butterfly," "Der Rosenkavalier."

COLETTE, *The Boy and The Magic*. Translated by Christopher Fry. New York: Putnam's 1964. $4.00. Gr. K–up. An adapted version of Colette's libretto for Ravel's opera.

CROZIER, ERIC, *The Magic Flute: Mozart's Opera & How It Was Written*. New York: Walck, 1965. $4.00. Gr. 4–6. Imaginary letters to his sister tell how Mozart's opera was written.

GIBSON, ENID, *The Golden Cockerel: Three Stories of Magic and Witchcraft from Russian Opera*. New York: Walck, 1963. $4.00. Gr. 4–6. Brief notes on the music as well as the stories of Glinka's "Ruslan and Ludmila," Prokofiev's "Love for Three Oranges," and Rimsky-Korsakov's "Golden Cockerel."

GRIMM, WILLIAM, *Hansel and Gretel*. New York: Knopf, 1944. $3.84. Gr. 3–5. Story of Humperdinck's opera—the poor woodcutter's children lost in the forest and their encounter with the witch. Illustrations by Warren Chappell contribute much to the book. Easy arrangements of selections are included.

HOSIER, JOHN, *Sorcerer's Apprentice and Other Stories*. New York: Walck, 1961. $4.00. Gr. 4–6. Information about composers and stories of "Lieutenant Kije," "Hary Janos," "Till Owlglass," "William Tell."

JOHNSTON, JOHANNA, *Story of the Barber of Seville*. New York: Putnam's, 1966. $3.95. Gr. 3–6. Story of Rossini's famous comic opera concerning Figaro, a clever barber. Delightful illustrations by Susan Perl.

MONTRESOR, BENI, *Cinderella*. New York: Knopf, 1965. $3.74. Gr. 2–4. Story and illustrations from Metropolitan Opera production of Rossini's opera in which Cinderella is transformed into a beautiful bride. A more sophisticated version of the usual story.

MORETON, JOHN, *The Love for Three Oranges*. New York: Putnam's, 1966. $3.64. Gr. 2–6. The delightful story of Prokofiev's fairy-tale opera, written especially for children. The illustrations add humor to this book.

ORGEL, DORIS, *The Story of Lohengrin: The Knight of the Swan*. New York: Putnam's, 1966. $3.95. Gr. 3–6. This opera appeals to children and has been retold in a simplified version by Doris Orgel. Based upon the opera by Richard Wagner.

SPENDER, STEPHEN, *The Magic Flute*. New York: Putnam's 1966. $3.86. Gr. 2–up. The story of Mozart's opera, retold by Stephen Spender and illustrated by Beni Montresor.

UPDIKE, JOHN, *The Ring*. New York: Knopf, 1964. $4.79. Gr. 4–7. The story of "Siegfried" including musical themes and illustrations.

Sound and Music

ALEXENBERG, MELVIN L., *Sound Science*. Englewood Cliffs, N.J.: Prentice-Hall, 1968. $4.75. Gr. K–3. An imaginary "gloop" character helps children through a series of experiments which demonstrates the "how" of sound and variances in pitch and volume.

ANDERSON, DOROTHY, *Junior Science Books Series*. Champaign, Ill.: Garrard, 1962. $2.39. Gr. 2–5. Simple experiments illustrate how sound is made and travels; how musical instruments create sound; even how a grasshopper sings.

BAER, MARION, *Sound: An Experiment Book*. New York: Holiday, 1952. $3.50. Gr. 4–6. Tells how to make high and low tones; how to transmit sound from one place to another; how to bounce sound using things around the house.

BRANLEY, FRANKLYN M., *High Sounds, Low Sounds*. New York: Thomas Y. Crowell, 1967. $3.50 Gr. 2–5. Experiments using spoons, strings, straws help the young reader understand sound.

FREEMAN, IRA M., *All About Sound and Ultrasonics*. New York: Random House, 1961. $2.50. Gr. 5–6. Science of sound including excellent illustrations and experiments.

HAWKINSON, JOHN, AND MARTHA F. FAULHABER, *Rhythms, Music and Instruments To Make.* Chicago: Whitman, 1965. $3.50. Gr. 3–6. How to make more advanced wind, string, and percussion instruments. Experimenting with pentatonic scale, rhythm & melody on various instruments.

HAWKINSON, JOHN, AND MARTHA FAULHABER, *Music and Instruments For Children To Make.* Chicago: Whitman, 1969. $3.50. Gr. K–3. How to experiment with rhythm and sound and create rhythm instruments. Illustrated.

*KRISHEF, ROBERT K., *Playback: The Story of Recording Devices.* Minneapolis: Lerner, 1962. $2.75. Gr. 4–7. A history of recording devices from Thomas Edison's first phonograph to the record player of today.

LOWRY, L. F., *Sounds Are High, Sounds Are Low.* New York: Holt, Rinehart & Winston, 1969. $1.50. Gr. 2–4. "I Wonder Why" series. This is a popular series of science books for elementary children. Series includes 24 books.

————, *Sounds Are For Listening.* New York: Holt, Rinehart & Winston, ND. $1.50. Gr. 2–4. "I Wonder Why" series.

MANDELL, MURIEL AND ROBERT E. WOOD, *Make Your Own Musical Instruments.* New York: Sterling, 1959. $3.99. Gr. 3–8. Use of easy to find articles such as bottle tops, cigar boxes, hose, rubber bands, and strings to make more than 100 musical instruments. Illustrations are helpful.

OLNEY, ROSS R., *Sound All Around. How Hi-fi and Stereo Work.* Englewood Cliffs, N.J.: Prentice-Hall, 1967. $3.75. Gr. 4–7. What hi-fi is all about; tells function of each basic part, such as amplifier, tuner, record player, tape recorder and speakers. A glossary of terms is included.

PINE, TILLIE S., *Sounds All Around.* New York: McGraw-Hill, 1958. $2.50. Gr. 2–5. Uses bottles, straws and the singing voice to show how sounds are made and varied.

SPIER, PETER, *Gobble, Growl, Grunt.* New York: Doubleday, 1971. $4.95. Gr. K–2. Easy fiction. Unpaged, illustrated. A Junior Literary Guild Book. Pictures of animals, birds and fish with dynamic printing of sounds they make provide material for exploring voice sounds in vocal range with different degrees of dynamics.

Stories

ABISCH, ROZ, *Twas in the Moon in Wintertime.* Englewood Cliffs, N.J.: Prentice-Hall, 1969. $4.95. Gr. 3–6. This song is the Indian story of the birth of Christ and comes from the Huron Indians. Illustrated with woodcut type pictures.

ADAMS, ADRIENNE, *Bring the Torch, Jeanette Isabella.* New York: Scribner's 1963. $3.25. Gr. 2–6. A picture book illustrating the old French carol telling of the villagers going with torch light to the creche.

BROWNE, C. A., *The Story of Our National Ballads.* Revised by Willard Heaps. New York: Thomas Y. Crowell Co., 1960. $5.00. Gr. 6–9. Each song discussed has found a place in the hearts of Americans. There are twenty-one chapters. Songs of the Civil War, the Spanish American War, World War I and World War II are included.

CHAPPELL, WARREN, *The Nutcracker* (adapted). New York: Knopf, 1959. $3.74. Gr. K–3. An illustrated version of the story of the Nutcracker. Lots of color. Includes familiar themes from the Tchaikovsky ballet.

DAVIS, KATHERINE, *The Little Drummer Boy*. New York: Macmillan, 1968. $3.95. Gr. K–3. A handsome picture book containing the lyrics of the song about the nativity and the drummer boy. This song was originally called "Carol of the Drum."

EMBERLEY, BARBARA, *One Wide River to Cross*. Englewood Cliffs, N.J.: Prentice-Hall, 1969. $3.95. Gr. K–3. Woodcuts illustrate the song story of Noah's ark and the animals coming two by two.

FREEMAN, LYDIA, *Pet of the Met*. New York: Viking, 1953. $3.95. Gr. K–3. Easy fiction. 63 pages illustrated. A delightful illustrated story about a family of mice who live in the Metropolitan Opera House and are harassed by an evil cat who lives there too. The cat comes under the spell of "The Magic Flute" and the story ends happily. Provides an excellent introduction to Mozart's "The Magic Flute."

KARASZ, ILONKA, *Twelve Days of Christmas*. New York: Harper, 1949. $4.95. Gr. 1–5. "A thing of beauty and a joy forever . . . The color is soft and rich and on the last two pages is the music for the song. Here are art and music and an old tradition for young and old all between the covers of one book." (Saturday Review)

KEY, FRANCIS SCOTT, *Star Spangled Banner*. New York: Thomas Y. Crowell, 1966. $3.75. Gr. 4–up. How our national anthem happened to be written. All stanzas of the song are included and colorfully illustrated.

LANGSTAFF, JOHN, *Frog Went A-Courtin'*. New York: Harcourt Brace Jovanovich, 1955. $3.99. Gr. K–3. (Caldecott Medal in 1956.) A picture book version of the favorite old ballad "Frog Went A Courtin'." Vivid colors.

LYONS, JOHN HENRY, *Stories of Our American Patriotic Songs*. New York: Vanguard, 1942. $3.95. Gr. 4–9. When, why and by whom ten American patriotic songs were written. Songs included are: "Star Spangled Banner," "Yankee Doodle," "Hail, Columbia," "America," "Columbia, The Gem of the Ocean," "Dixie," "Maryland, My Maryland," "Battle Cry of Freedom," "Battle Hymn of the Republic," "America, The Beautiful."

MENOTTI, GIAN-CARLO, *Amahl and the Night Visitors*. New York: Whittlesey, 1962. $3.75. Gr. 3–up. The story of the Christmas opera as adapted by Frances Frost. Can be used with the recordings of the opera.

MILLER, NATALIE, *Story of the Star Spangled Banner*. Chicago: Childrens Press, 1965. $3.00. Gr. 2–5. How a poem became a national anthem during a battle.

MONTGOMERY, ELIZABETH RIDER, *The Story Behind Popular Songs*. New York: Dodd, Mead, 1966. $3.75. Gr. 7–9. Sketches of popular composers and their lyricists from 1851–1943 and stories of how some of their songs came to be written. (Junior High School Library Catalogue)

PATERSON, A. B., *Waltzing Matilda*. New York: Holt, Rinehart & Winston, 1972. Gr. 3–6. Delightful book containing lyrics to the song, although they vary somewhat from the version we sing in the United States. Children will enjoy beautiful illustrations by Desmond Digby. Received the "Picture Book of the Year" award in Australia, where it was originally published.

PAULI, HERTHA, *Silent Night*. New York: Knopf, 1943. $3.64. Gr. 3–7. The story of this famous Christmas carol, written in a small Austrian village, and why it remained a mystery for so many years.

PROKOFIEV, SERGE, *Peter and the Wolf*. Edited by Warren Chappell. New York: Knopf, 1940. $3.84. Gr. 4–6. Delightful picture version of the Russian fairy tale about the boy and the wolf. Musical themes are included.

QUACKENBUSH, ROBERT, *Old MacDonald Had a Farm*. Philadelphia: Lippincott, 1972. $4.82. Gr. 1–4. Delightful book illustrating each verse of this old accumulative folk song. History and music of song are also included.

ROUNDS, GLEN, *The Boll Weevil*. Gold Gate Junior Books, Los Angeles, Calif.: 1967. $3.95. Gr. 3–5. The Boll Weevil is first printed as a story with appealing illustrations and then as a song made famous by Carl Sandburg.

SCHACKBURG, RICHARD, *Yankee Doodle*. Englewood Cliffs, N.J.: Prentice-Hall, 1965. $3.75. Gr. 1–7. Woodcuts in red, white and blue by Edward Emberley illustrate this song. Notes on the text are added by the author.

SCOTT, JOHN ANTHONY, *The Ballad of America*. New York: Grosset & Dunlap, 1967. $5.95. Gr. 6–up. A history of the United States in song and story. Stories, words, and music of more than 125 songs.

SPIER, PETER, *Erie Canal*. New York: Doubleday, 1970. $4.50 Gr. 4–8. Another book about a folk song that is interesting beyond description. This artist is outstanding.

————, *The Fox Went Out on a Chilly Night*. New York: Doubleday, 1961. $3.50. Gr. 1–5. A delightfully illustrated book about the adventures of a fox on a chilly night. This old folk song is printed at the end of the book. Illustrations are detailed beyond description.

————, *London Bridge is Falling Down*. New York: Doubleday, 1967. $3.95. Gr. K–2. "For the child who enjoys big pictures filled with small details, this version of the familiar verses should be a small treasure." (Saturday Review) A picture book with scenes of 18th century London. Musical score is included.

appendix b

Alphabetical Listing of Composers in *Adventures in Music*

Anderson: Irish Suite—THE GIRL I LEFT BEHIND ME, *GR. 5, Vol. 2*
Bach:
    Cantata No. 147—JESU, JOY OF MAN'S DESIRING, *GR. 5, Vol. 1*
    LITTLE FUGUE IN G MINOR (Arr. by L. Cailliet), *GR. 6, Vol. 1*
    Suite No. 2—BADINERIE, *GR. 3, Vol. 1*
    Suite No. 3—Gigue, *GR. 1*
Bartok:
    Hungarian Sketches—BEAR DANCE, *GR. 3, Vol. 2*
    Hungarian Sketches—EVENING IN THE VILLAGE, *GR. 5, Vol. 2*
    Mikrokosmos Suite No. 2—JACK-IN-THE-BOX, *GR. 2*
Beethoven: Symphony No. 8—SECOND MOVEMENT, *GR. 6, Vol. 1*
Berlioz: The Damnation of Faust—BALLET OF THE SYLPHS, *GR. 1*
Bizet:
    Arlesienne Suite No. 1, L'—MINUETTO, *GR. 4, Vol. 2*
    Arlesienne Suite No. 2, L'—FARANDOLE, *GR. 6, Vol. 1*
    Carmen—CHANGING OF THE GUARD, *GR. 3, Vol. 2*
    Children's Games—THE BALL; CRADLE SONG; LEAP FROG, *GR. 1*
Borodin: ON THE STEPPES OF CENTRAL ASIA, *GR. 6, Vol. 1*
Brahms: HUNGARIAN DANCE NO. *1, GR. 5, Vol. 2*

Cailliet: POP! GOES THE WEASEL—Variations, *GR. 4, Vol. 1*

Carpenter: Adventures in a Perambulator—THE HURDY-GURDY, *GR. 5, Vol. 2*

Chabrier:

ESPAÑA RAPSODIE, *GR. 5, Vol. 1*

MARCHE JOYEUSE, *GR. 4, Vol. 1*

Charpentier: Impressions of Italy—ON MULE-BACK, *GR. 5, Vol. 1*

Coates: London Suite—KNIGHTSBRIDGE MARCH, *GR. 5, Vol. 2*

Copland:

Billy the Kid Ballet Suite—STREET IN A FRONTIER TOWN, *GR. 6, Vol. 1*

The Red Pony Suite—CIRCUS MUSIC, *GR. 3, Vol. 1*

Rodeo—HOE-DOWN, *GR. 5, Vol. 2*

Corelli-Pinelli: Suite for Strings—SARABANDE, *GR. 6, Vol. 2*

Debussy:

Children's Corner Suite—THE SNOW IS DANCING, *GR. 3, Vol. 1*

La Mer—PLAY OF THE WAVES, *GR. 6, Vol. 2*

Delibes: Coppelia—WALTZ OF THE DOLL, *GR. 1*

Dvořák: SLAVONIC DANCE NO. 7, *GR. 4, Vol. 2*

Elgar:

Wand of Youth Suite No. 1—FAIRIES AND GIANTS, *GR. 3, Vol. 1*

Wand of Youth Suite No. 2—FOUNTAIN DANCE, *GR. 2*

Falla: La Vida Breve—SPANISH DANCE NO. *1, GR. 6, Vol. 1*

Faure: Dolly—BERCEUSE, *GR. 2*

Ginastera: Estancia—WHEAT DANCE, *GR. 4, Vol. 1*

Gliere: The Red Poppy—RUSSIAN SAILORS' DANCE, *GR. 6, Vol. 2*

Gluck: Iphigenie in Aulis—AIR GAI, *GR. 1*

Gottschalk-Kay: Cakewalk Ballet Suite—GRAND WALK-AROUND, *GR. 5, Vol. 1*

Gould: AMERICAN SALUTE, *GR. 5, Vol. 1*

Gounod: Faust Ballet Suite—WALTZ NO. 1, *GR. 3, Vol. 1*

Grainger: LONDONDERRY AIR, *GR. 4, Vol. 2*

Gretry:

Cephale et Procris—GIGUE (Arr. by Mottl), *GR. 1*

Cephale et Procris—TAMBOURIN (Arr. by Mottl), *GR. 2*

Grieg:

Lyric Suite—NORWEGIAN RUSTIC MARCH, *GR. 4, Vol. 1*

Peer Gynt Suite No. 1—IN THE HALL OF THE MOUNTAIN KING, *GR. 3, Vol. 2*

Griffes: THE WHITE PEACOCK, *GR. 5, Vol. 1*

Grofé: Death Valley Suite—DESERT WATER HOLE, *GR. 4, Vol. 1*
Guarnieri: BRAZILIAN DANCE, *GR. 6, Vol. 2*
Handel:
    Royal Fireworks Music—BOURREE MENUETTO NO. 2, *GR. 3, Vol. 2*
    Water Music—HORNPIPE, *GR. 2*
Hanson: Merry Mount Suite—CHILDREN'S DANCE, *GR. 3, Vol. 1*
Herbert:
    Babes in Toyland—MARCH OF THE TOYS, *GR. 2*
    Natoma—DAGGER DANCE, *GR. 3, Vol. 1*
Humperdinck: Hansel and Gretel—PRELUDE, *GR. 5, Vol. 2*
Holst: The Perfect Fool—SPIRITS OF THE EARTH, *GR. 6, Vol. 2*
Ibert:
    Divertissement—PARADE, *GR. 1*
    Histories No. 2—THE LITTLE WHITE DONKEY, *GR. 2*
Kabalevsky:
    The Comedians—MARCH, COMEDIANS GALOP, *GR. 3, Vol. 1*
    The Comedians—PANTOMIME, *GR. 1*
Khachaturian: Masquerade Suite—WALTZ, *GR. 4, Vol. 2*
Kodály:
    Hary Janos Suite—ENTRANCE OF THE EMPEROR AND HIS COURT,
        GR. 4, Vol. 2
    Hary Janos Suite—VIENNESE MUSICAL CLOCK, *GR. 2*
Lecuona: Suite Andalucia—ANDALUCIA, *GR. 4, Vol. 1*
Lully: Ballet Suite—MARCH, *GR. 3, Vol. 2*
McDonald:
    Children's Symphony (1st Movement)—LONDON BRIDGE; BAA, BAA,
        BLACK SHEEP, *GR. 3, Vol. 2*
    Children's Symphony (3rd Movement)—FARMER IN THE DELL; JIN-
        GLE BELLS, *GR. 2*
MacDowell: Second (Indian) Suite—IN WARTIME, *GR. 5, Vol. 1*
Massenet: Le Cid—ARAGONAISE, *GR. 1*
Menotti: Amahl and the Night Visitors—SHEPHERDS' DANCE, *GR. 4, Vol. 2*
Meyerbeer: Les Patineurs—WALTZ, *GR. 2*
Milhaud:
    Saudades do Brazil—COPACABANA, *GR. 4, Vol. 2*
    Saudades do Brazil—LARANJEIRAS, *GR. 2*
Moussorgsky:
    Pictures at an Exhibition—BALLET OF THE UNHATCHED CHICKS (Or-
        chestrated by Ravel) *GR. 1*
    Pictures at an Exhibition—BYDLO (Orchestrated by Ravel) GR. 2

Mozart:
Divertimento No. 17—MENUETTO NO. 1, *GR. 5, Vol. 2*
Eine kleine Nachtmusik—ROMANZE, *GR. 4, Vol. 1*
Offenbach: The Tales of Hoffmann—BARCAROLLE, *GR. 3, Vol. 1*
Prokofiev:
Children's Suite—WALTZ ON THE ICE, *GR. 3, Vol. 2*
Summer Day Suite—MARCH, *GR. 1*
Winter Holiday—DEPARTURE, *GR. 2*
Ravel:
Mother Goose Suite—THE CONVERSATIONS OF BEAUTY AND THE BEAST, *GR. 5, Vol. 1*
Mother Goose Suite—LAIDERONNETTE, EMPRESS OF THE PAGODAS, *GR. 4, Vol. 2*
Respighi:
Brazilian Impressions—DANZA, *GR. 5, Vol. 2*
Pines of Rome—PINES OF THE VILLA BORGHESE, *GR. 4, Vol. 1*
Rimsky-Korsakov: Le Coq d'Or Suite—BRIDAL PROCESSION, *GR. 4, Vol. 1*
Rossini: William Tell Overture—FINALE, *GR. 3, Vol. 1*
Rossini-Britten: Soirées Musicales—MARCH, *GR. 1*
Rossini-Respighi:
The Fantastic Toyshop—CAN-CAN, *GR. 2*
The Fantastic Toyshop—TARANTELLA, *GR. 3, Vol. 2*
Saint-Saens: Carnival of the Animals—THE SWAN, *GR. 3, Vol. 2*
Scarlatti-Tommasini: The Good-Humored Ladies—NON PRESTO MA A TEMPO DI BALLO, *GR. 4, Vol. 2*
Schubert: Symphony No. 5—FIRST MOVEMENT, *GR. 5, Vol. 1*
Schumann: Scenes from Childhood—TRAUMEREI, *GR. 4, Vol. 2*
Shostakovich:
Ballet Suite No. 1—PETITE BALLERINA, *GR. 2*
Ballet Suite No. 1—PIZZICATO POLKA, *GR. 1*
Sibelius: Karelia Suite—ALLA MARCIA, *GR. 5, Vol. 1*
Smetana: The Bartered Bride—DANCE OF THE COMEDIANS, *GR. 6, Vol. 2*
Sousa:
SEMPER FIDELIS, *GR. 3, Vol. 2*
STARS AND STRIPES FOREVER, *GR. 4, Vol. 2*
Strauss, R.: Der Rosenkavalier—SUITE, *GR. 6, Vol. 1*
Stravinsky:
The Firebird Suite—BERCEUSE, *GR. 1*

The Firebird Suite—INFERNAL DANCE OF KING KASTCHEI, *GR. 5, Vol. 2*

Taylor: Through the Looking Glass—GARDEN OF LIVE FLOWERS, *GR. 3, Vol. 2*

Tchaikovsky:

The Sleeping Beauty—PUSS-IN-BOOTS AND THE WHITE CAT, *GR. 3, Vol. 1*

The Sleeping Beauty—WALTZ, *GR. 4, Vol. 1*

Swan Lake—DANCE OF THE LITTLE SWANS, *GR. 1*

Symphony No. 4—FOURTH MOVEMENT, *GR. 6, Vol. 2*

Thomson:

Acadian Songs and Dances—THE ALLIGATOR AND THE COON, *GR. 3, Vol. 2*

Acadian Songs and Dances—WALKING SONG, *GR. 1*

Vaughan Williams:

FANTASIA ON "GREENSLEEVES," *GR. 6, Vol. 2*

The Wasps—MARCH PAST OF THE KITCHEN UTENSILS, *GR. 3, Vol. 1*

Villa-Lobos: Bachianas Brasileiras No. 2—THE LITTLE TRAIN OF THE CAIPIRA, *GR. 3, Vol. 1*

Wagner: Lohengfiin—PRELUDE TO ACT III, *GR. 6, Vol. 1*

Walton: Facade Suite—VALSE, *GR. 6, Vol. 2*

The content of two additional albums is as follows:

Album 2 (Grade 1, Vol. 2): (*LC #71-750850*) LES-1010 (stereo) $5.98

Arnold: English Dances—GRAZIOSO; Stravinsky: Petrouchka—RUSSIAN DANCE; Khachaturian: Gayne Ballet Suite—DANCE OF THE ROSE MAIDENS; McBride: Punch and Judy—PONY EXPRESS; Tchaikovsky: Nutcracker Suite—DANCE OF THE SUGAR PLUM FAIRY, DANCE OF THE REED PIPES; Hanson: For the First Time—BELLS; Menotti: Amahl and the Night Visitors—MARCH OF THE KINGS; Grieg: Peer Gynt Suite No. 1—ANITRA'S DANCE; Saint-Saens: Carnival of the Animals—THE ELEPHANT; Milhaud: Suite Provencale—MODERE No. 1; Moussorgsky-Ravel: Pictures at an Exhibition—PROMENADE; Rossini-Britten: Matinees Musicales—WALTZ; Bartok: Mikrokosmos Suite No. 2—FROM THE DIARY OF A FLY; German: Henry VIII Suite—MORRIS DANCE; Moore: Farm Journal—HARVEST SONG; Delibes: The King Is Amused—LESQUERCARDE; Mozart: THE LITTLE

NOTHINGS, No. 8; Kabalevsky: The Comedians—WALTZ; Liadov: Eight Russian Folk Songs—BERCEUSE

Album 4 (Grade 2, Vol. 2): (*LC #71-750850*) LES-1011 (stereo) $5.98 Arnold: English Dances—ALLEGRO NON TROPPO; Prokofieff: Lieutenant Kije—TROIKA; Schuller: Seven Studies on Themes of Paul Klee —THE TWITTERING MACHINE; Copland: The Red Pony Suite— DREAM MARCH; Elgar: Wand of Youth Suite No. 1—SUN DANCE; Rimsky-Korsakoff: The Snow Maiden—DANCE OF THE BUFFOONS; Delibes: Coppelia—SWANHILDE'S WALTZ; Bach: Suite No. 2 in B Minor—RONDEAU; Pierne: Cydalise Suite No. 1—ENTRANCE OF THE LITTLE FAUNS; Respighi: The Birds—PRELUDE; Rossini-Britten: Soirees Musicales—BOLERO; McBride: PUMPKIN EATER'S LITTLE FUGUE; Cimarosa-Malipiero: Cimarosiana—NON TROPPO MOSSO; Gluck: Armide Ballet Suite—MUSETTE; Bizet: Carmen—THE DRAGOONS OF ALCALA; Howe: SAND; Webern: Five Movements for String Orchestra —SEHR LANGSAM *appendix c*

Series 1

ANIMALS AND CIRCUS (BOL #51)

CARNIVAL OF THE ANIMALS, Saint-Saens. (Introduction, Royal March of the Lion, Hens and Cocks, Fleet Footed Animals, Turtles, the Elephant, Kangaroos, Aquarium, Long Eared Personages, Cuckoo in the Deep Woods, Aviary, Pianists, Fossils, The Swan, Finale)

CIRCUS POLKA, Stravinsky

UNDER THE BIG TOP, Donaldson. (Marching Band, Acrobats, Juggler, Merry-Go-Round, Elephants, Clowns, Camels, Tightrope Walker, Pony Trot, Marching Band.)

NATURE AND MAKE-BELIEVE (BOL #52)

MARCH OF THE DWARFS, Grieg

ONCE UPON A TIME SUITE, Donaldson. (Chicken Little, Three Billy Goats Gruff, Little Train, Hare and the Tortoise.)

THE LARK SONG (Scenes of Youth), Tchaikovsky

LITTLE BIRD, Grieg

DANCE OF THE MOSQUITO, Liadov
FLIGHT OF THE BUMBLE BEE, Rimsky-Korsakov
SEASON FANTASIES, Donaldson. (Magic Piper, The Poet and his Lyre, The
Anxious Leaf, The Snowmaiden)
TO THE RISING SUN (Fjord and Mountain, Norwegian Suite 2), Torjussen
CLAIR DE LUNE, Debussy

PICTURES AND PATTERNS (BOL #53)

PIZZICATO (Fantastic Toyshop), Rossini-Respighi
MARCH-TRUMPET AND DRUM (Jeux d'Enfants), IMPROMPTU-THE TOP
(Jeux d'Enfants), Bizet
POLKA (Mlle. Angot Suite), GAVOTTE (Mlle. Angot Suite), Lecocq
INTERMEZZO (The Comedians), Kabalevsky
GERMAN WALTZ-PAGANINI (Carnaval), Schumann-Glazounov
BALLET PETIT, Donaldson
MINUET, Mozart
A GROUND, Handel
CHOPIN (Carnaval), Schumann-Glazounov
VILLAGE DANCE, Liadov
EN BATEAU (In a Boat), Debussy
HARBOR VIGNETTES, Donaldson (Fog and Storm, Song of the Bell Buoy,
Sailing)

MARCHES (BOL #54)

ENTRANCE OF THE LITTLE FAUNS, Pierne
MARCH, Prokofieff
POMP AND CIRCUMSTANCE #1, Elgar
HUNGARIAN MARCH (Rakoczy), Berlioz
COL. BOGEY MARCH, Alford
MARCH OF THE LITTLE LEAD SOLDIERS, Pierne
MARCH (Love for Three Oranges), Prokofiev
CORTEGE OF THE SARDAR (Caucasian Sketches), Ippolitov-Ivanov
MARCHE MILITAIRE, Schubert
STARS AND STRIPES FOREVER, Sousa
THE MARCH OF THE SIAMESE CHILDREN (The King and I), Rodgers

DANCES, PART I (BOL #55)

DANCE OF THE CAMORRISTI, Wolf-Ferrari
DANCA BRASILEIRA, Guarnieri

GAVOTTE, Kabalevsky
SLAVONIC DANCE #1, Dvořák
HOE-DOWN (Rodeo), Copland
FACADE SUITE, Walton (Polka, Country Dance, Popular Song)
HUNGARIAN DANCE #5, Brahms
SKATER'S WALTZES, Waldteufel
MAZURKA (Masquerade Suite), Khatchaturian
GALOP (Masquerade Suite), Khatchaturian

DANCES, PART II (BOL #56)

FOLK DANCES FROM SOMERSET (English Folk Song Suite), Vaughan-Williams
JAMAICAN RUMBA, Benjamin
BADINERIE, Corelli
DANCE OF THE COMEDIANS, Smetana
CAN CAN (Mlle. Angot Suite), Lecocq
GRAND WALTZ (Mlle. Angor Suite), Lecocq
TRITSCH-TRASCH POLKA, Strauss
TARANTELLA (Fantastic Toyshop), WALTZ (Fantastic Toyshop), Rossini-Respighi
ESPAÑA WALTZES, Waldteufel
ARKANSAS TRAVELER, Guion
RUSSIAN DANCE (Gayne Suite #2), Khatchaturian

FAIRY TALES IN MUSIC (BOL #57)

CINDERELLA, Coates
SCHERZO (Midsummer Night's Dream), Mendelssohn
MOTHER GOOSE SUITE, Ravel (Pavane of the Sleeping Beauty, Hop o' My Thumb, Laideronette, Empress of the Pagodas, Beauty and the Beast, The Fairy Garden)

STORIES IN BALLET AND OPERA (BOL #58)

SUITE FROM AMAHL AND THE NIGHT VISITORS, Menotti (Introduction, March of the Three Kings, Dance of the Shepherds)
HANSEL AND GRETEL OVERTURE, Humperdinck
NUTCRACKER SUITE, Tchaikovsky (Overture Miniature, March, Dance of the Sugar-Plum Fairy, Trepak, Arabian Dance, Chinese Dance, Dance of the Toy Flutes, Waltz of the Flowers)

LEGENDS IN MUSIC (BOL #59)

DANSE MACABRE, Saint-Saëns
PEER GYNT SUITE #1, Grieg (Morning, Asa's Death, Anitra's Dance, In the Hall of the Mountain King)
SORCERER'S APPRENTICE, Dukas
PHAETON, Saint-Saëns

UNDER MANY FLAGS (BOL #60)

THE MOLDAU, Smetana
LAPLAND IDYLL (Fjord and Mountain, Norwegian Suite #2), Torjussen
FOLK SONG (Fjord and Mountain, Norwegian Suite #2), Torjussen
LONDONDERRY AIR, Grainger
FINLANDIA, Sibelius
LONDON SUITE, Coates (Covent Garden, Westminster, Knightsbridge March)

AMERICAN SCENES (BOL #61)

GRAND CANYON SUITE, Grofé (Sunrise, Painted Desert, On the Trail, Sunset, Cloudburst)
MISSISSIPPI SUITE, Grofé (Father of Waters, Huckleberry Finn, Old Creole Days, Mardi Gras)

Series 2

MASTERS IN MUSIC (BOL #62)

JESU, JOY OF MAN'S DESIRING, Bach
BOURREE FROM FIREWORKS MUSIC, Handel
VARIATIONS (from "Sunrise" Symphony), Haydn
MINUET (from Symphony #40), Mozart
SCHERZO (from Seventh Symphony), Beethoven
WEDDING DAY AT TROLDHAUGEN, Grieg
RIDE OF THE VALKYRIES, Wagner
TRIUMPHAL MARCH (Aida), Verdi
HUNGARIAN DANCE #6, Brahms
THIRD MOVEMENT, SYMPHONY #1, Mahler

CONCERT MATINEE (BOL #63)

CHILDREN'S CORNER SUITE, Debussy, (Doctor Gradus ad Parnassum, Jumbo's

Lullaby, Serenade of the Doll, The Snow is Dancing, The Little Shepherd, Golliwog's Cakewalk)
SUITE FOR STRING ORCHESTRA, Corelli-Pinelli (Sarabande, Gigue, Badinerie)
MINUET (from "Surprise" Symphony), Haydn
ANVIL CHORUS, Verdi ,"Il Trovatore")
NORWEGIAN DANCE IN A (#2), Grieg
TRAUMEREI, Schumann

MINIATURES IN MUSIC (BOL #64)

CHILDREN'S SYMPHONY, Zador
THE BEE, Schubert
GYPSY RONDO, Haydn
WILD HORSEMEN, Schumann
HAPPY FARMER, Schumann
LITTLE WINDMILLS, Couperin
ARIETTA, Leo
MUSIC BOX, Liadov
FUNERAL MARCH OF THE MARIONETTES, Gounod
DANCE OF THE MERRY DWARFS (Happy Hypocrite), Elwell
LITTLE TRAIN OF CAIPIRA, Villa-Lobos

MUSIC, USA (BOL #65)

SHAKER TUNE (Appalachian Spring), Copland
CATTLE & BLUES (Plow that Broke the Plains), Thomson
FUGUE AND CHORALE ON YANKEE DOODLE (Tuesday in November), Thomson
PUMPKIN EATERS LITTLE FUGUE, McBride
AMERICAN SALUTE, Gould
POP! GOES THE WEASEL, Cailliet
LAST MOVEMENT, SYMPHONY #2, Ives

ORIENTAL SCENES (BOL #66)

WOODCUTTER'S SONG, Koyama
THE EMPEROR'S NIGHTINGALE, Donaldson
SAKURA (folk tune), played by koto and bamboo flute

FANTASY IN MUSIC (BOL #67)

THREE BEARS, Coates

CINDERELLA, Prokofiev (Sewing Scene, Cinderella's Gavotte, Midnight Waltz, Fairy Godmother)

MOON LEGEND, Donaldson

SLEEPING BEAUTY WALTZ, Tchaikovsky

CLASSROOM CONCERT (BOL #68)

ALBUM FOR THE YOUNG, Tchaikovsky. (Morning Prayer, Winter Morning, Hobby Horse, Mamma, March of the Tin Soldiers, Sick Doll, Doll's Burial, New Doll, Waltz, Mazurka, Russian Song, Peasant Plays the Accordion, Folk Song, Polka, Italian Song, Old French Song, German Song, Neapolitan Dance Song, Song of the Lark, Hand-organ Man, Nurse's Tale, The Witch, Sweet Dreams, In Church)

OVER THE HILLS, Grainger

MEMORIES OF CHILDHOOD, Pinto (Run, Run; Ring Around the Rosie; March; Sleeping Time; Hobby Horse)

LET US RUN ACROSS THE HILL, Villa-Lobos

MY DAUGHTER LIDI, TEASING, GRASSHOPPER'S WEDDING, Bartok

DEVIL'S DANCE, Stravinsky

LITTLE GIRL IMPLORING HER MOTHER, Rebikov

Series 3

MUSIC OF THE DANCE: STRAVINSKY (BOL #69)

FIREBIRD SUITE (L'Oiseau de Feu) (Koschai's Enchanted Garden, Dance of the Firebird, Dance of the Princesses, Infernal Dance of Koschai, Magic Sleep of the Princess Tzarevna, Finale: Escape of Koschai's Captives.)

SACRIFICIAL DANCE from "The Rite of Spring" (Le Sacre du Printemps)

VILLAGE FESTIVAL from "The Fairy's Kiss" (Le Baiser de la Fée)

PALACE OF THE CHINESE EMPEROR from "The Nightingale" (Le Rossignol)

TANGO, WALTZ AND RAGTIME from "The Soldier's Tale" (L'Histoire du Soldat)

MUSIC OF THE SEA AND SKY (BOL #70)

CLOUDS (Nuages), Debussy

FESTIVALS (Fêtes), Debussy

MERCURY from The Planets, Holst

SEA PIECE WITH BIRDS, Thomson

OVERTURE TO "THE FLYING DUTCHMAN" (Der Fliegende Hollander), Wagner

DIALOGUE OF THE WIND AND SEA from The Sea (La Mer), Debussy

SYMPHONIC MOVEMENTS, NO. 1 (BOL #71)

FIRST MOVEMENT, SYMPHONY No. 40, Mozart
SECOND MOVEMENT, SYMPHONY No. 8, Beethoven
THIRD MOVEMENT, SYMPHONY No. 4, Tchaikovsky
SECOND MOVEMENT, SYMPHONY No. 4, Schumann
THIRD MOVEMENT, SYMPHONY No. 3, Brahms
FOURTH MOVEMENT, SYMPHONY No. 3, Saint-Saëns

SYMPHONIC MOVEMENTS, No. 2 (BOL #72)

FIRST MOVEMENT, SYMPHONY No. 9, ("From the New World"), Dvorak
FIRST MOVEMENT, SYMPHONY No. 5, Beethoven
FIRST MOVEMENT, (Boisterous Bourrée), A SIMPLE SYMPHONY, Britten
SECOND MOVEMENT, SYMPHONY No. 2, Hanson
FIRST MOVEMENT, SYMPHONY No. 2, Sibelius

SYMPHONIC STYLES (BOL #73)

SYMPHONY No. 99 ("Imperial"), Haydn (Adagio: Vivace Assai, Adagio, Minuetto, Vivace)
CLASSICAL SYMPHONY, Prokofiev (Allegro, Larghetto, Gavotte: Non troppo allegro, Molto vivace)

TWENTIETH CENTURY AMERICA (BOL #74)

EL SALON MEXICO, Copland
DANZON from "Fancy Free," Bernstein
EXCERPTS, SYMPHONIC DANCES from "West Side Story," Bernstein
AN AMERICAN IN PARIS, Gershwin

U.S. HISTORY IN MUSIC (BOL #75)

A LINCOLN PORTRAIT, Copland
CHESTER from NEW ENGLAND TRIPTYCH, Schumann
PUTNAM'S CAMP from "Three Places in New England," Ives
INTERLUDE from FOLK SYMPHONY, Harris
MIDNIGHT RIDE OF PAUL REVERE from Selections from McCuffey's Readers, Phillips

OVERTURES (BOL #76)

OVERTURE TO "THE BAT" (Die Fledermaus), Strauss
ACADEMIC FESTIVAL OVERTURE, Brahms
OVERTURE TO "THE MARRIAGE OF FIGARO," Mozart
ROMAN CARNIVAL OVERTURE, Berlioz
OVERTURE TO "WILLIAM TELL," Rossini (Dawn, Storm, Calm, Finale)

SCHEHERAZADE BY RIMSKY-KORSAKOV (BOL #77)

The Sea and Sinbad's Ship, Tale of the Prince Kalendar, The Young
Prince and the Princess, The Festival at Bagdad

MUSICAL KALEIDOSCOPE (BOL #78)

ON THE STEPPES OF CENTRAL ASIA, Borodin
IN THE VILLAGE FROM CAUCASIAN SKETCHES, Ippolitoff-Ivanoff
EXCERPTS, POLOVTSIAN DANCES FROM "PRINCE IGOR," Borodin
RUSSIAN SAILORS' DANCE FROM "THE RED POPPY," Gliere
L'ARLESIENNE SUITE No. 1, Bizet (Carillon, Minuet)
L'ARLESIENNE SUITE No. 2, Bizet (Farandole)
PRELUDE TO ACT *1*, "CARMEN," Bizet
MARCH TO THE SCAFFOLD, from Symphonie Fantastique, Berlioz

MUSIC OF THE DRAMA: WAGNER (BOL #79)

"LOHENGRIN" (Overture to Act 1, Prelude to Act 3)
"THE TWILIGHT OF THE GODS" (Die Götterdämmerung) (Siegfried's Rhine
Journey)
"THE MASTERSINGERS OF NUREMBERG" (Die Meistersinger von Nürnberg)
(Prelude, Dance of the Apprentices and Entrance of the Mastersingers)
"TRISTAN AND ISOLDE" (Love Death)

PETROUCHKA BY STRAVINSKY (BOL #80)

COMPLETE BALLET SCORE WITH NARRATION

ROGUES IN MUSIC (BOL #81)

TILL EULENSPIEGEL, Strauss
LIEUTENANT KIJE, Prokofiev Birth of Kije, Troika
HARY JANOS, Kodály (Viennese Musical Clock, Battle and Defeat of Napo-
leon, Intermezzo, Entrance of the Emperor)

MUSICAL PICTURES: MOUSSORGSKY (BOL #82)

PICTURES AT AN EXHIBITION (Promenade Theme, The Gnome, The Old Castle, Tuileries, Ox-Cart, Ballet of Chicks in Their Shells, Goldenberg and Schmuyle, The Market Place at Limoges, Catacombs, The Hut of Baga Yaga, The Great Gate of Kiev)
NIGHT ON BALD MOUNTAIN

ENSEMBLES, LARGE AND SMALL (BOL #83)

YOUNG PERSON'S GUIDE TO THE ORCHESTRA, Britten
CANZONA IN C MAJOR FOR BRASS ENSEMBLE AND ORGAN, Gabrieli
CHORALE: AWAKE, THOU WINTRY EARTH, Bach
FOURTH MOVEMENT, "TROUT" QUINTET, Schubert
THEME AND VARIATIONS FOR PERCUSSION QUARTET, Kraft
THEME AND VARIATIONS from SERENADE FOR WIND INSTRUMENTS, Mozart (K361)

CONCERTOS (BOL #84)

FIRST MOVEMENT, PIANO CONCERTO, Grieg
FOURTH MOVEMENT, PIANO CONCERTO No. 2, Brahms
THIRD MOVEMENT, VIOLIN CONCERTO, Mendelssohn
SECOND MOVEMENT, GUITAR CONCERTO, Castelnuovo-Tedesco
THIRD MOVEMENT, CONCERTO IN C FOR TWO TRUMPETS, Vivaldi

MUSICAL IMPRESSIONS: RESPIGHI (BOL #85)

PINES OF ROME (Pines of the Villa Borghese, Pines Near a Catacomb, Pines of the Appian Way)
FOUNTAINS OF ROME (The Fountain of Valle Giulia at Dawn, The Triton Fountain at Morning, The Trevi Fountain at Midday, The Villa Medici Fountain at Sunset)
THE BIRDS (Prelude)

FASHIONS IN MUSIC (BOL #86)

ROMEO AND JULIET (Fantasy-Overture), Tchaikovsky
LITTLE FUGUE IN G MINOR, Bach
SUITE No. 2 FROM "DAPHNIS AND CHLOË," Ravel
ROMANZE FROM A LITTLE NIGHT MUSIC (Eine kleine Nachtmusik), Mozart
PERIPETIA FROM FIVE PIECES FOR ORCHESTRA, Schoenberg

appendix d

Publishers of Recent Music Series

Allyn and Bacon, Inc., Boston 02210. THIS IS MUSIC FOR TODAY.
American Book Company, New York 10003. NEW DIMENSIONS IN MUSIC.
Follett Publishing Company, Chicago 60607. DISCOVERING MUSIC TO-
    GETHER.
Ginn and Company, Boston 02117. THE MAGIC OF MUSIC.
Holt, Rinehart and Winston, Inc., New York 10017. EXPLORING MUSIC.
Macmillan Publishing Co., Inc., New York 10022. THE SPECTRUM OF
    MUSIC.
Prentice-Hall, Inc., Englewood Cliffs, N.J. 07632. GROWING WITH MUSIC.
Silver Burdett Company, Morristown, N.J. 07960. MAKING MUSIC YOUR
    OWN.
Summy-Birchard, Evanston, Illinois 60204. BIRCHARD MUSIC SERIES.

index of songs

Are You Sleeping? 199
Christmas Bells, 187
Come, Ye Thankful People, Come, 190
Follow On! 139
Gerakina, 126
Go Tell Aunt Rhody, 172
Hot Cross Buns, 171, 172
June, Lovely June, 146
Little Tom Tinker, 198
London Bridge, 212
Love Somebody, 135, 172
Me He Manu Rere, 121
Merrily We Roll Along, 171
Nobody Home, 186
Old Texas, 203
Row Your Boat, 184
Sandy Land, 200
Skip to My Lou, 202
Sleep, Baby, Sleep, 155
Streets of Laredo, 151
Three Blind Mice, 201
Trampin', 140
Wayfaring Stranger, 188
Whistle, Daughter, Whistle, 171

general index

A

Accent, 74, 81–84, 124, 248-R
African music, 270–71, 274-R
American Indian music, 271
Animals described in music, 247-R, 295-R
Art and music, 255-R
Articulation, 248-R
  Asian and African, 270–71, 274–75-R
Atonal music, 100
Augmentation, 85, 86
Autoharp, 173–80
  instruction book, 216
  tuning, 178, 257-R
  types of accompaniments, 179

B

Bacon, Denise, 88, 215
Ballet, 269-R, 300-R
Beat (pulse), 70–74, 67-R, 142, 246-R
  divisions of, 71–79
Bells, 164–67
  discoveries with, 164
  glockenturm, 167
  numeral notation with, 166
  resonator, 165
  step,166
Bongo drum, 121
Books, children's, 277–88
Bottles, 162–63
Bruner, Jerome, 19

C

Cadence, 208
Chant, 197–204
Child development, 3
Children's chant, 92
Child voice, the, 115
Chord, 135, 148
  common, 157-R
  inversions, 136
  piano, 152
  quintal and quartal, 149
  tone cluster, 107
Chording:
  with bells, 189
  piano, 184–89
Chord root, 151
Chorus, 155–56
Clapping:
  in canon, 80

Clapping (*cont.*)
    echo, 79
    question-and-answer, 80
Classroom:
    open, 8
    ungraded, 8
Cognitive process skills, 30–35
Composers' devices, 85–86
Composing music, 56, 100, 104, 105, 109,
        153, 155, 191, 211–15, 258-F
    haiku, 214
    opera, 214
    song-writing, 212–14
Concepts, 19–20
Conducting, 63–64, 83
Conga drum, 121
Contour, melodic, 142
Curriculum:
    cyclic, 64
    spiral, 64

D

Dalcroze, Emil Jaques, 83
Dance:
    creating, 119
    ethnic, 121–22
    Latin-American, 120–21
    patterns, 120–21, 251-R
    recordings of, 252–53-R, 296–97-R
    traditional, 120
Data, 19
Descant, 146, 256-R
Diminution, 85, 86
Doolin, Howard, 160
Dramatization, 71
Drum:
    bongo, 121
    conga, 121
    talk, 72
Dynamics, 23, 69, 116, 143

E

Ear training, 93, 127, 141, 193–94
Echo clapping, 79
Evaluation, 46–47

F

Film Guide for Music Educators, 255, 275

Films and filmstrips, 216-F, 218–20
        234-F, 239–40-F, 254-F, 258-F,
        266–69-F
    Churchill, 217
    general, 217
    suggestions for use, 219
Folk music, 279–81
Form, 28–29, 107–8, 119, 207–8,
        259–69-RF
    compound ternary, 264-R
    multiple concepts of, 268-R
    in music, 259–61
    of music, 261–69-RF
    repetition and change in, 261
    sonata-allegro, 267-R
    suite, 267
    three-part, 263–64-R
    tone poem, 267–68-R
    two-part, 263-R
    unity and variety in, 261
Fugue, 256-R

G

Generalization, 20
Grouping, 9–13
Guitar, 182–83
    instruction books, 217

H

Halloween, music for, 268-R
Hand signs, 91–97
Harmony, 104–7, 147–54, 257–58-R,
        258–59-F
Harmony, contemporary, 257–58-R
    bitonality, 148
    chords, 149
    dissonance, 147
Harmony, polyphony, and texture, 26–28,
        255–58
Hawaiian music, 271–72
Home tone, 93, 100

I

Improvisation, 58, 62–63, 76, 93, 106,
        107, 108, 119, 150, 192
Instruments:
    children's books about, 282–84
    harmony, 173–89

Instruments (*cont.*)
  melody, 162–73
  orchestra, 232–39
  percussion, 117
Interval, 133–35
  less common, 192
  minor third, 90–95
  sixth, 154
  third, 153–54

K

Keynote, finding the, 143–44
Keys, major and minor, 257-R
Key signatures, 101, 124, 136, 196
Kodály, Zoltan, 88, 216

L

Learning:
  center, 5–6
  contract, 12
  emotional setting for, 4
  establishing conditions for, 4–14
  general principles of, 13–14
  materials for, 7–8
  organizing the classroom for, 4–14
  package, 12–13
  physical factors for, 6–7
  pictorial description of, 18
  types of classroom organization for,
    8–13
Leonhard, Charles, 47–48
Lesson plan:
  for cognitive process skills, 32–34
  criteria for, 45–46
  for music skills, 36
  other plans, 44–45, 60–67, 93–96
  for teaching concepts, 44
Listening. *See* Sounds and Tone Qualities;
  Tone Quality

M

Machines, described in music, 247-R
Manhattanville Music Curriculum Program,
  54, 57–67
  MMCP Interaction, 57–64
  MMCP Synthesis, 64–67
Maracas, 121
Mazurka, 120

Melody, 25–26, 87–108
  analyzing, 157
  atonal, 100
  contour of, 99
  instruments, 162–73
  modulating, 100
  retrograde, 197
Melody and harmony, 104–7
Meter, 81–84, 124, 211, 249–50-R
Meter signature, 101, 124, 136, 196
Modulation, 137
Movement, 240–47
  free rhythmic responses, 241-R
  fundamental movements, 72, 241–45-R
  rhythmic dramatization, 245–46-R
Music:
  absolute, 227
  art and, 255-R
  atonal, 100
  contemporary, 227–29
  program, 226
  stories in, 269-F
Music concepts and generalizations, 21–29
  dynamics, 23
  form, 28–29
  harmony, polyphony, texture, 26–28
  melody, 25–26
  rhythm, 23–25
  sounds and tone qualities, 21–22
Music content, selection of, 18–30
Music learning. *See* Learning
Music of other cultures, 121–22, 125–27,
  269–75
  American Indian, 271
  analysis of, 272–73
  Asian and African, 270–71, 274–75-R
  generalizations about, 269–70
  Hawaiian, 271–72
  recordings of, 273–75-R
Music programs, guides for, 13–14
Music textbooks, 7

N

Nature, described in music, 247-R, 295-R
Notation, 156, 166, 192, 193
  invented, 59, 71
  learning, 208–11
  numeral, 166
  of pitch, 99–100
  rhythmic, 118

Note memory, 77
Note names, 99
Note reading, 77, 78, 111, 193

O

Objectives, 34–38
  for music attitudes, values, behaviors,
    36–38
  for music skills, 34–36
Objectives, areas of, 15–17
  as a basis for planning, 38–42
  behavioral, 39–42
  drill for writing, 40–41
  guide to formulating, 39
  performance, 39–42
Opera, 268-R, 269-F
  children's books about, 284–85
Orchestra:
  classroom, 189–91
  symphony, 269-F
Orff, Carl, 204–7
  related recording, 206-R
Ostinato, 119, 197, 256-R

P

Partner songs, 149
Part singing, 259-F
  harmonic, 149–55
  male teacher and, 155
  steps in learning, 154
Percussion instruments, 177
  classified, 56
Percussion score, 68
Phrase, 107–8, 140, 142, 260, 261–62
Piano, 159, 167, 194–95
  chording, 184–89
  easy uses of, 194–95
  substitute for voice, 159
  use as melody instrument, 167
  use in teaching, 159
Pitch, 97
  establishing for singing, 141
  matching, 87–90, 168
Plainsong, 132
Plans:
  criteria for, 45–46
  daily, 42–46
  designing, 42–45

  for teaching and evaluating, 38–48
  weekly, 42
Polka, 120
Polyphony, 145–46, 255-R
Polyphony, harmony, and texture,
  255–58-R, 258–59-F
Polyrhythms, 84
Pulse. *See* Beat

Q

Questioning strategies, 30–31

R

Range of children's voices, 87–88
Recorder, 168–73
  fingering chart, 173
  instruction books, 217
Recordings:
  available today, 229–30
  cataloging, 221
  catalogs of, 222
  of familiar songs, 223–25-R
  in lesson plans, 62, 66, 67, 87
  selection of, 221–26
  of songs, 157–58-R
References, 15, 49, 110, 215, 275–76
Rest, 73
Rhythm, 23–25, 67–87, 116–23, 240–51,
  251–54-RF
Rhythm pattern, 72–79, 250–51-R
Rhythm-related concepts, 248–51-R
Roll call, 93–95
Rondo, 108, 262, 264–65-R
Rote singing, teaching of, 138–43
Round, 145
Rounds and canons, 256-R

S

Scale:
  ethnic, 104
  invented, 104
  major, 100
  major and minor, 128
  modal, 130–32
  natural minor, 101
  pentatonic, 101, 129
  tonal center and, 100–4

Scale (*cont.*)
  tone row, 102
Schottische, 120
Sequence, 133, 263-R
Singing, independence in, 142
Singing classroom orchestra, 189–90
Skills:
  cognitive process, 30–34
  music, 34–36
Songs, 111–14
  I-chord, 177
  II-chord, 178
  III-chord, 178
  activities with, 137–38
  echo-type, 115–38
  of limited range, 112
  motivating interest in, 142
  partner, 149
  repititious, 114, 139
  selection of, 7
Sound, children's books about, 285–86
Sounds and tone qualities, 21, 54–69, 63-R,
    67-R, 230–40
  brass, 236, 237–38-R
  brass sound, 161
  electronic, 231-R, 232
  orchestra instruments, 239-R, 239–40-F
  percussion, 238–39-R, 246-R
  science of, 160–63
  string, 232–34-R
  string sound, 160
  unconventional, 230–31-R
  woodwind, 234, 235–36-R
  woodwind sound, 161
Stories, 286–88
String bass, 182–83
Syncopation, 83, 86

T

Tape recorder, composing with, 87
Teaching:
  guides of, 13–14
  with instruments, 119–97, 204–7
Tempo, 22, 69, 116, 246-R, 248-R
Texture, 26–27, 143, 158-R
Thematic development, 261, 263-R
Time signature. *See* Meter
Tonal memory, 96, 97, 98, 116, 118, 127,
    193
Tone cluster, 107
Tone matching, 87–90, 98, 168
Tone pattern, 97, 132
Tone quality, 54–69, 89, 115, 143. *See
    also* Sounds and tone qualities
Transparencies, 220–21
Transposition, 195–96
Triplet, 73, 78

U

Ukulele, 180–83

V

Variation, 108, 208, 265–66-R
Voice, child, 115
  of 5th-and 6th-grade children, 154–55
Voice range of children, 87–88

W

Water glasses, 162–63

X

Xylophone, 166